The Better Part:
Sitting at the Feet of Jesus

The Better Part:
Sitting at the Feet of Jesus

366 Daily Devotions
for New Christians

John Burns

To:

_____

From:

_____

Date:

_____

Cover photo from Shutterstock

Editor: Dona Watson, Silver Fox Productions LLC

ISBN 979-8391750673 (paperback)
ISBN 979-8391813552 (hardcover)

Dedication

Dedicated to the students in Adult and Teen Challenge centers worldwide finding freedom from addiction through a personal relationship with Jesus Christ.

"...being confident of this, that he who began a good work in you will carry it on to completion until the day of Christ Jesus."
Philippians 1:6

Foreword

Welcome to a fresh easy to read and understand captivating devotional for new Christians! For more than two decades, John Burns has dedicated his life and ministry to serve those whose lives have been shipwrecked by addiction.

It's my great privilege to serve with John and observe first-hand his commitment to disciple new believers in the Christian faith. As a servant leader of the ministry of Teen Challenge, his caring heart has been used by God to change lives through the power of the Holy Spirit, the ministry of the Word of God, and fellowship of the community of believers. This carefully framed devotional guide is filled with practical insights and an instructive approach to the scriptures that is easy to read and apply.

The heart of John's work in this anointed offering is to continue to point the believer to the Author and Perfecter of their Christian faith, Jesus Christ.

Whether the lesson comes from the Old or New Testament, it flows from a heart whose wellsprings are connected to the Giver of all life. The vibrancy of John's faith can be felt in every page as he desires his readers to connect daily with the Word of God.

This act of worship prayerfully read each day will inspire the reader to live within the boundaries of God's Word. And they will grow to be stable, steadfast, strong, and immovable; always abounding in the work of the Lord.

Ron Brown
Executive Director/CEO
Teen Challenge of Southern California
An International Conference Speaker for Pastors and
Christian Leaders

Introduction

"Therefore every teacher of the law who has become a disciple in the kingdom of heaven is like the owner of a house who brings out of his storeroom new treasures as well as old."
Matthew 13:52

This book is based on the value of having regular devotional and prayer time with the Lord and studying the Word of God in our quiet time in God's presence. I hope to bless and encourage you by sharing the Word of God in this devotional format. I want to share how the Word of God applies to our everyday lives and helps us to grow spiritually and closer to the Lord in our relationship with him. I want to help new believers understand some of the foundational teachings of Christianity and how they apply to faith and life. I want to pass on the truths that the Lord and others have shared with me that have impacted my life and my relationship with Jesus. I desire to share a comprehensive presentation of Scripture emphasizing Christian discipleship.

This devotional is intended to supplement involvement in a local church, regular prayer time, and personal Bible study. It is not my intention to promote or argue denominational interpretations, but to share the gospel of Jesus Christ and to focus together with you on the common ground of Bible-based, Christ-centered, and God-honoring application of biblical principles.

I pray that the Word of God can bless and help you as it has helped me. I invite you to fellowship with me as we pray and reflect on the Word of God together. I pray that you will experience a closer relationship with the Lord through the Word of God and the ministry of his Holy Spirit. God bless you.

Dear Heavenly Father, I pray for those who read this devotional that they will be blessed by your Word and the ministry of your Holy Spirit. I pray that you will draw close to them in the name of Jesus. Amen.

January 1

A New Beginning

"In the beginning God created the heavens and the earth."
Genesis 1:1

Genesis is the first book of the Bible. The Bible begins with a narration of how God created the earth. The creation story depicts the creative power of our eternal God. The Bible goes on to tell the story of how God has powerfully interacted with the world he created throughout the centuries. The focus of the Bible is on God, not his creation. God is there working in the beginning, the middle, and the end.

January 1 is also the beginning of a new year. God is a God of new beginnings. As we start a new beginning today, we pay attention to how God is doing new and powerful things in our lives. We can participate in the Lord's purpose and plan for our lives by focusing on him in a fresh new way. Our past is behind us. Our future with God is in front of us, starting with today. God is real and he is actively working in the world today as much as he did in the beginning of the book of Genesis. As we turn to the Lord and focus on him, we will experience new and marvelous beginnings.

Dear Lord, you are the creator of the universe, I turn to you and invite you to do new and marvelous works in my life. I thank you for a new beginning and I focus my heart on you in a new way today. In Jesus' name, amen.

January 2

The Better Part

"'Martha, Martha,' the Lord answered, 'you are worried and upset about many things, but few things are needed—or indeed only one. Mary has chosen what is better, and it will not be taken away from her.'" Luke 10:41–42

Jesus was in Bethany at the home of his friends—a brother named Lazarus and two sisters, Martha and Mary. Jesus was fellowshipping with them. He was sitting, relaxing, and visiting, just as we like to do with our friends. Mary was sitting at the feet of Jesus, quietly listening as Jesus was talking with his friends in the house. She was enjoying having time with Jesus, being close to him, soaking it in. Martha was busy with all of the preparations that had to be made. She was probably making lunch and she wanted everything perfect. After all, Jesus was there visiting and he deserved the best. Martha was getting stressed out by all the preparations. She looked across the room and saw her sister Mary there, just sitting at Jesus' feet. Martha must have been a close friend of Jesus. She had no problem telling him what to do: "Lord, don't you care that my sister has left me to do the work by myself? Tell her to help me!" Jesus probably smiled when he lovingly and gently responded: "Martha, Martha, you are worried and upset about many things, but few things are needed—or indeed only one. Mary has chosen what is better, and it will not be taken away from her." Jesus loved Martha and appreciated all that she was doing, but he wanted her, and all of us, to know that we can get caught up in a lot of activity, even good things, that take away from our opportunity to spend time with him. It is better to spend time with Jesus than to become busy and worried and upset about so many things.

Dear Jesus, help me to choose the better part and spend time with you rather than become worried and upset about everything I have to do today. In your name, amen.

January 3

Look Up and Live

"The LORD said to Moses, 'Make a snake and put it up on a pole; anyone who is bitten can look at it and live.' So Moses made a bronze snake and put it up on a pole. Then when anyone was bitten by a snake and looked at the bronze snake, they lived."
Numbers 21:8–9

Moses was leading the Israelites along the Red Sea when the people began to complain and speak against Moses and the Lord. The Lord then sent venomous snakes among them. Many of the people were bitten by the snakes and died. The people confessed their sins to Moses for speaking against him and the Lord. Moses prayed for the people and the Lord told Moses to make a bronze snake, put it on a pole, and lift it up. Whoever looked up at the snake would live. This account of the bronze snake is a foreshadowing and type of what Jesus did on the cross. Just as the sin of the Israelites caused them to be bitten by venomous snakes, our sin brings eternal death and separation from the Lord. Just as the Lord made a way for the Israelites to be delivered from death through the bronze snake, the Lord made provision for us by giving his Son Jesus, that whoever believes in him, shall not perish but have everlasting life. Just as the snake was lifted up on a pole in the wilderness, so was Jesus lifted up on a cross to die for our sins. In the same way that all the Israelites had to do was look up at the snake to live, we too have the gift of eternal life when we look up to Jesus, ask him for the forgiveness of our sins, and accept him as our Lord and Savior. Thank God for the healing, forgiveness, deliverance, and salvation that we have through Jesus Christ.

Dear Lord, today I choose to look up to Jesus and live. Thank you for your forgiveness and healing from the venom of sin in my life. In Jesus' name, amen.

January 4

Jesus Saves

"If you declare with your mouth, 'Jesus is Lord,' and believe in your heart that God raised him from the dead, you will be saved." Romans 10:9

Jesus saves us from the power and the penalty of our sins. Jesus always was and always will be God. He became a man and lived a sinless life on earth. Jesus sacrificed his own life to take the punishment of our sins that we deserved. He saved us from that punishment by dying on the cross in our place. He shed his blood for the forgiveness of our sins. All we have to do is confess and believe. We confess that Jesus is Lord and ask him to forgive us for our sins. We believe in our hearts by faith that Jesus is God and ask him to be the Lord of our lives. When we believe in Jesus in our hearts, we put our faith and our trust in him. We surrender our lives to him. This simple experience of confessing and believing in Jesus Christ allows us to receive his gift of salvation. Once we experience this, we are saved. We are forgiven for our sins. We receive the Holy Spirit. Our eternal destination is changed from condemnation to heaven. This is an immediate change that takes place in our lives regarding our standing with God, our relationship with Jesus, and our eternal destiny. We may not "feel saved," but this reality is based on the Word of God, not on our feelings. We have assurance of our salvation based on the Word of God. We stand on God's Word. The changes in our lives often take time, but the biggest change and greatest miracle of salvation already occurred when we confessed that Jesus is Lord, and believed in our heart that God raised him from the dead.

Dear Heavenly Father, I confess that Jesus is Lord. I believe in my heart that you raised Jesus from the dead. Thank you for forgiving me and saving me from my sin. In Jesus' name, amen.

January 5

Morning Prayer

"In the morning, LORD, you hear my voice; in the morning I lay my requests before you..." Psalm 5:3

This psalm, written by David, expresses his commitment to pray to God in the morning. The Lord's mercies are new every morning; our prayers should also be new every morning. This keeps our relationship with the Lord current and fresh. We thank the Lord for the new day of life and the many blessings he has given us. We worship him because of his lordship in our lives and his great love for us. We make a small sacrifice to wake up early to spend time with him. He is worth it. We give the Lord the first fruits of our day by spending time with him in the morning. He is more important to us than all the other things on our minds that we have to do. We can tell the Lord all that is on our hearts and minds. We take the time to pray for those we know who have needs before we begin our day. In the quiet of the morning, we are still before the Lord and we take the time to listen to the Lord for what he is speaking through his Word or the gentle whisper of his Spirit. Before our day begins, we submit ourselves new to the Lord and we commit the day to him. We want to honor the Lord through-out our day. We may have things on our minds that we want to accomplish, but we lay those things before the Lord. We are dependent on the Lord for anything we do during the day. May the Lord's will be done in our lives every new day.

In the morning, Lord, you hear my voice; in the morning I lay my requests before you. In Jesus' name, amen.

January 6

Love God with Everything You Have

"Love the Lord your God with all your heart and with all your soul and with all your mind and with all your strength."
Mark 12:30

Jesus said that to love the Lord with all your heart and with all your soul and with all your mind and with all your strength is the first and greatest commandment. Jesus makes loving God our priority. This is more important than anything else. This biblical description of how we should love God also shows that our love for God encompasses our whole being: our heart, our soul, our mind, and our strength.

To love the Lord with our heart includes the emotional aspect of our love. Love is certainly a deep-seated and strong emotion. Yet love is not merely an emotion. The fact that loving God and others is a commandment in the Bible indicates that love is also a choice. We can decide to love or not to love. To love the Lord with all of our minds is to have knowledge and understanding of God's love and our love for him and to make a decision to love God to the full extent. We can decide to hold back love. However, the Lord wants us to love him all the way; to hold nothing back. To love the Lord with all of our strength includes those things we do to show our love to God. Love is an action when we show God our love through our lifestyle. Loving the Lord with all our strength also includes our perseverance. When we become tired and weary, we can continue to love the Lord with everything we have.

Dear Heavenly Father, I love you so much. Help me to love you more with all my heart, all my soul, all my mind, and all my strength. In Jesus' name, amen.

January 7

God-Breathed

"All Scripture is God-breathed and is useful for teaching, rebuking, correcting and training in righteousness, so that the servant of God may be thoroughly equipped for every good work." 2 Timothy 3:16–17

The Bible is the inerrant, infallible rule of faith and conduct. To say that Scripture is God-breathed is to say that it is inspired by God. The Holy Spirit moved in the minds and hearts of the men who wrote the Bible so that they wrote what God wanted them to write. The Bible is true. We can count on God's Word. We can stand on the promises of God.

The Bible is God's manual for living. It tells us how to live our lives the way God intended us to. It teaches us new things about God, others, and ourselves. The Bible sets forth standards of what is right and what is wrong. It corrects us when we are wrong so that we can get back on track with what is right. The Bible is useful for training in righteousness because it keeps us on track. Like a train that runs best when it is on the rails, we can live a successful life by living according to the principles of the Bible and following its commands. Every area of life is addressed in the Bible so that we may be equipped for every good work.

There are so many voices in the world screaming for our attention. Television, radio, social media, public opinion, style, fads, and trends all may influence our thoughts and our lives. However, God wants to influence our thoughts and our lives by his Word. Styles, trends, and fads will come and go, but the Word of God remains the same and endures forever.

Dear Heavenly Father, thank you for your Word. I pray that you will use your Word to teach me, to correct me, and to train me in righteousness. In Jesus' name, amen.

January 8

Called to Be Separate

"I am the Lord, who brought you up out of Egypt to be your God;
therefore be holy, because I am holy."
Leviticus 11:45

The Lord challenges us when he says that we should be holy because he is holy. Just as the Israelites were called out of slavery in Egypt and were destined for the Holy Land, we are called out of the slavery of sin and worldliness to be destined for the Promised Land in heaven with Jesus for eternity. Until then, we are living in this world, but we are called out of sin and worldliness into God's holiness. This makes us different than the world. Our aim is not to seek worldly success or pleasure, but to please and honor the Lord. Our holiness, or separateness, is based on our commitment to our relationship with Jesus Christ and to God's Word. We live by the principles and commands of the Bible. We base our worldview on the Bible, not on worldly philosophies and ideas. As Christians, we are called to be different from the world yet we are still in the world to show God's love to others. We should be an influence on the world around us rather than the world influencing us in an ungodly way. We make the decision to honor the Lord and his Word in our lifestyle. We do what the Bible says we should do, and we do not do what the Bible says not to do. We practice holiness when we say "No" to ungodliness in our lives. God helps us with this. The Holy Spirit is inside of us, which is a source of holiness. The Holy Spirit cleanses us of impure thoughts and habits and helps us to make God-honoring choices. The fruit of the Spirit in our lives reflects holiness. As we grow as Christians, God helps us to be more like him. God is holy, and with his help and strength from the Holy Spirit, we have God's holiness in our lives as well.

Dear Lord, you are holy. Help me to have your holiness in my
life. Lead me and empower me to be holy for you.
In Jesus' name, amen.

January 9

Mending Broken Relationships

"All this is from God, who reconciled us to himself through Christ and gave us the ministry of reconciliation."
2 Corinthians 5:18

Reconciliation describes the process of mending broken relationships. We all had a broken relationship with God that needed reconciliation. Our sins separated us from God. When we were in our sinful life, our sins put a wall between us and God. Jesus came to knock that wall down. Another way to describe this is that we were on one edge of a cliff. The Lord was on another cliff. There was a huge chasm between us. There was no way to get across that chasm to be with God. The cross of Christ is the bridge over that chasm. When Jesus died on the cross, he took the penalty of sin for us so that we no longer were separated from God. Jesus bridged the chasm that separated us from God through his death on the cross. After three days Jesus rose from the dead, victoriously defeating death, hell, and the grave.

God always wants reconciliation with us. Even if we feel a separation between ourselves and God, the Lord has already opened the door for reconciliation. He sent his Son, Jesus, to die for us. His arms are open wide. The Lord desires a right relationship with us. The ball is in our court. We can just turn to him and ask for forgiveness. Forgiveness is the threshold to reconciliation. Reconciliation is always God's will. Once we have that reconciliation in our relationship with God, he will help us to be reconciled in our relationship with ourselves, as well as others. We can also be reconcilers and help other people experience his reconciliation.

Dear Heavenly Father, thank you for reconciling me to yourself through Christ and thank you for giving me the ministry of reconciliation. In Jesus' name, amen.

January 10

Walking in Agreement

"Do two walk together unless they have agreed to do so?"
Amos 3:3

To be in one accord and to have mutual understanding and consent is important in any relationship. If two people are walking together, they should agree on why they are walking together and where they are going. When we work together with others, we need to share a common goal as to what we are trying to accomplish, or else we will be all over the place and not be able to accomplish the goal we had in mind. Relationships work when people are in agreement. If all parties in a relationship do not want the same thing, the relationship will not work. A relationship is not healthy if one person wants the relationship and the other does not. God has already shown us that he wants a relationship with us by giving his Son, Jesus, so that we may have eternal life by believing in him. Jesus gave it all to show us how much he wants a relationship with us. While we were still sinners, Jesus died for us. When we confess our sins to Jesus and ask for forgiveness through his shed blood, we are agreeing with God that we are sinners in need of a Savior. When we ask Jesus to be the Lord and Savior of our lives, we are agreeing with God that we are surrendering our will and our lives to the lordship of Jesus Christ. The Lord has shared his goals and his expectations for our relationship through his Word. When we have a personal relationship with Jesus, we are agreeing to live in obedience to his Word. We agree to do things God's way instead of our way. We agree to seek God's will to be done in our lives rather than imposing our own will on the Lord. Walking in a personal relationship with Jesus Christ means submitting and surrendering to him.

Dear Heavenly Father, help me to walk in agreement with you as I surrender my will and my life to you today and every day. In Jesus' name, amen.

January 11

God's Greatest Gift

"For God so loved the world that he gave his one and only Son, that whoever believes in him shall not perish but have eternal life." John 3:16

God's greatest gift was the gift of his one and only Son, Jesus. God gave his Son, Jesus, to save the world from the penalty of our sins and to provide eternal life. The gift of God's Son was an expression of his love. God's love is generous; he gives the best. God's love is universal; he gave his Son to the world, not just one group of people. God's love is sacrificial; he gave at a great cost and hurt to himself. God's love is unconditional; we did nothing to earn this gift, we did nothing to receive it. All we have to do is just believe. This portrays the simplicity of the gospel message: "that whoever believes in him shall not perish but have eternal life." This good news is for everyone in the world. There is no one whom the Lord does not love. No one is beyond the redemption of Jesus.

Once we have received God's love and forgiveness, we have the promise of eternal life through Jesus. Others still need to hear the simple gospel message. Others need God's greatest gift of love. God gave the gift to everyone. We can share the good news message and share the generous, universal, sacrificial, unconditional love of God with others as well. Once we have received God's love, he wants us to share it with others. We need to love others the same way God loved us. Showing God's love is the most powerful way to share God's good news. Let's show someone God's love today.

Dear Heavenly Father, thank you for sharing the greatest gift of your Son, Jesus, to save me from my sin and bring me eternal life. Help me to share your love and good news with someone else today. In Jesus' name, amen.

January 12

In God We Trust

"Trust in the LORD with all your heart and lean not on your own understanding; in all your ways submit to him, and he will make your paths straight." Proverbs 3:5–6

When we trust in the Lord, we place our full confidence in him. God is the Creator of the universe. We are amazed at the miracles we read about in the Bible. He has the power and ability to handle any situation we may be facing. God also created each of us and cherishes us more than we can understand. He loves us so much that he gave his Son, Jesus, to die on the cross to save us from the penalty of our sins. We trust God because of his awesome power and his great love.

He is our Rock and our Refuge. We have safety and security in him. When we place our trust in the Lord, he dispels our fears, worries, and anxiety. We can take a sigh of relief putting our lives in his hands. We resist the temptation to do things our way and lean on our own understanding. We seek his Word for truth regarding whatever we are facing in life. We also trust the Lord by waiting on him. We resist the urge to grow impatient and want to do something now. We have learned that our efforts to solve problems have at times even made things worse. We wait on the Lord to take care of things in his way and in his time. He comforts and assures us that he is trustworthy. We look back and see his faithfulness in our lives and know that as he has been faithful in our past situations, that he will be faithful in whatever situation we are facing today. We place our trust in him.

Dear Heavenly Father, I trust in you with all of my heart, leaning not on my own understanding, but submitting to you in all my ways, trusting that you will make my paths straight.
In Jesus' name, amen.

January 13

Born Again

"Jesus replied, 'Very truly I tell you, no one can see the kingdom of God unless they are born again.'" John 3:3

Jesus taught that we must be born again. Jesus was talking about the spiritual renewal that takes place in our lives when we believe in him. Jesus made this possible for us because he, who always was and always will be God, became a man to save us from the penalty of our sins. Jesus took the penalty of our sins when he shed his blood and died on the cross. On the third day after he died, Jesus rose from the dead to lead the way for us in victory over sin and into eternal life.

When we ask Jesus to forgive us of our sins and accept him as our Lord and Savior, our sins are forgiven and the Holy Spirit comes inside of us. There is a spiritual regeneration that takes place in our spirits through the power of the Holy Spirit. We experience a new birth into a living hope through Jesus Christ. To be born again is a spiritual experience. When we become Christians, we have a new life in Christ. Our sins are forgiven and cleansed through the blood of Jesus. Just as Jesus died and was buried in the tomb, our old life before Christ is dead and buried. Jesus makes us a new creation. Our past is behind us and does not define us. We are new people in Christ and the Word of God defines us as loved sons and daughters of our Lord. When we accept Jesus as Lord and become born again, our eternal destiny has changed and we enter the kingdom of God in this life and for eternity. When we become born again, our future will be with Jesus forever in heaven.

Dear Lord Jesus, thank you that I am born again because of your death on the cross and resurrection to life. Thank you for your Holy Spirit inside of me to give me a new life.
In Jesus' name, amen.

January 14

Unity in Christ

"How good and pleasant it is when God's people live together in unity!" Psalm 133:1

The Lord is pleased when we live together in unity. Our unity as Christians is found in Jesus Christ. He is the head; we are the body. The body is functioning best when all the parts work together in unity. Jesus has called us to love one another and he said that others will know we are his disciples if we have love for one another. The divinity of Jesus Christ is the common ground on which we stand. Our relationships with other Christians are Christ-centered. The love of Jesus Christ binds us together. Therefore, we should not allow denominational differences to cause division among us. We can live in unity when we have love. God's love is gracious and forgiving, patient, and enduring. We can live in unity when we are humble. Humility does not have to win the argument or have the last say. We practice humility when we are willing to put our differences aside and submit to each other rather than insisting that we are right and everyone else is wrong. Living in unity takes active effort on our part. Rather than passively accepting the way things are, we stand up and reach out to others. The important thing is that we serve together and get along with each other. We are better together. The Lord wants us to build bridges, not walls, with each other. We live in unity when we build each other up. There is no place for us to tear each other down. Let us reach out to each other with the love of Jesus and live together in unity today!

Dear Heavenly Father, use me to build a spirit of unity today. Help me to be part of "how good and pleasant it is when God's people live together in unity!" In Jesus' name, amen.

January 15

We Are All One in Christ Jesus

"There is neither Jew nor Gentile, neither slave nor free, nor is there male and female, for you are all one in Christ Jesus."
Galatians 3:28

Martin Luther King, Jr., was a civil rights activist who opposed racial discrimination in our country. His birthday was on January 15th. Our nation observes the third Monday in January as a national holiday to commemorate the work of Dr. King to facilitate racial equality and civil rights.

Our country has come a long way in developing racial equality and civil rights, but there is still work to be done. The destructive influence of racism in our country still exists. The Bible states that we are all one in Christ Jesus. Jesus has made us one by destroying the barrier, the dividing walls of hostility between us. We are the spiritual family of God. All people are created in God's image. We are equal to each other. One racial or ethnic group is not better than or superior to the other. We respect, love, value, and honor all people regardless of the racial, ethnic, cultural, social, or gender distinctions between us. The Lord has created humankind with the beauty and wonder of diversity. Diversity does not become a dividing wall between us; it makes us stronger in our purpose to serve and honor the Lord as we lock arms together in unity. We can be part of the solution and not part of the problem of racial division still present and causing harm in our society. We can show God's love in such a way that brings unity, healing, and reconciliation.

Dear Heavenly Father, I thank you for the diversity you created in the body of Christ. Help me today to be an instrument of your love, peace, and unity. Have mercy and bring repentance, healing, and racial reconciliation in our society.
In Jesus' name, amen.

January 16

Return to the Father

"When he came to his senses, he said, 'How many of my father's hired servants have food to spare, and here I am starving to death! I will set out and go back to my father and say to him: Father, I have sinned against heaven and against you."
Luke 15:17–18

In the parable of the lost son, the son demanded his inheritance from his father. He set out for a distant land and wasted his wealth on wild living. When he had lost everything, he hired himself out as a worker and was sent to feed pigs. He was so hungry that he longed to eat the food the pigs ate. It was then that he came to his senses and decided to return to his father and ask for forgiveness.

What a great decision! When we decidedly leave or unintentionally drift away from our relationship with our Heavenly Father, we need to come to our senses and return to our Heavenly Father. The son came to his senses when he hit bottom. The Lord used that scenario to get his attention. This was a wake-up call for him. When we experience negative results in our life because we too do things our own way, we need that same spiritual awakening, that epiphany, to see and understand that we are separating ourselves in our relationship with our Heavenly Father. Whenever we sense that we are drifting off from the Lord's best plans and purposes for our lives, even the smallest compromise of obedience to his Word, we need to come to our senses and return to the Father.

Dear Heavenly Father, I pray that I will not allow disobedience or compromise in my relationship with you. When I allow myself to drift from you in any way, help me come to my senses and return to you, my loving Heavenly Father. In Jesus' name, amen.

January 17

He Cares for You

"Cast all your anxiety on him because he cares for you."
1 Peter 5:7

Our anxiety, worries, and cares can weigh us down. We think about things over and over again. This constant process preoccupies us. We are distracted from the here and now. We even become disheartened, afraid, or frustrated, because as much as we think and worry about something, it does not change or resolve anything!

Becoming a Christian does not mean we will not have any more anxiety. God can help us cope with anxiety when we do feel anxious. The Lord can help us so that anxiety does not overwhelm us and impair our ability to live life. The Lord brings comfort through the presence of his Holy Spirit. His Word also brings comfort and renewal to our minds when our thoughts are troubled. We can stand on the promises of God to assure us and hope as we trust in him. His love brings security to our fears. There is a supernatural peace that God provides to us through our relationship with him. With God's help, anxiety can become less intense, less frequent, and less enduring. We can pray about whatever is bothering us and ask God to receive it and ask him to deal with it. We are never alone. God cares for and loves us so much that he wants to help us. He is also big enough and strong enough to handle the problems that are so overwhelming to us. Our biggest problems are easy for God to solve. He is the Creator of the universe. We can have his peace as we trust the Lord through faith that he will be with us to walk through whatever happens. We do not have to deal with our problems on our own anymore.

Dear Heavenly Father, today I cast my cares on you because I know you care for me. Help me with my anxious thoughts. My trust and faith are in you. Thank you for taking my anxiety and giving me your peace. In Jesus' name, amen.

January 18

God Gives Hope

"'For I know the plans I have for you,' declares the LORD, 'plans to prosper you and not to harm you, plans to give you hope and a future.'" Jeremiah 29:11

The difficulties and challenges of life can become so over-whelming that we may experience hopelessness and despair. There is no light at the end of the tunnel. There is no expectation that things will get better. The only expectation is that things will continue to get worse. This hopelessness seems unchanging, especially when our failures led to this place. We feel terrible and blame ourselves.

The good news is that no one is beyond God's hope. God gives hope when we are in despair. No one has gone too far down the slope of hopelessness that God is not able to reach them and turn their life around. The biblical concept of hope is described as a confident expectation rather than an uncertain wishy-washy "hope so but I am not sure." When we put our faith and trust in God, he gives us hope. We know we can count on him. We know he has mighty power to work miraculous change in our circumstances. Hope starts in our inner person as strength in our soul. God will never leave us nor forsake us. He sent his Son, Jesus, to die on the cross to save us from the penalty of our sins. Jesus rose from the dead and ascended to heaven. He is alive in heaven praying to the Father on our behalf. Jesus will return for us. He is our blessed hope. No matter what happens here on earth we know that we will have eternity in heaven with Jesus.

Dear Lord, thank you for the plans that you have for me, to prosper me and not to harm me, plans to give me hope and a future. Thank you that you are the God of hope. In Jesus' name, amen.

January 19

Yet I Will Rejoice in the Lord

"Though the fig tree does not bud and there are no grapes on the vines, though the olive crop fails and the fields produce no food, though there are no sheep in the pen and no cattle in the stalls, yet I will rejoice in the LORD, I will be joyful in God my Savior."
Habakkuk 3:17–18

Tragedy, injustice, personal setbacks, periods of financial challenges, or spiritual dryness can bring discouragement and doubt. Our faith can be tested during difficult times. We can become tempted to lose hope and allow challenging or negative circumstances to interfere with our relationship with God and with our spiritual disciplines of prayer, Bible reading, and church attendance.

Rather than allowing challenging times to pull us away from the Lord, it is when we face difficulties that we should be pressing into the Lord! It is during our difficult times that the Lord wants to draw close to us. Although we may be facing a terrible situation, it does not change the reality of God's love, faithfulness, goodness, and mighty power. Material possessions and prosperity may come and go, but the love of God endures forever. He is faithful and he does not change. Although our circumstances may not be good, God is good all the time.

We do not worship God based on our circumstances. We do not only praise the Lord when things are going well. We praise the Lord in the good times and the hard times.

Dear Lord, I praise you because of who you are, my mighty loving Heavenly Father. I will praise you not only in the good times but help me to rejoice in your presence when times are tough. In Jesus' name, amen.

January 20

Keep the Fire Burning

"The fire must be kept burning on the altar continuously; it must not go out." Leviticus 6:13

The priests were given instructions regarding the altar for burnt offerings. It was their responsibility to keep the fire burning. The fire was never to go out. Because of Jesus' sacrifice on the cross, we no longer need to make burnt offerings to the Lord. However, just as the priests were responsible for keeping the fire on the altar burning, we need to keep the fire of our love relationship with Jesus burning with passion.

When people are passionate about the Lord, we describe them by saying that they are "on fire for God." God does not want that fire to go out. When we first become saved and experience the love of God, there is often great joy and peace, followed by zeal and passion to serve the Lord. That passion and zeal can grow, rather than it being a temporary "honeymoon" experience with God that just goes away in a short period of time. That fire is God's love and the presence of his Holy Spirit inside of us. God wants to keep that fire of love and spiritual power burning inside of us. We keep the fire burning when we spend time in the Lord's presence through worship, prayer, Bible study, and fellowship with other believers. We can also quench the fire by neglecting our relationship with the Lord. The quickest way to put out God's fire is when we are disobedient to the Word of God. When we live in love and trust by obeying God's Word and spending time with him, we are stoking up the fire of God in our lives.

Dear Lord, I thank you for the fire of love and spiritual power in my heart through my relationship with you. Help me to keep that fire burning continuously. It must not go out.
In Jesus' name, amen.

January 21

A New Creation

"Therefore, if anyone is in Christ, the new creation has come: The old has gone, the new is here!" 2 Corinthians 5:17

It feels great to get something new: some new clothes, a new car, a new house. How about a new life? This is what God offers us through Jesus Christ.

It does not matter who we are or what we have done in the past. God loves us and brings miraculous transformation to our lives when we come to him in repentance. God can put our past behind us and give us a brand-new life. People who come from backgrounds of addiction, sin, crime, abuse, brokenness, and hurt can receive forgiveness, deliverance, healing, and wholeness through Jesus Christ. Jesus sacrificed his own life on the cross so that we may have new life. This experience that the Lord does inside of us is called "regeneration." This describes the spiritual experience of being "born again." When we ask Jesus to forgive us of our sins and accept him as our Lord and Savior, this spiritual transformation takes place. We are forgiven of our sins. The Holy Spirit resides in us. Our eternal destination is changed from condemnation to eternal rest in the presence of Jesus. God makes this immediate change in our lives and then continues to change us and work in us to conform us to the image of Christ for the rest of our lives. Let us celebrate our new life in Christ today!

Dear Father in heaven, thank you for the new creation you have made in my life. Thank you that the old life has gone and the new life has come through Jesus Christ my Lord. Continue to change me and make me more like him.
In Jesus' name, amen.

January 22

Overcome Evil with Good

"Do not repay evil with evil or insult with insult. On the contrary, repay evil with blessing, because to this you were called so that you may inherit a blessing." 1 Peter 3:9

When someone insults us or hurts us, our first reaction may be to want to insult or hurt them right back. This is not what the Lord wants from us.

The first response we can have when we are wounded is to draw close to God. We can let God know our feelings in prayer. We can receive his love, comfort, and healing for our hurt. Jesus knows what it is like to be betrayed and hurt by others.

The second response we can have is to forgive those who hurt us the same way the Lord forgives us. To forgive is not to deny the wrongdoing or to condone or excuse the offense. To forgive is not to pretend we were not hurt. To forgive is not to trust again blindly. Trust needs to be earned. To forgive is to make a promise that we are releasing the person from the debt they owe us and that we are entrusting the person and the matter into the Lord's hands.

The third response we can have when others hurt us is to bless them and do good. With God's help, we can channel the energy of our pain and anger to do good. We practice the love of God when we respond to offenses with kindness and prayer. We build relationships by doing good. When we do good, we bless others and ourselves.

Dear Heavenly Father, I bring you my hurts and ask for your healing. I forgive those who hurt me. Please help me to walk in that forgiveness and to show your love and do good.
In Jesus' name, amen.

January 23

Strength Within

"We are hard pressed on every side, but not crushed; perplexed, but not in despair; persecuted, but not abandoned; struck down, but not destroyed." 2 Corinthians 4:8–9

Life brings challenges, stresses, and difficulties. When faced with these challenges, we experience the temptation to think the worst and feel like we are defeated. But we are not defeated! We may get knocked down, but we are not knocked out! A Christian is either up or getting up! When we experience discouragement and have the temptation to think the worst, that is when we turn to the Word of God and read the truth to overcome our self-defeating thoughts. God's Word encourages us to persevere. We can stand on the promises of God! The Holy Spirit inside of us is the source of the inner strength that we maintain no matter what the world or the devil throws at us. The same Spirit that raised Jesus from the dead is inside of us. We have the power of the Holy Spirit to keep us strong during difficult times. During our difficult challenges, we turn to our Lord Jesus in prayer. We draw close in our relationship with Jesus Christ. Because of his great love for us, he is close to us in the time of trial. We are not alone. We are encouraged by his love and presence. Yes, we do face difficulties, stress, and hardship, but the promises of God, the power of God, and our personal relationship with Jesus Christ always give us strength.

Dear Heavenly Father, I thank you that when I am hard-pressed on every side, I am not crushed. When I am perplexed, I am not in despair. When I am persecuted, I am not abandoned. I may get struck down, but I am not destroyed because of the strength within that comes from you. In Jesus' name, amen.

January 24

God Gives Wisdom

"If any of you lacks wisdom, you should ask God, who gives generously to all without finding fault, and it will be given to you." James 1:5

A contemporary definition of wisdom is "the practical application of knowledge." Wisdom may be attained by experience and by learning from our own mistakes and the mistakes of others. It is for this reason that wisdom is often associated with maturity and old age. Our "wisdom teeth" are named such because they are the last teeth to grow just as wisdom is often a quality that comes later in life.

However, wisdom from God is available to all believers regardless of age. Spiritual wisdom from God lies in contrast to worldly wisdom. The wisdom of the world will contradict the principles of godliness and love for the Lord and others that the Bible is based on. Wisdom in the Bible is associated with the fear of the Lord, obedience, knowledge, understanding, and prudence, which is consequential thinking or the ability to think things through to see how our decisions will play out. The Bible describes a wise person as someone who is patient, who keeps their emotions under control, holds their tongue, and listens to counsel.

When faced with the many choices and decisions we have today, we need God's wisdom! It is available to us; we need to ask the Lord and he will give us his wisdom. Rather than make impulsive decisions, speak hastily, or react emotionally, we need to pause and pray and ask the Lord for his wisdom in the choices we make today.

Dear Heavenly Father, I ask you for your wisdom today, because I lack wisdom. I thank you that you give wisdom generously without finding fault. I need your wisdom today.
In Jesus' name, amen.

January 25

Press On

"Brothers and sisters, I do not consider myself yet to have taken hold of it. But one thing I do: Forgetting what is behind and straining toward what is ahead, I press on toward the goal to win the prize for which God has called me heavenward in Christ Jesus." Philippians 3:13-14

Our Christian life is not a sprint; it's a marathon. The apostle Paul describes himself as a runner running a race. He pushes forward and does not look back. His focus is on the finish line. Although it takes everything he's got, he does not give up.

We can learn from our past, but we do not have to carry it with us. It would be like running a race while carrying a heavy weight. Jesus forgave us and freed us from our past because of what he did on the cross. Our sinful life in the past is dead just as Christ died on the cross. We also follow Christ in his resurrection with a new life free from the past.

Paul describes himself as straining toward what is ahead and pressing on toward the goal. This reflects the reality that the race is not easy; it takes perseverance and endurance to continue. Such is the Christian life. We do not give up. When we are tired and weary, we know that God is with us. He gives us strength. Paul is motivated by the goal to win the prize at the finish line. Our finish line is in heaven where we will be with Jesus for all eternity. When we are heavenly minded and focused on our Lord Jesus, we have the strength to press on and not give up.

Dear Heavenly Father, today I need your strength and perseverance. I will not give up. Forgetting what is behind and straining toward what is ahead, I press on toward the goal to win the prize for which God has called me heavenward in Christ Jesus. In Jesus' name, amen.

January 26

Our Loving Heavenly Father

"...But while he was still a long way off, his father saw him and was filled with compassion for him; he ran to his son, threw his arms around him and kissed him." Luke 15:20

This parable told by Jesus is commonly called the Parable of the Prodigal Son, or The Lost Son. This parable is also about the loving father. The father in this story reflects the love of God.

The father had generous love. He gave his son the inheritance when he demanded it. Our Heavenly Father also generously lavishes his love on us. The greatest expression of God's love is that he gave his one and only Son, Jesus, to become a man to save us from the penalty of sin and to make a way for us to have eternal life.

The father also had permissive love. He let the son take his inheritance and leave. Our Heavenly Father loves us so much that he gives us free will. He does not force us to obey him. He wants us to choose to follow him. He longs for a love relationship with us. He wants us to choose to love him back.

The father was also merciful, compassionate, and forgiving. When the son returned, the father received him back with open arms without criticism or condemnation, simply love. Our Heavenly Father also waits with open arms for us. When we return to him, his grace runs out to meet us. He longs to hold us close to him.

Dear Heavenly Father, thank you so much for your love, for your compassion, and for your forgiveness, I love you, Lord. Help me today and every day to remain in your embrace and love you more. In Jesus' name, amen.

January 27

Love and Worship

"I am a rose of Sharon, a lily of the valleys."
Song of Songs 2:1

The Song of Songs is a love story between a husband and his wife written by Solomon. This story can be interpreted as an allegory or an illustration of the love that we as Christians have in our personal relationship with Jesus Christ. In the New Testament, Jesus is depicted as the bridegroom and we the church as the bride of Christ. The intimate covenant love between a husband and wife is a mere expression of the intimate covenant love that Christ has for us. The sign of his covenant love with us is the blood he shed on the cross.

Just as husbands and wives can speak intimately, tenderly, and affectionately to each other, we can share our tender love with our Lord Jesus as we share our hearts with him in prayer. He has already written a love letter to us, the Bible. We can direct the terms of affection, the "love-talk," between the husband and wife in the Song of Songs to Jesus as words of love and worship. He is the rose of Sharon, the lily of the valley. We are telling Jesus how beautiful and precious he is to us, how much we love him, and how close he is in our hearts.

We can grow closer to the Lord and experience intimacy in our love relationship with Jesus as we allow ourselves to feel his deep love and learn to express our love to him with affection and intimacy in regular devoted quiet times of worship and prayer alone with him.

Dear Jesus, you are the rose of Sharon, you are the lily of the valley, you are the fairest of ten thousand. I worship you in the beauty of your holiness. I thank you for your love. I love you so much. Help me to draw closer to you in love.
In Jesus' name, amen.

January 28

Strength in Weakness

"But he said to me, 'My grace is sufficient for you, for my power is made perfect in weakness.' Therefore, I will boast all the more gladly about my weaknesses, that Christ's power may rest on me." 2 Corinthians 12:9

This verse provides the Lord's response to Paul when Paul asked the Lord to remove the "thorn" from his flesh. The Bible does not specify exactly what Paul's thorn in his flesh was. The good thing about that is that we can personalize and identify with this exchange between Paul and the Lord. We all may have a "thorn in the flesh"—a problem, an issue, a shortcoming, or a weakness that we struggle with—and we like Paul, want God to take this problem or weakness away from us.

God does not always take away our problems or weaknesses. He gives us the grace to carry on while still having them. A contemporary description of the biblical concept of grace is "God's unmerited favor." He gives us his goodness, his strength, and his love even though we do not deserve it. There is nothing we can do to earn it. That is the nature of God's grace. He empowers us to accomplish his will and purposes even though we have problems, weaknesses, and issues. We do not accomplish his purposes in our own strength. When we are at the end of ourselves, God can begin. When we come to terms with our weaknesses, we can receive his strength. Then we can say along with Paul, "When I am weak, then I am strong," because of God's strength.

Dear Heavenly Father, I thank you that your grace is sufficient for me. I will boast about my weakness so that Christ's power may rest on me. For when I am weak, then I am strong with your strength. In Jesus' name, amen.

January 29

Jesus Is Knocking

"Here I am! I stand at the door and knock. If anyone hears my voice and opens the door, I will come in and eat with that person, and they with me." Revelation 3:20

This Scripture presents a beautiful picture of Jesus' active desire to have a personal relationship with each one of us. He announces his presence, "Here I am!" He does not just come in on his own. He does not break the door down, even though he could if he wanted to. No, he stands at the door and knocks. He waits for us to hear his voice and to open the door. He does not come in to inspect the house or interrogate, evaluate, or castigate us. No, just to eat and fellowship with us, to spend time with us. This is what Jesus wants. It is up to us to hear his voice, open the door, let him in, and take the time to sit and eat with him. Like any other relationship, our personal spiritual relationship with Jesus develops when we spend quality time in his presence and when we open up to him in prayer. To take this illustration one step further, when Jesus comes into our house, he wants access to every room in the house. He does not want to find a locked door and hear that he can go anywhere in the house except that one room.

When Jesus knocks on the door of hearts, we let him in to abide in our hearts. We allow Jesus to have access and free reign over every area of our lives. We don't hold back any area of our lives from him. We have completely surrendered our hearts, our wills, and our lives to him.

Jesus, I have opened the door of my heart and have invited you into my life. I give you access and free reign over every area of my heart and my life. I trust you. I surrender my life to you. In Jesus' name, amen.

January 30

The Body of Christ

"And let us consider how we may spur one another on toward love and good deeds, not giving up meeting together, as some are in the habit of doing, but encouraging one another—and all the more as you see the Day approaching."
Hebrews 10:24–25

Let us not give up meeting together in church! For a disciple of Jesus, church attendance is a foundational spiritual practice, right up there with personal time in prayer and Bible study. The model of the church is outlined in the New Testament. The church is the body of Christ and Jesus is the head.

It is so important for us to belong to a local church. We are not supposed to live as Christians alone and isolated, but to come together as a body of believers to worship the Lord together. We are under the spiritual covering and leadership of the church and our pastor. The Lord anoints the pastor of the church to lead the church and minister through the teaching and preaching of the Word of God. We are connected in our fellowship with Christ and our fellow believers. We pray for each other, encourage each other, and love each other with the love of Christ.

The church is not only a place for us to receive, but to give. We give of our finances and also of our service to the Lord at our church. We serve the Lord in ministry in our local church to worship the Lord, minister to others, and reach out to the lost. The ministry of the church is God's ordained pattern for Christians to worship, grow, and minister together.

Dear Heavenly Father, I thank you for your church, the body of Christ. As I follow you, show me how I can be more involved in your church. In Jesus' name, amen.

January 31

God Is Love

"Dear friends, let us love one another, for love comes from God.
Everyone who loves has been born of God and knows God.
Whoever does not love does not know God, because God is love."
1 John 4:7–8

God is love! Love is God's outstanding attribute. To know God is to know love. Everything God does comes from his love. When we have a relationship with God, we experience his love. The love of God will change our lives if we let him. God loves each of us so much. He fills us with his love in such a way that gives us fulfillment and purpose in life. He created us to enjoy a loving relationship with him and with each other.

This presents simple logic. If God is love, and Christians have God in our lives, then Christians will show love. In other words, show me a Christian, and I will show you someone who loves God and loves other people. This is the statement that John brings out. A person who does not love does not know God because God is love.

The closer we get to God, the more of his love we will receive. God's love will bring healing to our hearts when we are hurt by others. God wants us to know how much he loves us and how much we deserve to be loved; not hurt, not abused, not neglected, but loved with everlasting love. God's love will fill us in such a way that he helps us to love ourselves. God's love will fill us up and run over into our relationships with others so that we will show God's love to others in the same way God loves us.

Dear Heavenly Father, you are love! I thank you for your love
in my life. I love you, Lord! Help me to love you more, to love
myself, and to share your love with others. In Jesus' name, amen.

February 1

Like a Tree Planted by Streams of Water

"Blessed is the one who does not walk in step with the wicked or stand in the way that sinners take or sit in the company of mockers, but whose delight is in the law of the LORD, and who meditates on his law day and night. That person is like a tree planted by streams of water, which yields its fruit in season and whose leaf does not wither—whatever they do prospers."
Psalm 1:1–3

As we walk with Christ on our faith journey, we cannot allow ourselves to be deterred or distracted by people in the world who do not share our faith or commitment to Jesus. We need to be careful about who we spend time with and how they impact our faith journey.

In contrast to being distracted and dissuaded by other people, we are blessed and nourished by the Word of God. To meditate on the Word day and night indicates how essential the Word of God is in our personal faith journey and spiritual growth. Rather than rushing through chapters of the Bible, we take the time to think about how God's Word applies to us and our daily situation. We mull the Word over in our minds. We allow the Word to be hidden in our hearts and impact who we are and what we do. As a result, we grow strong in our faith like a tree planted by streams of water. Just as the water provides sustenance for the tree to be strong and healthy, we receive spiritual strength from the Word of God. God's Word will nourish our spirit so that our lives will be fruitful and prosperous. Meditate on God's Word today!

Dear Heavenly Father, today I choose not to be distracted or deterred by the influences of the world. Instead, I will meditate on your Word day and night. Help me to grow and become strong like a tree planted by streams of water.
In Jesus' name, amen.

February 2

Return to God

"'Ever since the time of your ancestors you have turned away from my decrees and have not kept them. Return to me, and I will return to you,' says the LORD Almighty."
Malachi 3:7

A lifestyle pattern of disobedience and turning away from the commandments in the Bible is to turn away from God himself. To have a right relationship with the Lord we need to have a lifestyle of obedience to him and his Word. Although it is our behavior that is the measuring rod for our obedience, behavior is just the tip of the iceberg. The key to our right relationship with the Lord is what is in our hearts. In order to change our behavior, we need to change our hearts: our beliefs, our attitudes, and our desires. When we set our hearts on the Lord, he will draw close to us and help us to change our thinking, heal our emotions, and change the way we act. The Lord changes us from the inside out! The Holy Spirit will help us to understand the Word of God and empower us to apply God's Word to our lives and practice it in our behavior and lifestyle. Changing patterns of disobedient behavior is often a process that takes time and requires the Lord's help. We can do our part to return to the Lord and he will return to us. When we set our hearts on our relationship with the Lord, we will take steps to live that out by spending time in prayer, reading the Bible, fellowshipping with other Christians, and living in obedience to his Word. But it starts with our heart. When we return to the Lord, he will return to us.

Dear Heavenly Father, I thank you that when I return to you, that you return to me. Change my heart, Lord, and draw me closer to you today. In Jesus' name, amen.

February 3

Dimensions of Growth

"And Jesus grew in wisdom and stature, and in favor with God and man." Luke 2:52

This statement captures four different dimensions of growth: wisdom, stature, favor with God, and favor with man. With God's help, we can continue to grow in these dimensions on our journey as Christians.

To grow in wisdom refers to intellectual or mental growth. We grow mentally when God helps us to change the way we think. We grow in wisdom when we learn from our mistakes, listen to wise people, and maintain a teachable spirit.

To grow in stature refers to physical growth. Our focus on physical growth is on health and wellness. We need to take care of our bodies and ensure a healthy lifestyle with proper sleep, diet, and exercise.

To grow in favor with God refers to our spiritual growth. None of us have arrived at the height of our spiritual growth until we arrive in heaven. We continue to focus on our personal relationship with Jesus.

To grow in favor with man refers to social or relational growth. The Lord wants us to enjoy loving relationships with other people. God wants us to forgive others as he has forgiven us.

Each day brings new growth opportunities. Let's be aware of how the Lord is helping us to grow today.

Dear Heavenly Father, help me to grow in these different dimensions of my life: mentally, physically, spiritually, and relationally. Show me how I can be the person you want me to be. Conform me into the image of Christ. In Jesus' name, amen.

February 4

God's Good Gifts

"Every good and perfect gift is from above, coming down from the Father of the heavenly lights, who does not change like shifting shadows." James 1:17

The good gifts we have in life are gifts from God, whether these gifts are material blessings, personal attributes or abilities, or even those relationships in our lives that are important to us.

Good gifts come from a good God. Goodness is an attribute of God. God is good all the time! God does not have evil or badness in him. The goodness we experience in life is a reflection of who God is and how he relates to us with his goodness.

God is the Father of the heavenly lights, the creator of the sun, the moon, and the stars in the sky. He is almighty and all-powerful. His almighty power is over all things; his sovereignty is another of God's attributes. He has the power to bring his goodness and love to us in such a way that overcomes darkness and evil.

God does not change like shifting shadows. Faithfulness is another attribute of God. We can count on him. He is stable, consistent, and reliable. He does the things he promises. He is true to his Word. He is not unstable. He is faithful, not flakey!

Let us thank the Lord today for his good gifts in our lives and his goodness, his power, and his faithfulness!

Dear Lord, you are a good God! Every good and perfect gift in my life is from you. You are the Father of the heavenly lights; you do not change like shifting shadows. Thank you for your goodness, your power, and your faithfulness in my life.
In Jesus' name, amen.

February 5

The Lord Who Heals You

"He said, 'If you listen carefully to the Lord your God and do what is right in his eyes, if you pay attention to his commands and keep all his decrees, I will not bring on you any of the diseases I brought on the Egyptians, for I am the Lord, who heals you.'" Exodus 15:26

Jehovah-Rapha is a Hebrew compound name for God translated as "the Lord who heals you." The Lord brings us healing and health in our bodies, our minds, our spirits, and our souls. This verse reveals that one of the ways God provides healing for us is outlined in a healthy way of life contained in the commands and the principles of the Bible. The Bible addresses every aspect of life, including how to live healthy. Some illnesses come as a direct result of disobedience and sinful living. However, this does not mean that every sickness is a result of sin. It also does not guarantee that we as Christians will be free of all illnesses. This world has sickness and our bodies will break down at some point. The Lord has the supernatural power to bring healing to our lives. In the New Testament, Jesus went around healing many people. Jesus is our Great Physician. He continues to bring healing to our lives today. The Bible makes it clear that God can heal and that we should pray for his healing for others and ourselves. The Bible shows that faith in God is a factor in his healing. However, our faith is not what brings healing, God does. Our faith is not in our faith, but our faith is in the Lord who heals. As Christians, we will receive our ultimate healing when we go to be with Jesus. In heaven there will be no more sickness, sin, or sadness forever.

Dear Heavenly Father, you are Jehovah Rapha, the Lord who heals. I pray for your healing in my own life and the lives of those who are on my heart. Help me to live a healthy life according to the principles in your Word. In Jesus' name, amen.

February 6

Just for Today

"Two things I ask of you, Lord; do not refuse me before I die: Keep falsehood and lies far from me; give me neither poverty nor riches, but give me only my daily bread. Otherwise, I may have too much and disown you and say, 'Who is the Lord?' Or I may become poor and steal, and so dishonor the name of my God."
Proverbs 30:7–9

This "Prayer of Agur" is rich in wisdom and has insight into areas of weakness in our human nature. It is interesting that when Jesus taught the disciples to pray, he also said we should pray for our daily bread. Agur prayed that God would not give him too much or too little, but just what he needed for the day.

When we give our lives to the Lord, God blesses us with a good lifestyle. However, we cannot allow the comforts of God's blessing to decrease the passion we have for the Lord or our dependency on him. Just because we have security and prosperity in our lives, it does not mean we no longer need and hunger for the Lord. We need God as much now as we did when we cried out to him in despair!

When we feel our needs are not being met, we may experience a sense of urgency, which influences us to break God's laws to meet that need or desire in our life. We need to slow down and pray rather than make impulsive, emotional, or hasty decisions that break God's laws. God helps us to trust in him and allow him to meet our needs his way.

Dear Lord, today I pray that you give me neither poverty nor riches, but give me only my daily bread. Help me not to forget you because of the blessings and comfort in my life. Help me to trust in you to meet my needs. In Jesus' name, amen.

February 7

Arise, Shine

"Arise, shine, for your light has come, and the glory of the LORD rises upon you." Isaiah 60:1

We can arise by becoming more aware of the Lord's presence, plans, and purposes today. God is actively moving in our midst and he wants us to move with him and be part of what he wants to do in our lives and the lives of those around us. We need to wake up from our comfort zone. We need to pull away from the worries of life that preoccupy us and ask the Lord what he is doing and how we can be a part of it. We need to rise to the realm of the Spirit and the kingdom of God rather than being caught up in an earthly mindset and worldliness. The Lord wants us to go through the day with the eyes of our hearts opened and enlightened to him and his purposes.

God is the light in whom there is no darkness. He wants to shine his light on the world and bring light to the darkness around us. He wants to use us so that his light shines through us as we live out godly lives, obey his Word, and share his Word and his love with others. The glory of the Lord rises upon us today to accomplish his purposes. We cannot accomplish his will on our own. He anoints us and equips us to do his will and accomplish his purposes. We are sensitive to his leading as we stand on his Word and are attentive to the guidance of the Holy Spirit. God is on the move to accomplish great things. We should be on the move with him! Arise and shine!

Dear Heavenly Father, thank you for your light which has come through your presence and for your glory that rises upon me. Help me to arise to your presence, plans, and purposes and to shine your light and love on others today.
In Jesus' name, amen.

February 8

My Soul Thirsts for God

"As the deer pants for streams of water, so my soul pants for you, my God. My soul thirsts for God, for the living God. When can I go and meet with God?" Psalm 42:1–2

There is a thirst in our souls that only God can quench. There is an emptiness inside of us that only he can fill. We try to fill that emptiness by other means: relationships, material things, pleasure, drugs, and alcohol. All these things fall short and leave us still thirsting for more. In the past, we kept trying but were never filled; like a dog chasing its tail, going round and round but never getting anywhere. It's time to stop looking in all the wrong places and turn to the Lord.

The Lord can fill us with his love to meet that deep need inside of us. He fulfills a need that cannot be met anywhere else. He created us with that need and the capacity to have a loving relationship with Jesus Christ. When the Lord fills us with his love, we experience peace and satisfaction. There is an enduring joy that lasts in contrast to the fleeting pleasures of sin that end up taking a destructive toll on our lives. There is a fulfillment in our relationship with the Lord that gives us strength in the difficulties and stress of this life. The world will drain us of our strength, but the presence of the Lord will fill us up. The approval of people will come and go, but the Lord's love endures forever. Our time in prayer and the study of his Word is a time to allow him to fill us with his presence and satisfy the thirst in our souls.

Dear Lord, as the deer pants for streams of water, so my soul pants for you, my God. My soul thirsts for God, for the living God. Help me to stop turning to anyone or anything else. Only you can satisfy my soul. In Jesus' name, amen.

February 9

Share the Word

"These commandments that I give you today are to be on your hearts. Impress them on your children. Talk about them when you sit at home and when you walk along the road, when you lie down and when you get up." Deuteronomy 6:6–7

When the Lord's Word is on our hearts it becomes part of who we are, how we act, and what we say. For those of us who are parents, we are responsible for sharing God's Word with our children. We can teach them about the truth in God's Word as we share everyday life with our children. When we do share the Word of God with our children, it is like planting seeds of truth in their minds. We want those seeds to grow and take fruit so that our children develop their own relationship with the Lord and are committed to living godly lives. We leave a legacy to our children by sharing the Word of God with them.

The Lord may also bring others into our lives with whom we can share the Word of God. As we naturally go through the day, we can bring up the Word of God in our conversations with others. Whether they are believers or not, they will be blessed and enlightened by the Word of God. When we are going through our day today and a Scripture comes to mind, we can speak it out and share it with whomever we are with. Others will be blessed as we have been by God's Word, and the Lord will be glorified.

Dear Heavenly Father, I pray that your Word is on my heart as I go through my day. Please give me Scriptures to share to impress them on my children and others with whom I spend time. Help me to talk about your Word when I sit at home, and when I walk along the road, when I lie down, and when I get up. In Jesus' name, amen.

February 10

Rubble Removal

"Meanwhile, the people in Judah said, 'The strength of the laborers is giving out, and there is so much rubble that we cannot rebuild the wall.'" Nehemiah 4:10

When the Babylonian army attacked Jerusalem, they demolished the walls that surrounded the city. The book of Nehemiah tells the story of how Nehemiah led the people to rebuild the walls around the city. In order to build the new walls, they had to remove the rubble from the old walls. There was so much rubble that the people got tired and discouraged. In our walk with Christ, we also may become tired and discouraged when faced with the rubble from our past. We want to build a new life in Christ, yet we become discouraged when faced with the reality of the rubble from our past such as failures, broken commitments, personal loss, and broken relationships. We may still be directly dealing with consequences or results from our past mistakes.

Be encouraged! God has forgiven us for our past mistakes. The Lord sees us through the blood of Jesus. We need to see ourselves the way God sees us. God will help us clean up any rubble from our past that we are still dealing with. We need to keep our focus on the Lord and do what we need to do each day. God will clean up the rubble of our past one day at a time. We do not look back. We keep moving forward. God can clean up the rubble from our past so that we may walk fully in our new life in Christ. We do not give up!

Dear Heavenly Father, I thank you for the rebuilding that you are doing in my life. Thank you for your forgiveness and for setting me free from my past. I pray that you will help me clean up the rubble from my past so that I may walk in my new life in Christ. In Jesus' name, amen.

February 11

Bitter or Better

"David was greatly distressed because the men were talking of stoning him; each one was bitter in spirit because of his sons and daughters. But David found strength in the LORD his God."
1 Samuel 30:6

When David and his army returned to their camp, they found that the camp had been attacked by the Amalekites; their wives and children had been taken captive. The men became embittered with David and wanted to stone him, but David found strength in the Lord. When we are faced with hardships and difficulties, we have a choice as to how we will respond. We can become bitter or better.

When we hold on to anger and dwell on how bad our situation is, those negative thoughts and feelings build up inside of us. We can become resentful and bitter. We may seek to blame others for our situation and then hold it against them. We can become overwhelmed with negative thoughts and feelings. We can begin to lose control.

We have a better choice. We can turn to the Lord and ask for his help with our anger. He can give us the grace to forgive and let go of toxic negative thinking and feelings. The Lord can heal our hurts. We can submit our emotions to the Holy Spirit. We also can turn to the Word of God to help renew our thinking. With God's help, we can go through tough times without falling apart or losing control. We can find strength in the Lord.

Dear Heavenly Father, when faced with difficulties I pray that I will be better, not bitter. Help me to forgive others, let go of resentment, and submit my thoughts and emotions to your Holy Spirit. Help me to find strength in you. In Jesus' name, amen.

February 12

One Body, Many Parts

"Now you are the body of Christ, and each one of you is a part of it." 1 Corinthians 12:27

The church is the body of Christ. Jesus is the head. Each of us is part of the same body. Each part of the body is necessary and important. One part of the body is not better than the other parts. We are all important. Everyone has a place to serve in the body. Not everyone is called to be the pastor. There are so many roles necessary in the body of Christ including teachers, ushers, greeters, musicians, and maintenance workers. Some people are prayer warriors, others are great at witnessing and evangelizing, others cook for special occasions, some give an encouraging word, and others are great listeners. We each have a gift and talent that is unique that the Lord wants to use to build up the body of Christ by serving Christ and serving others.

As members of the body of Christ, it is so important that we serve in unity. We esteem others greater than ourselves. We have an attitude of humility wanting to have a servant spirit and giving God the glory. We love each other as fellow members of the family of God. We glorify the Lord when we work together for his purposes and his glory.

We all can find a place of service in the body of Christ to use our God-given gifts to serve the Lord and others.

Dear Jesus, you are the head of the church. I am grateful to be part of your body. Show me how I can better serve you in the body of Christ. Help me to have a spirit of unity with the other members of your body. Use us to serve together to accomplish your purposes. In Jesus' name, amen.

February 13

Always Keep On Praying

"And pray in the Spirit on all occasions with all kinds of prayers and requests. With this in mind, be alert and always keep on praying for all the Lord's people." Ephesians 6:18

Prayer is a vital part of our Christian life. Prayer is the key to communicating with the Lord and developing our personal relationship with Jesus Christ. Like any other relationship, it is developed by spending quality time together. Our prayer time is quality time spent with the Lord.

We are to pray on all occasions. Prayer to the Christian is like breathing to the body. There are many different kinds of prayers: worship, thanksgiving, confession, repentance, and forgiveness for ourselves and others. We pray for our own needs as well as for the needs of others. There is individual prayer and corporate prayer with other believers. Our prayer time also includes listening. We should be practicing all of these different kinds of prayers.

We also need to practice perseverance in our prayers. The Lord may not answer our prayers the first time we pray about something. We may have to wait on the Lord for his will to be done regarding our prayer requests. God works in mysterious ways. He also does things in his own time. We pray for his will to be done. Prayer is not about us imposing our own will on the Lord, but submitting our requests in faith and trusting him with the results. Our part is to always keep on praying and not give up.

Dear Heavenly Father, help me to remember to pray on all occasions with all kinds of prayers and requests. Help me to be alert and always keep on praying. Enrich my relationship with you and my prayer time in your presence. In Jesus' name, amen.

February 14

Celebrate God's Love

"For I am convinced that neither death nor life, neither angels nor demons, neither the present nor the future, nor any powers, neither height nor depth, nor anything else in all creation, will be able to separate us from the love of God that is in Christ Jesus our Lord." Romans 8:38–39

Valentine's Day is celebrated on February 14 in many parts of the world. It is that special day to tell the people we love just how much we love them. We buy gifts for the person we love: a card, flowers, chocolates, maybe jewelry. The people we love are important to us. Expressing and celebrating that love is important to us. As powerful and meaningful as our love relationships are, this love we feel for others is yet a smaller reflection of the great love that the Lord has for us.

Nothing can separate us from the love of God that is in Christ Jesus our Lord! No circumstance can interfere with God's love. No power or force can take God's love away. There is nothing that we have done or can do to change God's love for us. God is not like us; he will not get mad at us or tired of us and one day decide to stop loving us. His is an everlasting supernatural love like we have never and will never experience anywhere else from anyone else! Our life will change when we experience the love of God. God's love is so powerful that we will want to love him back with our lives. We also can turn his love on ourselves and learn to love ourselves the way that God loves us. God fills us up with his love to overflowing so that we can share his love with others. Let's celebrate God's love today!

Dear Heavenly Father, thank you that nothing shall separate me from your love that is in Christ Jesus my Lord. I receive your love today. I love you, Lord. Help me to live in your love and reflect your love in my relationship with you, with myself, and with others. In Jesus' name, amen.

February 15

Look to Jesus

"I made a covenant with my eyes not to look lustfully at a young woman." Job 31:1

Job describes a "covenant with his eyes" to prevent him from looking at a woman lustfully. This is a creative way for him to say that he was already prepared for how to handle himself when he did see a pretty woman. He was committed to purity and integrity with his eyes and his thoughts. Our purity and integrity before the Lord are not limited to our behavior. It is neither healthy for us nor honorable in our relationship with Christ to dwell on impurity or any other sinful thoughts. We are responsible for our thought lives as well as our actions. We cannot allow our eyes to wander and our thoughts to just run wild. We should be fixing our eyes on Jesus. We know that Jesus meets the desires of our hearts. Our integrity and right relationship with the Lord are more important than the fleeting pleasures of sinful fantasies. Our actions are a result of our thoughts, so if we want to act right, we need to think right. With God's help, we can be aware of our thought life and take responsibility for our thoughts. Self-control is a fruit of the Holy Spirit. The Holy Spirit can help us to be aware of our wandering eyes and ungodly thoughts. The Lord can turn our eyes away from worthless things and turn our eyes and our hearts toward him. We can stay focused on the Lord and his plans and purpose for our lives. We do not have to be wandering in the wilderness of pleasure-seeking and self-satisfaction through sinful thoughts. The Lord will help us keep our eyes on Jesus.

Dear Heavenly Father, I make a covenant with my eyes not to look lustfully at other people. Help me to keep my eyes, my thoughts, and my heart focused on you.
In Jesus' name, amen.

February 16

The Gift of Creativity

"See, I have chosen Bezalel son of Uri, the son of Hur, of the tribe of Judah, and I have filled him with the Spirit of God, with wisdom, with understanding, with knowledge and with all kinds of skills—to make artistic designs for work in gold, silver and bronze, to cut and set stones, to work in wood, and to engage in all kinds of crafts." Exodus 31:2–5

The Lord describes how he filled Bezalel with the Holy Spirit to work with his hands with creativity and craftsmanship. God is the Creator of the universe. Creativity is one of his spiritual attributes. When we accept Jesus Christ as Lord, the Holy Spirit of God indwells within us and we will reflect the Lord's attributes. We are made in his image, and we can reflect his love, his goodness, and his creativity. Since creativity is an attribute of God, our participation in creative acts can be a spiritual connection between us and the Lord, where he meets us while imparting this spiritual attribute. One of the strengths of creativity is that it can bypass our understanding. We at times may think too much and allow our thinking to be a spiritual stumbling block. When we engage in creativity, we can practice a free flow of expression that is not hindered by our thoughts. Our creativity can be an expression of worship. The Lord does not give spiritual gifts to us, but moves through us to benefit him and others. Now that we are new creations in Christ, do not be surprised to discover new creative gifts, qualities, or interests. It is never too late to discover creative gifts we never knew we had. We can benefit by trying new things and discovering creative abilities that the Lord has given us.

Dear Heavenly Father, you created the heavens and the earth. I pray that you help me to be creative to glorify you and to serve others. In Jesus' name, amen.

February 17

A Cool Head and a Warm Heart

"And the Lord's servant must not be quarrelsome but must be kind to everyone, able to teach, not resentful."
2 Timothy 2:24

"It takes two to tango." When we engage in an argument with another person, we have become participants and are responsible for the outcome. We cannot blame the other person for being argumentative because we were there, arguing right along with them. Arguing is not productive. Both parties are trying to force each other to see things their way. There is often more speaking than listening as we try to talk over each other. Arguments often become heated. Frustration and anger begin to rise. Hurtful things may be said.

As followers of Christ, we are not quarrelsome and argumentative, but kind and gentle. These qualities are the fruit of the Holy Spirit. Rather than become defensive when we hear something we do not agree with, we can remain gentle and kind. Rather than oppose another person, we come alongside them to understand them. It also takes humility on our part to have the self-control to resist the temptation to prove ourselves right. When we are kind to another person we can minister to them. Our goal is not to force someone to change their mind or their point of view. We can argue until we are blue in the face and it will not change the other person's mind. Instead, by responding with kindness and gentleness we can show the other person the love of God. Only the Lord can change a person's heart. We need to get out of the way and allow the Lord to minister to that person. We need to keep a cool head and a warm heart.

Dear Heavenly Father, I pray for your help today that I will not be quarrelsome, but kind to everyone, able to teach, not resentful. In Jesus' name, amen.

February 18

Deep Calls to Deep

"Deep calls to deep in the roar of your waterfalls; all your waves and breakers have swept over me."
Psalm 42:7

The deep things of God can minister to the deep things inside of us. We can go deeper still in both directions. We can grow to a deeper place in our relationship with the Lord, and we also can allow him to minister to a deeper place within us. The Holy Spirit and the Word of God go hand in hand in our pursuit to have a deeper spiritual relationship with the Lord. The ways of the Lord are mysterious and unfathomable. Yet as we grow closer to him, the Lord gives us more understanding of who he is. Our mindset shifts from natural to spiritual. We gain deeper insight into the depths of the riches of his Word. The Lord leads us further in our journey of spiritual growth. We can overcome falsehoods in our beliefs that we were previously blind to. The Lord continues to help us grow and change in new ways as he is conforming us to the image of Christ. We allow this mutual closeness to continue by dedicating ourselves wholly to our relationship with the Lord. The psalmist mentions the roar of his waterfalls, and waves and breakers sweeping over him. This is not achieved by just stepping ankle-deep into the waters of our spiritual relationship with the Lord. We need to take the full plunge and immerse ourselves in his presence, in his Word, and in his ways. This applies to our willingness to surrender our lives to him, to love him with all of our hearts, and to be dedicated to spending time in his presence.

Dear Heavenly Father, deep calls to deep in the roar of your waterfalls; all your waves and breakers have swept over me. I pray that you lead me into a deeper relationship with you today and every day. In Jesus' name, amen.

February 19

Health and Wellness

"Dear friend, I pray that you may enjoy good health and that all may go well with you, even as your soul is getting along well."
3 John 1:2

We are blessed when we can enjoy good health. Good health enables us to have a fulfilled quality of life. Although health issues develop that are out of our control, we also have the responsibility to make choices and take care of ourselves in such a way that supports a healthy lifestyle. The Lord created us in these bodies and he wants us to take care of them.

It is right for us to consider how we can make choices to improve our health. Getting adequate sleep, eating a healthy and balanced diet, and staying active are foundational components of a healthy lifestyle. We need to have balance in our lives so that we are not overworking, even when doing the Lord's work. We take steps to monitor the amount of stress in our lives because too much stress can cause health problems.

When we are healthy, we can enjoy life more the way that God intended us to. We also can do more for the Lord and the kingdom of God when we have good health. God wants us to go into all the world, so we need to get off the couch! Our good health will also determine how much we can do as we get older and help us to enjoy a longer life with our loved ones. With God's help, we can make choices to improve our health today!

Dear Heavenly Father, I pray for good health for myself and my loved ones today. Help me to make choices to live a healthy life. In Jesus' name, amen.

February 20

Pray for Our Leaders

"I urge, then, first of all, that petitions, prayers, intercession and thanksgiving be made for all people—for kings and all those in authority, that we may live peaceful and quiet lives in all godliness and holiness." 1 Timothy 2:1–2

Presidents' Day is a holiday in the United States observed on the third Monday of February. This holiday commemorates and honors the leadership of the men who led our country as presidents. We worship the Almighty Sovereign God who is the King of Kings and Lord of Lords. No power or ruler is greater than God. The Lord is over all governments. He sets one leader up and sets another down. He reigns over all. The authorities that exist have been established by God. As Christians, we must pray for our presidents as well as all of our leaders on a national, state, and local level. The hearts of our leaders are in the hands of the Lord. We can pray that the Lord directs the hearts of our leaders according to his will. Our leaders make decisions that affect all of our lives. We need to pray that our leaders have wisdom and can make decisions according to the will of God. Our leaders can make an impact on the social, and economic issues of our lives. We need to pray that the Lord's will be done here on earth as it is in heaven. We can come alongside our leaders by praying for them. There is power in prayer and there will be an impact on the lives of our leaders and those whom they serve when we are committed to praying for them.

Dear Heavenly Father, I pray for our president as well as all of our leaders in our federal, state, and local government. I pray for your will to be done in their lives and in our land according to your great love and power. In Jesus' name, amen.

February 21

The War Within

"So I say, walk by the Spirit, and you will not gratify the desires of the flesh. For the flesh desires what is contrary to the Spirit, and the Spirit what is contrary to the flesh. They are in conflict with each other, so that you are not to do whatever you want."
Galatians 5:16–17

A man had two dogs. They were always fighting each other. A neighbor asked the man, "I noticed your dogs are always fighting, which dog wins?" The man replied, "The dog that I feed the most wins." So it is with our Christian experience. The flesh and the Spirit are in conflict with one another, and the one that we feed the most wins.

The flesh wants to fill our natural desires. The flesh would lead us by our feelings, to do whatever we feel like doing. The flesh reacts impulsively and hastily acts without regard for consequences. The flesh leads to the attitude of doing "what I want when I want." Following the flesh leads us to sinful territory such as selfishness, pride, unforgiveness, anger, excess, and addictions. When we give in to our flesh, it becomes stronger and gains more control in our lives.

However, when we deny our flesh and feed the Spirit, we can walk in freedom and victory over the flesh that hinders our spiritual growth. We can feed the Spirit through prayer, Bible study, and Christ-centered fellowship with other believers. When we follow the leading of the Holy Spirit, then the Spirit becomes stronger inside of us. With God's help, we can deny the flesh and keep in step with the Spirit.

Dear Heavenly Father, I pray for your help that I may walk by the Spirit and that I will not gratify the desires of the flesh. In Jesus' name, amen.

February 22

Putting Others First

"Do nothing out of selfish ambition or vain conceit. Rather, in humility value others above yourselves, not looking to your own interests but each of you to the interests of the others."
Philippians 2:3–4

We tend to look out for ourselves first. We work hard to get ahead. There is nothing wrong with having goals to do better for ourselves. However, there is a mindset that can develop wherein we think only of ourselves and do not care about others. This attitude of just looking out for number one is worldly. As Christians, our primary purpose is not to serve ourselves but the Lord first and others as well. It is our selfishness that keeps us thinking about what is best for ourselves. Selfish ambition will lead us to push our own interests forward with no concern for others. It is like running people over on our road to success. Vain conceit is that desire to pump up our ego about what a great person we are or how great an accomplishment we have achieved. It can lead us to seek our own glory when our goal should be to glorify God!

Selfishness is the opposite quality of love. To love the Lord and others as ourselves is our high calling as Christians. We cannot allow the attitude of selfish ambition to creep into our lives. We need to be intentional about putting others first. This takes humility as well as love. We can still work hard while being mindful of other people and intentionally bless others instead of seeking to bless ourselves first. With God's help, we can value others above ourselves.

Dear Heavenly Father, help me today to do nothing out of selfish ambition or vain conceit. Help me to value others above myself, not looking to my own interests but also to the interests of others. In Jesus' name, amen.

February 23

Water Baptism

"We were therefore buried with him through baptism into death in order that, just as Christ was raised from the dead through the glory of the Father, we too may live a new life."
Romans 6:4

Water baptism is one of two ordinances that are based on Scripture and practiced in the church. The other is communion or the Lord's Supper. They are symbolic representations of spiritual realities practiced prayerfully and reverently in the church, following the teaching of Scripture and by Jesus' words and example. After we become Christians, we need to be water baptized because it is something that Jesus said to do.

Water baptism is an outward expression of an inward spiritual reality. When we asked Jesus to forgive us of our sins and we accepted Jesus as our Lord and Savior, we followed him in death to our sinful life. Just as Jesus died on the cross, we died to our life of sin. Just as Jesus rose from the dead, we have followed him in new life, gaining victory over sin in this life and the promise of eternal life in heaven. Water baptism symbolizes this miraculous salvation that has taken place in our lives as a public testimony of the saving grace of our Lord Jesus. We go down submerged in the water to symbolize death and burial. We come up out of the water to symbolize the resurrection of Jesus and the new life we have in Christ. Once we have become water-baptized, every day is a celebration of the new life we have in Christ. We can celebrate the new life we have in Jesus today.

Dear Jesus, I thank you that you died on the cross for my sins and rose from the dead for my new life into eternity. Help me to celebrate the new life you have given me today by bringing you glory. In your name, amen.

54

February 24

God Will Never Leave You

"Keep your lives free from the love of money and be content with what you have, because God has said, 'Never will I leave you; never will I forsake you.'" Hebrews 13:5

We do not need to be chasing after money or anything else to make us happy because we have God in our lives! We can experience true contentment in our personal relationship with Jesus Christ. God can satisfy the longings of our souls. We try to fill that hunger in our soul by different means such as wealth, relationships, or pleasure, only to find that those things do not truly satisfy us and we will always want more. We can experience true contentment and peace through the love of God in our lives. That relationship with the Lord is more valuable than riches or anything else that this world can offer. We may not be rich with material possessions but we have the riches of God's steadfast love in our lives.

It is a rare treasure to find someone who will never leave us nor forsake us. We have had our share of fair-weathered friends, those who were there for us when we were doing good, but then were nowhere to be found when we were in our time of need. God is not like that. He is always there for us. In our darkest moments, when we feel that we are all alone, we are *not* alone because God will never leave us. Despite our failures or shortcomings, no matter how bad we mess things up, in the midst of our failure, God is there. He will never forsake us. We may have burned all of our bridges and pushed everyone who cared for us away, but God's love never fails. His love endures forever. God's love does not quit! We can be comforted and strengthened today knowing that God will never leave us nor forsake us.

Dear Heavenly Father, I thank you that you will never leave me nor forsake me. I love you Lord and I thank you for your steadfast love. In Jesus' name, amen.

February 25

New Every Morning

"Because of the LORD's great love we are not consumed, for his compassions never fail. They are new every morning; great is your faithfulness." Lamentations 3:22–23

No matter how difficult life may be, we can always be grateful for God's great love. God loved us so much that he sent his Son, Jesus, to die on the cross to save us from our sins. He rose from the dead to give us new life and hope for eternity. We are not judged for our sins because Jesus saved us. We are not getting the punishment our sins deserve. Because of God's great love, we are not consumed. That places the challenges of our day in perspective. We can walk in God's love today and love him back with our lives.

The Lord's compassions never fail. His love is steadfast and unconditional. We do not have to earn the love of the Lord. His compassions are new every morning. As the dew refreshes the grass each morning, God's new mercies and compassions refresh us and renew us each day. They are new every morning. This is not the compassion from yesterday, God has new mercy for us every new day. It does not matter what happened yesterday. Every day is an opportunity for a new beginning with God. He does not hold on to resentment or bitterness, criticism or condemnation toward us; he has new mercies for us today. We do not have to walk in the guilt and shame of our sins. We are free from the power of sin in our lives because of the love of God and the forgiveness we have received through Jesus Christ.

Dear Heavenly Father, I thank you that because of your great love we are not consumed, for your compassions never fail. They are new every morning. Great is your faithfulness.
In Jesus' name, amen.

February 26

Dedicated and Devoted

"They devoted themselves to the apostles' teaching and to fellowship, to the breaking of bread and to prayer."
Acts 2:42

This description of the early church sets an example for Christians today. There are four elements of their participation mentioned: the apostles' teaching, fellowship, the breaking of bread, and prayer. The apostles' teaching is a reference to the proclamation and teaching of the Word of God and the gospel of Jesus Christ. Fellowship signifies the Christ-centered relationships they shared. The breaking of bread is likely a reference to the Lord's Supper. The last element mentioned is prayer. Prayer is a key practice in the Christian life. We pray individually as well as corporately, together as a body of believers. These four practices are not an exhaustive description of the Christian church but remain key elements in our Christian life today. The members of the early church were devoted to these practices. We need to be devoted to our relationship with Jesus and to our spiritual disciplines such as those described here. To be devoted Christians means that our relationship with the Lord is a top priority in our lives. We will miss out on other less important activities and interests because our relationship with God comes first. To be devoted means we have a strong commitment to our adherence to the Word of God, our relationship with God, and our Christian life. To be devoted means that we do not give up during difficult times, but we continue in faithfulness no matter what may interfere with our abilities because our relationship with the Lord and participation in the church is extremely valuable to us. Our heart is in it. We are all in. We are devoted.

Dear Lord, I am devoted to you. Help me to practice that devotion in my spiritual disciplines, my lifestyle, and my participation in church. In Jesus' name, amen.

February 27

A Complete Turnaround

"From that time on Jesus began to preach, 'Repent, for the kingdom of heaven has come near.'" Matthew 4:17

Repentance was a theme in Jesus' message and continues to be a relevant theme for us today. This message, simply put, is to say, "Stop sinning and turn to God!" Repentance is a process of turning away from sin and toward God. Repentance is much more than saying "I am sorry." It goes beyond the feeling of remorse for our sin and expressing an apology. That may be a good place to start, but it is just the beginning of repentance. To repent is to make a "U-turn," to go in the opposite direction than we were going. It is not about simply stopping the sinful behavior, but most importantly, now turning to the Lord and strengthening that relationship with him. Repentance involves change. The changes we make when we repent are not limited to our behavior or how we act but involve changes in the way we think. Repentance is "an inside job." God changes us from the inside out. When God changes the way we think, then he will change the way we act. Yes, there is an effort on our part, but repentance and change are not experiences we can muster up in our own strength. It is a spiritual phenomenon that comes from the Spirit of God. God can change our hearts. Our behavior is just the tip of the iceberg. Repentance is better understood as a process than as a single act. We may say, "I messed up, but I repented." However, that repentance needs to be demonstrated in a lifestyle. Repentance will change the way we live! God wants to help us in this process. We are not alone. The Lord will bless our effort to stop sinful behavior and receive strength from him to persevere in a new way of life and not turn back!

Dear Lord, I repent from my sin. I pray for your help to continue to turn from sin and draw closer to you. Change my heart by your Holy Spirit. In Jesus' name, amen.

February 28

Reverse the Cycle

"When tempted, no one should say, 'God is tempting me.' For God cannot be tempted by evil, nor does he tempt anyone; but each person is tempted when they are dragged away by their own evil desire and enticed. Then, after desire has conceived, it gives birth to sin; and sin, when it is full-grown, gives birth to death." James 1:13–15

God will not tempt us. He is good, not evil. He has no evil in him. He loves us and brings good, not evil into our lives. Our temptation to sin does not come from God. Our sinful temptations may be coming from within ourselves, from our own sinful nature and desires. When we dwell on our desires rather than turning to the Lord for fulfillment and trusting him to meet our needs, those desires grow stronger. Desires can become strong enough that we give in to them even when we know the desire is sinful. Then sin itself also grows. It has a progressive nature to it. Like a snowball starting to roll down a hill, it gets bigger and faster as it goes. The sin in our lives will also grow to the point of no control. Like cancer that spreads throughout the body, sin spreads to the different areas of our lives. It affects our relationships, our jobs, our health, and more. The path of sin leads to death.

The good news is that just as sin leads to death; God brings life through Jesus Christ. Just as sin brings destruction, the Lord brings restoration. He can turn our lives around when we turn to him. The Lord will help us to resist the evil desires that lead to sin when we turn to him. With God's help, we can be free from the bondage of sin.

Dear Lord, I pray for your help to resist the evil desires that lead to sin. I turn to you to meet my needs. I trust you and I find satisfaction in your love. In Jesus' name, amen.

February 29

Words and Thoughts

"May these words of my mouth and this meditation of my heart be pleasing in your sight, Lord, my Rock and my Redeemer."
Psalm 19:14

We can please and honor the Lord not just by what we do, but also by what we say and what we think. This prayer focuses on pleasing and honoring the Lord with our words and our thoughts. With God's help, we can be more aware of our words and our thoughts. We can recognize thoughts and words that are not pure and godly. Examples of words that would not please the Lord include complaining, gossip, unwholesome or crude talk or jokes, offensive words, divisive words, insults, and explicit details of violence, sex, or evil. With God's help, we can stop ourselves before ungodly words roll out of our mouths. We can check our hearts and turn to the Lord for help in prayer even as we struggle with our words. Instead of saying unwholesome words, we can say things that honor the Lord and build up and positively bless other people. We can be a blessing and an encouragement to others with our words rather than be a stumbling block and bring other people down.

With the Lord's help, we can also monitor our thoughts. Our words and our actions begin in our thoughts so we need to be aware of our thought life and take responsibility to cast down ungodly or unwholesome thoughts. We can overcome ungodly thoughts with the Word of God to think pure, positive, and productive thoughts that will lead to words and actions that please the Lord as well.

Dear Lord, may these words of my mouth and this meditation of my heart be pleasing in your sight, Lord, my Rock, and my Redeemer. In Jesus' name, amen.

March 1

Blessed in Brokenness

"My sacrifice, O God, is a broken spirit; a broken and contrite heart you, God, will not despise." Psalm 51:17

We are not going to win God over by trying to impress him with good deeds. We will not gain his favor through our accomplishments. We will not gain his compassion or earn his forgiveness by making sacrifices. The sacrifice for our sins has been made through the death of our Lord and Savior Jesus Christ. We need to come to the Lord with the honest need for which that sacrifice was made. The Lord already knows our sins. He knows everything about us. We are being honest with ourselves when we admit our brokenness and our need for the Lord's love and compassion. To be broken before the Lord is to let go of our pride and any façade that we have it all together. We become transparent before the Lord and admit what a mess we are and how much we need him. It takes humility to experience brokenness, to admit to ourselves and God that we have problems and that we need help. It does not feel pleasant at the time, but broken before the Lord is a wonderful place to be. God is so rich in love and compassion for us that our brokenness draws him to us. He wants to draw near to us and love us when we are in a place of brokenness before him. On the contrary, we keep him at a distance when we act like we do not need him. Jesus came for broken people, not for people who have it all together. God specializes in healing brokenness and putting back together the pieces of broken lives. We are blessed in our brokenness because of his great mercy, compassion, and love.

Dear Lord, you do not delight in sacrifice or I would bring it; you do not take pleasure in burnt offerings. My sacrifice to you, God, is a broken spirit; a broken and contrite heart, O God, you will not despise. In Jesus' name, amen.

March 2

The Mother Heart of God

"As a mother comforts her child, so will I comfort you; and you will be comforted over Jerusalem." Isaiah 66:13

Much is said about the Father heart of God. He is our Creator. He has authority. He has wisdom. He provides for us. He is strong and faithful. He disciplines us like a loving father does. He loves us with the heart of a father. The Lord is also capable of loving us with the heart of a mother. There is a unique love that a mother has for her children. Nobody's love can compare to the endearing love that a mother has for her child. This love is unashamedly, very clearly, and emotionally expressed. There is no mistaking a mother's love because she will not hold back. A mother's love is compassionate, comforting, and nurturing. Even when that child becomes an adult, a mother's love does not change. That adult will always be her child whom she loves. God also loves us with this motherly love. When we are hurting, he wants to be close to us and bring healing to our hurts with his love. His loving presence also comforts us when we are afraid or feel alone. His love casts away all our fears. He wants us to know that we are never alone and that his presence can comfort us. As a mother lovingly comforts a child and wipes the child's tears away, God also gently and lovingly comforts us with tenderness when we are weak and fragile. He knows what we need and is there with nurturing love when we need that. Just as a mother's love is faithful, God's love does not change. We will always be his children that he loves. He will always see and believe in our good. He always wants and believes in the best for us. A father's love and a mother's love are mere reflections of the unfathomable, everlasting love that God has for us.

Dear Lord, I thank you that as a mother comforts her child, you love and comfort me. Thank you for your love that endures forever. In Jesus' name, amen.

March 3

Our True Friend

"I no longer call you servants, because a servant does not know his master's business. Instead, I have called you friends, for everything that I learned from my Father I have made known to you." John 15:15

Jesus calls us friends. He said that everything that he learned from the Father he shared with us. This describes some of the characteristics of friendship: sharing and communicating.

Friends share things in common. Jesus can identify with us because he became a man and lived life on Earth. He is not detached from us or our lives. He knows what it is like to live and love and have friends. He also knows what it is like to be hurt. He was tempted in every way that we are, yet he was without sin. He gave his life to save us from our sins. He knows what it is like to go through struggles. Jesus desires to share those experiences with us and be there with us as our friend as we share life with him.

Jesus has communicated with us through his story in the Gospel accounts. We can read all of his teachings and understand how he wants us to live life. He helps us to make decisions because of the values we learn from his teaching. Jesus also led by example. We get to know how he lived and he helps us to become more like him. He continues to communicate in our hearts through the Holy Spirit. We communicate with him every day through our prayer and Bible reading. We know he is present with us throughout the day. We share life with Jesus as we do with a close friend. Jesus is there for us. He wants to have a closer friendship with us today.

Dear Jesus, I worship you as my Lord and Savior. Thank you that you have called me your friend. Help me to have a closer friendship with you today. In your name, amen.

63

March 4

A Hedge of Thorns

"Therefore I will block her path with thornbushes; I will wall her in so that she cannot find her way." Hosea 2:6

The prophet Hosea's wife left him to go back to her life of prostitution. In this verse, the Lord states that he would block her path with thornbushes and wall her in so she could not find her way. The Lord can make the way of the transgressor hard so that person will stop in their rebellious ways and return to the Lord. The Lord desires for those who turn from him in rebelliousness to turn back to him in repentance and be restored to a right relationship with him.

The Lord can place "thornbushes" in the path of the person who has turned from him. These thornbushes may come in many ways, such as relationship problems, financial ruin, or an arrest. The Lord can provide an intervention in the path of the rebellious person to get their attention so they will stop in their rebellious ways and turn back to him.

If we are praying for a loved one who has turned from the Lord, we can pray that the Lord will put a hedge of thorns in their path so that they will stop in their sin and return to the Lord. We also need to pay attention to the thornbushes the Lord may put in our paths if we are getting off track with him.

Dear Heavenly Father, I thank you that you love me so much that you place thornbushes in my path when I wander from you. Dear Lord, I pray for the person that has turned away from you, that you would block their path with thornbushes and that you will wall them in so that they cannot find their way. I pray that you will draw them back to you with your love.
In Jesus' name, amen.

March 5

Formula for Success

"Keep this Book of the Law always on your lips; meditate on it day and night, so that you may be careful to do everything written in it. Then you will be prosperous and successful."
Joshua 1:8

The Lord emphasizes three practices regarding his Word in this verse: talk about it; think about it; and just do it! Talking about the Word of God is a spiritual strength in building healthy Christ-centered relationships with others. Talk about what you are reading in devotions, or the passage you heard taught in church. We need to bring God's Word out in the open in our conversations with other people.

When we think about God's Word, we increase the effect of God's Word on our lives. The Lord will use his Word to impact our daily lives and become the basis of our decisions. The more we think about the Word of God, the greater the influence his Word can have on our beliefs and attitudes. The more we meditate on the Word of God, the more it can be hidden in our hearts and be part of who we are.

When we are practicing God's Word in our daily lives, we are taking the important step of obedience. The other two practices lead to this. Application is the most important step in our Bible study! This is the key to our success. The Lord will help us to live our lives according to his Word. Talk about it, think about and then just do it!

Dear Heavenly Father, help me today to keep your Word always on my lips, to meditate on it day and night so that I may be careful to do everything written it. Help me today to talk about your Word, to think about your Word, and then just do it!
In Jesus' name, amen.

March 6

You Are Invited

"Come to me, all you who are weary and burdened, and I will give you rest. Take my yoke upon you and learn from me, for I am gentle and humble in heart, and you will find rest for your souls. For my yoke is easy and my burden is light."
Matthew 11:28–30

Life is not easy. The responsibilities and difficulties of life can wear us down. We do not have to deal with life alone and in our own strength. When we are tired and worn out, Jesus invites us to come to him and he will give us rest. Jesus says, "Take my yoke upon you...." A yoke is a piece of farm equipment that keeps two animals connected to each other. Jesus is simply describing the connection that we have in a personal relationship with him. When we become connected with Jesus, he makes life easier for us, not harder. He makes our burdens lighter, not heavier. He connects with us to help us, not hurt us. He is humble and gentle in heart. He loves us and wants to help us. He will give us rest, not only in our bodies but in our souls as well. There is a place deep within us that Jesus will heal and love and refresh when we accept his invitation to come to him. When we become exhausted because we are trying to do things with our own strength, when we are so discouraged that we feel like we just cannot go on, when we become tired of feeling sick and tired, Jesus invites us: "Come to me."

Dear Jesus, I am tired and weary. I come to you today and ask for rest in my soul. Put your yoke on me, for you are gentle and humble in heart. Your yoke is easy and your burden is light. In Jesus' name, amen.

March 7

Beauty for Ashes

"The Spirit of the Sovereign Lord is on me, because the Lord has anointed me to proclaim good news to the poor. He has sent me to bind up the brokenhearted, to proclaim freedom for the captives and release from darkness for the prisoners, to proclaim the year of the Lord's favor and the day of vengeance of our God, to comfort all who mourn, and provide for those who grieve in Zion—to bestow on them a crown of beauty instead of ashes, the oil of joy instead of mourning, and a garment of praise instead of a spirit of despair...."
Isaiah 61:1–3

In the Gospel according to Luke, Jesus reads this passage from the prophet Isaiah aloud in the synagogue. When Jesus was done, he said, "Today this scripture is fulfilled in your hearing." In other words, Jesus was saying, "This was written about me!" Jesus came to fulfill the ministry described in this passage. This was accomplished for us when Jesus, the eternal God, became a man, lived a sinless life, died on the cross for the penalty of our sins, and rose from the dead victoriously over death, sin, and Satan.

When we ask Jesus to forgive us of our sins and accept him as Lord and Savior, he begins this transformation in our lives: he sets us free, he heals our broken hearts, he comforts us for our sorrow and loss; he turns the ashes of our past into beauty with a new life. He gives us joy for our sadness, and praise instead of despair! This is usually a process that does not happen overnight. It occurs through the Holy Spirit as we develop a personal relationship with Jesus. Our trust and hope are in the Lord as he makes this beautiful transformation in our lives. Jesus is making it happen!

Dear Jesus, I thank you that you heal my broken heart and that you set me free from the captivity and darkness of sin. I thank you that you give me beauty for ashes, joy for mourning, and praise for despair. In your precious name, amen.

March 8

Stay at Your Post

"If a ruler's anger rises against you, do not leave your post; calmness can lay great offenses to rest." Ecclesiastes 10:4

It is easy to become upset when another person is angry with us. When we react emotionally, this often intensifies the situation. Our emotions may get the best of us and we might make hasty decisions. With the Lord's help, we can respond calmly rather than react emotionally.

In a workplace scenario, a boss or supervisor may be correcting us for something we did or did not do correctly. We can help resolve this situation by remaining calm and staying at our post. We do not react by quitting our jobs! We prayerfully keep doing what we have always done.

When we are in conflict situations with family or friends, we may want to stop doing things we would normally do because we are upset. This reaction adds life to the conflict and makes the situation worse, not better. We continue to do what we have always done. We avoid the temptation to pull back and withdraw. We do not start canceling plans. If we have always done nice things, we continue to do those things even when the other person is angry with us. If we always say, "Good morning!", we keep saying it. If we have plans for lunch, we do not cancel them. We keep doing what is right. We stay at our post. Calmness can lay great errors to rest.

Dear Lord, when another person's anger rises against me, I pray for your help to stay at my post and remain calm. I pray for your peace and calmness to lay offenses to rest.
In Jesus' name, amen.

March 9

Our Triune God

"May the grace of the Lord Jesus Christ, and the love of God, and the fellowship of the Holy Spirit be with you all."
2 Corinthians 13:14

We believe in the Holy Trinity. God eternally co-exists in the Father, the Son, and the Holy Spirit. These three members of the Godhead are separate but equal in authority. The word "trinity" is not used in the Bible, but the reality of this concept is presented and described throughout the Scriptures. We accept the reality of the Holy Trinity by faith and believe in the teaching of the Scripture in this matter. We also experience the existence of the three members of the Trinity in our spiritual relationship with God.

In his letter to the church in Corinth, Paul wrote a benediction, or a closing prayer and blessing. Rather than simply writing "God bless you," Paul specified a blessing from each member of the Holy Trinity. He prayed for the grace of Jesus Christ, the love of God, and the fellowship of the Holy Spirit. Paul was calling out for a specific attribute from each member of the Holy Trinity. Each member of the Trinity has his distinct attributes and ministry in our lives. God is three in one. He has a relationship with us through the Father, the Son, and the Holy Spirit. As we study the Scriptures, and develop our spiritual relationship with the Lord, we draw closer to each of the three members of the Trinity and their distinct roles in the Bible and our lives.

Dear Lord, I pray for the grace of my Lord Jesus Christ, the love of God, and the fellowship of the Holy Spirit in my life today. In Jesus' name, amen.

March 10

Jesus Gets Us

"For we do not have a high priest who is unable to empathize with our weaknesses, but we have one who has been tempted in every way, just as we are—yet he did not sin."
Hebrews 4:15

There is a powerful connection between two people who have had the same experience. A person recovering from drug addiction has a connection with another person struggling with drug addiction. A person who has survived cancer has a unique connection with another person who is fighting cancer. Jesus has a similar powerful connection with us when it comes to our struggle against sin. It is awesome that this is identified in Scripture because even some people come across like they do not struggle with sin as much as we do. That is one of the reasons why it is difficult to talk about our struggle with sin. We feel embarrassed or ashamed of ourselves. It seems like others do not have these same problems so we feel like maybe there is something wrong with us. Let's get the record straight. We all have struggles with sin. We are all messed up without the grace of God in our lives. The Bible does not shy back from saying that Jesus was tempted in every way that we are, yet he remained without sin. He understands our struggles and our temptations. He loves us. He is on our side. He came to help us with our struggles. He died on the cross to forgive us for our sins. He wants to help us overcome them. We can live free from the bondage of sin with his help. Jesus is present for us to pray and talk about our struggle because he knows what that temptation feels like. Jesus gets us.

Dear Jesus, I thank you that you are able to empathize with my weaknesses, that you were tempted in every way, just as I am, yet you were without sin. I confess my sin to you and I pray for your help to overcome the temptation to sin in my life.
In Jesus' name, amen.

March 11

Gateway to Victory

"No temptation has overtaken you except what is common to mankind. And God is faithful; he will not let you be tempted beyond what you can bear. But when you are tempted, he will also provide a way out so that you can endure it."
1 Corinthians 10:13

Temptation is the thought we have before we follow through with the action. Even if it was for a split second, we thought about what we were going to do before we did it. Temptations are deceiving. Somehow we think it is okay, even beneficial, to do something even when it will cause us to break God's laws. Temptation is like the bait on the fisherman's hook. The sin seems desirable at the moment. Only after the fact do we realize we have become disobedient and set ourselves up for negative consequences.

With God's help, we can overcome temptation. We do not have to give in every time we are tempted to do something wrong. Everyone has temptations, they are common to all people. The Lord provides help to overcome temptation. God can help us to stop and consider our thoughts before acting impulsively. We can overcome temptation with the Word of God. We can prepare ourselves by memorizing Scripture that deals with the area we get tempted in. The Holy Spirit inside of us will also develop the fruit of self-control. We can be mindful of the Lord's way out of the temptation. He will always make a way for us. God is faithful. Temptation does not have to be the gateway to sin. Temptation is our gateway to victory.

Dear Lord, I thank you that no temptation has taken me except what is common to man. And you are faithful, God, you will not let me be tempted beyond what I can bear. But when I am tempted, you will also provide a way out so that I can endure it. In Jesus' name, amen.

71

March 12

Stay Focused

"Let your eyes look straight ahead; fix your gaze directly before you. Give careful thought to the paths for your feet and be steadfast in all your ways. Do not turn to the right or the left; keep your foot from evil." Proverbs 4:25–27

It is so easy to become distracted. Whether we are at work, in school, or in a conversation with a friend or loved one, we do best when we are fully focused on what we are doing. We can become distracted by things we see around us, things we hear, or even thoughts that pop up in our minds that cause us to think about something other than what we are doing. Media and electronics such as the TV, our phones, and computers are huge sources of distraction for many of us. Even when our task at hand requires electronics, we can become distracted by social media, videos, or news stories online. We are better at whatever we are doing when we are 100% focused on it, instead of our thoughts being distracted and divided.

Similarly, staying focused is very important in our spiritual walk and relationship with Jesus. The world around us and our flesh will try to distract us from the things of God. We need to be intentional about keeping in step with the Spirit of God and also basing our thoughts, decisions, and actions on the Word of God. We need to stay focused to avoid getting off track of God's path of victory and success. A distraction could be the beginning of losing victory in an area of our lives. We need to keep our eyes on Jesus and stay focused on his will for us today.

Dear Lord, help me to keep my eyes focused straight ahead, to fix my gaze directly before me. Help me to give careful thought to the paths of my feet and to be steadfast in all of my ways. Help me to not turn to the right or the left. Keep my feet from evil. In Jesus' name, amen.

March 13

Freedom from Worrying

"So do not worry, saying, 'What shall we eat?' or 'What shall we drink?' or 'What shall we wear?' For the pagans run after all these things, and your heavenly Father knows that you need them. But seek first his kingdom and his righteousness, and all these things will be given to you as well."
Matthew 6:31–33

Jesus exhorts us to stop worrying! We think so much about our concerns that it preoccupies us. Worrying can have a negative impact on us. It affects our mood; we are stressed out instead of peaceful because we think too much about things. This could even lead to health issues such as muscle tension, headaches, or stomach problems, all because we worry so much. Our worrying does not solve anything. It only has a negative impact, not a positive impact.

We do not have to worry because our loving Heavenly Father knows about our needs and he can meet those needs. We can pray and cast our cares onto the Lord. Then we trust his goodness, his love, and his faithfulness to meet our needs. Our faith will help us to entrust our concerns to the Lord and have his peace. Our fears and doubts will tempt us to worry. Jesus presents this spiritual principle: seek God and his kingdom first, and then all these things will be added to you. He is a powerful and loving God. He knows all of our needs and loves us so much that he will take care of those needs. When we put God first in our lives, he takes care of everything else. We can trust him. We can stop worrying! When we can give him our worries, he can give us his peace.

Dear Heavenly Father, help me to stop worrying. You know my needs and the concerns in my heart. Today I seek first your kingdom and your righteousness, trusting all my concerns into your hands. I love you and I trust you. In Jesus' name, amen.

March 14

Choose What's More Important

"Do not wear yourself out to get rich; do not trust your own cleverness. Cast but a glance at riches, and they are gone, for they will surely sprout wings and fly off to the sky like an eagle."
Proverbs 23:4–5

Material things come and go. It is not worth it to wear ourselves out for the sake of money or material things. A person who struggles with greed or selfish ambition may wear themselves out to get rich. This person thrives on materialism, money, or ambition to find a sense of happiness. It is as if money or work becomes a drug that people can get addicted to. However, our society has also adopted a work-driven culture that has made it the norm for us to become worn out for the sake of work. We can make the mistake of seeking a sense of identity from our work. Our job is what we do, it is not who we are. It is great to have a sense of fulfillment or satisfaction in our work, but as Christians, our identity is in Christ, not in our jobs.

It may feel like we need to wear ourselves out at our jobs just to make a living and support our family. We can make choices to live a balanced life so that our job is not interfering with our health, our faith, or our relationships with our loved ones. We can keep our lifestyle in congruence with our values. We will pour our time and effort into that which is most important to us. We do not want to allow our jobs to interfere with our faith or our family. We need to remember our priorities: our relationship with God needs to come first, then our family, then our job or ministry. Let's remember what's most important.

*Dear Heavenly Father, help me to live a balanced life and not wear myself out to get rich, help me to focus on the true riches I have in my relationships with you and with my family.
In Jesus' name, amen.*

March 15

More of Him, Less of Me

"He must become greater; I must become less."
John 3:30

These words of John the Baptist are a call for all Christians. God must become greater; we must become less. When we ask Jesus to forgive us of our sins and accept him as our Lord and Savior, we are forgiven, we are freed from the penalty of our sins, and we become citizens of heaven. There is also a process of transformation that takes place in our lives and will continue until we are in the Lord's presence. God changes us and conforms us to his image. This is a spiritual transformation that takes place through the power of the Holy Spirit in our lives. This is also a collaborative process that we participate in with the Lord. We choose to surrender our lives totally to him. We choose to stop doing things our way and agree to do things God's way. We commit to live in obedience to his Word. We allow the truth in his Word to change the way we think. We choose to cultivate our relationship with the Lord through the practice of our spiritual disciplines such as prayer, Bible reading, and church attendance. The Lord blesses that position by working in our lives by his grace. We cannot live this Christian life without his grace and his help. The Holy Spirit cleanses us and helps us stop selfish habits. The Lord develops the fruit of his Holy Spirit in our lives. The Lord gives us his attributes so that we are more like him. The Lord cleanses us of unrighteousness and he imparts his love, his goodness, his patience, and his kindness in our lives. The Lord gives us fulfillment in our souls that we could never experience on our own. Our attitude changes from "It's all about me" to "It's all about you, Lord." He must become greater; we must become less.

Dear Lord, today I pray for more of you and less of me. You must become greater; I must become less. In Jesus' name, amen.

March 16

God Is Faithful

"The one who calls you is faithful, and he will do it."
1 Thessalonians 5:24

Faithfulness is an attribute of God. The faithfulness of God means that we can count on him. God does not say one thing and then do another. God is not a human who would not follow through with his Word for some reason. We can stand on the promises of God because of God's faithfulness. He is reliable and dependable. People change their minds about things, but God does not change. The Lord will not wake up in a bad mood and decide not to be faithful one day. He is stable and steadfast. God's faithfulness means he is loyal and trustworthy. We can trust in the Lord. We feel safe trusting him because he has already proven to be faithful. When we know we can trust God we have peace because we have placed our concerns and our lives into his hands. It is freeing to trust in his faithfulness because we do not have to worry or fret about things. When we look back at our lives and the trials that God has brought us through, we see that it was his faithfulness that got us through difficult times. Just as the Lord was faithful in those trials in our past, he is faithful to handle the trials we are facing today and he will be faithful to handle our future. We do not have the resources to tackle the challenges in front of us in our own strength. We wonder how we will ever make it through some challenges. The answer is God's faithfulness! He will see us through whatever challenges we face. Nothing is impossible with God. God's faithfulness is our resource to walk forward in faith with peace and confidence in him.

Dear Heavenly Father, you are faithful. You do not change. Your Word is true. My heart is at peace because I trust in you.
In Jesus' name, amen.

March 17

Blessed

"The LORD bless you and keep you; the LORD make his face shine on you and be gracious to you; the LORD turn his face toward you and give you peace." Numbers 6:24–26

The Lord gave this prayer to Moses to share with his brother Aaron to share with the priests to pray over the people. It is known as the priestly prayer or the priestly blessing. As God's people, we can read this in God's Word and receive it in our lives. We can have God's blessing on our lives every day! God has blessed us so much! God's blessings are new every morning. He blesses us with prosperity in our lives. We prosper beyond material blessings with the fullness of life and love in our relationships with God and others. When God keeps us, we have perseverance to not give up and we do not turn back! When God's face turns toward us and shines on us, we have his light and love and favor. The favor of God in our lives brings supernatural blessings for us that are unexplainable. Results that seem impossible are easily accomplished because God makes them happen in our lives. When God is gracious to us, we enjoy good things in life that we did not earn and do not deserve. We are blessed with the grace of God in our lives every day. When God blesses us with his peace, we can face difficult and busy days with strength in our hearts that God is with us and he will see us through whatever we are facing. We have these blessings from God every day in our relationship with him. We can receive these blessings from the Lord, and then let our lives be a reflection of God's blessing that in turn blesses God and blesses other people.

Dear Heavenly Father, I thank you that you bless me and keep me, that you make your face shine upon me, and you are gracious to me, that you turn your face toward me, and give me your peace. In Jesus' name, amen.

March 18

Hungry for God

"So we fasted and petitioned our God about this, and he answered our prayer." Ezra 8:23

The practice of fasting is found throughout the Bible. Fasting refers to skipping meals as a spiritual discipline. The spiritual strength of fasting is found when it is accompanied by prayer. Without prayer, fasting is just a diet. The time normally spent for a meal can be spent in extra time of focused prayer. Fasting is an expression of self-denial. It is to say, "God, I need you right now more than anything else, I hunger for you more than I hunger for food." Fasting can strengthen our ability to deny the appetite of our sinful desires by putting our flesh in check. Fasting can be practiced personally on our own, or corporately with others. Fasting is an expression of humbling ourselves before the Lord and expressing our dependence on him. Occasions for fasting in the Bible include repentance, mourning, seeking guidance, seeking favor, and seeking God in a closer way. Fasting can be a part of our spiritual practice today. The principle of fasting may be carried out in areas of our lives other than meals. For example, we can practice self-denial by fasting from TV or social media. We can also practice a partial fast by fasting certain foods like meats or desserts. Fasting from all foods can be practiced by fasting just one meal, rather than taking on long-term fasts. Before fasting, it is important to consider our health and any limitations fasting would bring about physically that may interfere with our abilities during the day. Whatever way we choose to fast becomes empowered when it is accompanied by extra time in prayer.

Dear Lord, I hunger for you, God. I desire you more than anyone or anything else in this life. Fill the hunger in my soul with more of you. In Jesus' name, amen.

March 19

To Be Like Jesus

"In your relationships with one another, have the same mindset as Christ Jesus" Philippians 2:5

To be Christlike in our relationships with others is the challenge and the goal for all Christians. Jesus sets an example for us of how he interacted with others. Jesus loved people. He was criticized for being a friend of "sinners." Jesus was accepting of others; he was not judgmental. He was approachable and took time for others. Jesus was kind and forgiving toward others. He was compassionate toward others when they needed help. He had the gift of mercy and he showed grace to people who had problems.

Jesus is alive today and we are blessed to have a relationship with him. We know his love, mercy, and forgiveness firsthand. These qualities that Jesus has are qualities that we can share with others as well. We can be a reflection of the love of Christ by becoming more Christlike ourselves. We can show others the same love, mercy, and forgiveness that Jesus has shown us. God will help us to develop Christlike qualities toward other people. We can learn to slow down and take time for people. We can be more accepting of others for the sake of Christ even when they seem different from us. Those who are different from us are still people that Jesus loves. We can practice compassion and mercy toward others rather than being caught up in our own world and not seeing the needs of others around us. We can show the grace of Jesus Christ by blessing others with kindness and goodness when they do not deserve it. After all, that is the way he treated us.

Dear Jesus I want to be more like you. Help me to have your mindset in my relationships with others. Help me to share your love. I pray that others will see you in me by the way I treat them. In Jesus' name, amen.

79

March 20

The Springtime of Life

"See! The winter is past; the rains are over and gone. Flowers appear on the earth; the season of singing has come, the cooing of doves is heard in our land." Song of Songs 2:11–12

The beauty of springtime inspires us by the majesty of God's creation. We stand in awe and wonder at the handiwork of God our creator. Lyricist Henry Van Dyke wrote these words set and sung to Beethoven's *Ode to Joy*: "Field and forest, vale and mountain, flowery meadow, flashing sea; chanting bird and flowing fountain, call us to rejoice in thee." Springtime explodes as a celebration of the new life we have in Christ.

The contrast between winter and spring compares to our life before Christ and the new life we have in Christ. We were like winter in our sin: dark and dreary, cold and lifeless. Receiving God's gift of salvation through Jesus Christ brings springtime to our lives. We have a new life in Christ. The Holy Spirit resides in our spirit and brings renewal and hope to our souls. In the same way that springtime brings fresh air, the Holy Spirit refreshes us with new life. We were dead in our sin, now we are alive in Christ. We have a new life in victory over the despair of sin, not only in this life but for eternity.

*Dear Lord, I thank you that the winter of my sinful life has passed and that you have given my life the refreshing beauty of springtime through the new life I have in Jesus Christ.
In Jesus' name, amen.*

March 21

Character Counts

"But Ruth replied, 'Don't urge me to leave you or to turn back from you. Where you go I will go, and where you stay I will stay. Your people will be my people and your God my God.'"
Ruth 1:16

Ruth was a young woman when her husband died. Her mother-in-law, Naomi, also lost her husband. Naomi, who now had neither husband nor sons to provide for her decided to travel from Moab back to Judah to be closer to relatives. She tried to convince Ruth to go back to her parents' house in Moab so that she could be provided for and perhaps find another husband. Ruth refused to leave Naomi. She expressed her dedication and loyalty to stay with Naomi and not leave her during this difficult time in their lives. Rather than thinking about what was best for herself, Ruth was dedicated to supporting her mother-in-law. This selflessness and sacrifice on Ruth's part reveals her godly character. Ruth went on to stay by Naomi's side. Her dedication was noticed by a landowner named Boaz who ended up marrying Ruth and providing for Ruth and Naomi. Boaz and Ruth had a son named Obed, who in turn had a son named Jesse, who was the father of David, king of Israel. It was from David's ancestry that the Messiah, Jesus our Savior, was born. Ruth is an ancestor of Jesus. Ruth's character exemplified her loyalty, dedication, sacrifice, and humility. These core qualities were her strength that impacted her destiny. Our gifts and talents may provide opportunities for us, but it is our character that will sustain us in the long run. The Lord will grant us the fruit of his Spirit and the image of Christ to mold our inner core to be a person of godly character. Our identity is in Christ.

Dear Lord, change me from the inside. Give me the qualities of Christ. Make me a person of godly character.
In Jesus' name, amen.

March 22

Cry Out to the Lord

"Then they cried out to the LORD in their trouble, and he delivered them from their distress." Psalm 107:6

Psalm 107 is a Wisdom Psalm. This is a psalm that teaches a lesson. This psalm is interesting because it tells four stories, one after the other. The four scenarios describe four different types of trouble: banishment, imprisonment, affliction, and storms. In each scenario, the people cry out to the Lord for help and he saves them and delivers them out of trouble.

The first lesson worth noting is that disobedience leads to consequences. We set ourselves up for negative consequences when we become disobedient to the Lord. When we stop doing things God's way and begin doing things our own way, we always get in trouble! God help us to remember that! God helps us to prevent negative consequences and trouble in our lives by staying obedient to God and his Word.

This psalm also teaches us that God is there for us when we cry out to him. It does not matter what type of trouble we are in, or how far down the path of trouble we are. God hears us when we cry out to him and he can deliver us from any trouble. We are never alone. God loves us and he will always be there for us. He will never leave us nor forsake us. When we are hurting, tempted, or in a big mess, we need to remember to cry out to God and he is there for us.

Lord, I thank you that when I cried out to you in my trouble you delivered me from my distress. I give you thanks because you are good and your love endures forever. In Jesus' name, amen.

March 23

Giving to God

"'Bring the whole tithe into the storehouse, that there may be food in my house. Test me in this,' says the LORD Almighty, 'and see if I will not throw open the floodgates of heaven and pour out so much blessing that there will not be room enough to store it.'" Malachi 3:10

One of the ways we worship the Lord is through our giving. Tithing is a biblical measure of giving back to the Lord from the finances he is blessing us with and entrusting to us. To tithe means to give ten percent of our income back to the Lord. This is a trusted biblical guideline and practice in churches today. Our regular tithe is best given to our home church, where we receive our spiritual covering and ministry. Giving to good causes and ministries outside of that is referred to as our offerings. Some people can give more than ten percent. To give sacrificially is to express our worship to the Lord because our giving is valuable to us and means something. Our giving to the Lord will challenge us to live within our means rather than using up all that we have on ourselves. When we give to the Lord, we are thanking him for the many blessings in our lives. Without the blessing and the generous provision of the Lord, we would not have anything. When we give to the Lord, we are trusting him to continue to provide for us. It is at this point that the Lord challenges us. He says, "Test me in this..." Our motive for tithing is not to be blessed, but we are assured of the Lord's blessing as we trust in him. Tithing to our church is an expression of our faith and worship.

Dear Lord, I worship you through my giving. I thank you for your provision. I give my tithe back to you because it is already yours. My faith and trust are in you. In Jesus' name, amen.

March 24

Faithful, Not Flaky

"His master replied, 'Well done, good and faithful servant! You have been faithful with a few things; I will put you in charge of many things. Come and share your master's happiness!'"
Matthew 25:21

Faithfulness is a quality that we, as Christians should demonstrate in our lives. Faithfulness is an attribute of God that should be reflected in our lives as well. In addition, faithfulness is a fruit of the spirit, so this quality will develop as we develop our relationship with the Lord. Christians need to be faithful, not flaky! This is part of our Christian witness. Our reputation as believers should be that people can rely on us and that we do the things we say we will do. This is something we can accomplish with God's help. We can develop consistency and stability in our lives. As Christians we should be reliable in our jobs, showing up on time every day. We also need to develop faithfulness concerning our spiritual relationship with the Lord. We practice faithfulness in our prayer and Bible reading as well as our church attendance.

Jesus brought out a spiritual principle. The one who was faithful with a few things was put in charge of many things. This emphasizes the importance for us to be faithful in the little things. This also shows us that when we have proven faithful with what God has given us, then he can entrust us with more. For example, if we desire a different job, we need to be faithful to the job the Lord has given us; then he can bless us with that new job we want. With the Lord's help, we can develop the quality of faithfulness in our lives!

Dear Lord, I pray that you would develop the fruit of faithfulness in my life. May my life reflect your faithfulness to others. In Jesus' name, amen.

84

March 25

The King of Kings

"Rejoice greatly, Daughter Zion! Shout, Daughter Jerusalem! See, your king comes to you, righteous and victorious, lowly and riding on a donkey, on a colt, the foal of a donkey."
Zechariah 9:9

In the week before his crucifixion, Jesus rode into Jerusalem and was publicly acknowledged as king for the first time. This event, known as the triumphal entry, is recorded in all four Gospel accounts. This event fulfilled the prophecy of Zechariah, written in the Old Testament about 500 years before it took place. Jesus came humbly, not with displayed authority and majesty, not with a lot of pizzazz, not with bling or swag. He came riding on a donkey, a beast of burden, not a magnificent white stallion like a general of an army would ride. This displays the very different nature of Jesus the King and his kingdom. Jesus came to serve and not be served, unlike the majority of leaders in world politics who seek power and prestige for themselves. Jesus' kingdom is not of this world. The kingdom of God is an everlasting kingdom. The crowds gathered and placed their cloaks in front of Jesus and waved palm branches, as was the practice of honoring royalty. This event is recognized in our church calendar as Palm Sunday because of the use of the palm branches to honor Jesus the King. The people shouted "Hosannah," an Aramaic term that means "Save now!" The crowds intended Jesus to save them from the rule of the Roman Empire. Jesus did not come to save them from the tyranny of the Roman rule. Jesus came to save the world from the tyranny of the devil and sin. Jesus is truly our King! He is the King of Kings and Lord of Lords!

Dear Jesus, you are the King of Kings and Lord of Lords! You rule and reign over my life. Your kingdom is an everlasting kingdom. In Jesus' name, amen.

March 26

The Last Supper

"For I received from the Lord what I also passed on to you: The Lord Jesus, on the night he was betrayed, took bread, and when he had given thanks, he broke it and said, 'This is my body, which is for you; do this in remembrance of me.' In the same way, after supper he took the cup, saying, 'This cup is the new covenant in my blood; do this, whenever you drink it, in remembrance of me.'" 1 Corinthians 11:23–25

On the night he was betrayed and arrested, Jesus had this Last Supper with his disciples. This event indicates a major change in the Lord's relationship with mankind. Jesus introduced a new covenant. This marks the difference between the Old Testament and the New Testament. Because of the New Covenant, our right standing with God no longer depends on adherence to the law. The system of sacrificing animals and shedding their blood was done away with. Jesus shed his blood and sacrificed his life for the remission of the sins of the world once and for all. The Last Supper also instituted the practice of Holy Communion as an ordinance of the church. Jesus instructed his disciples to eat the bread and drink the wine in remembrance of his body that was broken and his blood that was shed on the cross. We reverently remember what Jesus did for us on the cross. We prayerfully examine our lives and our relationship with God and others. We also look forward to Jesus' return. We thank God for what Jesus did on the cross to give us new lives here on earth and the promise of eternal life with him in heaven.

Dear Jesus, thank you for sacrificing your life on the cross. I thank you that you gave your body to be broken and that you shed your blood for the forgiveness of my sin. Help me to live my life to honor the sacrifice that you made for me. In your name, amen.

March 27

The Lamb of God

"The next day John saw Jesus coming toward him and said, 'Look, the Lamb of God, who takes away the sin of the world!'"
John 1:29

It is not a coincidence that the death of Jesus on the cross took place during the time that the Passover was being observed. The Passover, celebrated by Jewish people to this day commemorates the miraculous freedom of the Israelites from slavery in Egypt. The Lord inflicted ten plagues upon Egypt to persuade Pharaoh to let the Israelites go. The tenth plague was the death of the firstborn in all of Egypt. The Israelites were instructed to kill a lamb without blemish and put the blood of the lamb on the doorposts of their homes. When the plague of death came through Egypt, it would "pass over" the homes that had the blood of the lamb on their doorposts.

Jesus is the fulfillment of the Passover lamb. He is without spot or blemish because he was without sin. Just as the Passover led to the freedom of the Israelites from their slavery in Egypt, Jesus' death on the cross brought freedom from the power and penalty of sin to the world. Just as death passed over the homes that had the blood of the Passover lamb on their doorposts, those of us who apply the blood of Jesus on the doorposts of our hearts have eternal life. Jesus sacrificed his life to save us and he shed his blood for the forgiveness of our sins. After Jesus died on the cross, he rose from the dead, rising victoriously over death and leading the way for us to have a new life in him. Jesus brought us salvation to eternal life through his death and resurrection.

Dear Jesus, I love you and I worship you! You are the Lamb of God, who takes away the sin of the world! I thank you for your forgiveness, for freedom from the slavery of sin, and for eternal life. In your name, amen.

March 28

A Cross to Bear

"Then he said to them all: 'Whoever wants to be my disciple must deny themselves and take up their cross daily and follow me.'"
Luke 9:23

These words of Jesus are his invitation and description of the Christian life. Jesus identifies three disciplines of the Christian life: deny ourselves, pick up our cross daily, and follow him. To deny ourselves is to say "No" to the desires and temptations that are self-satisfying for the sake of honoring the Lord and being set apart for him. As Christians, we do not seek to please ourselves first, but the Lord.

To pick up our cross daily takes self-denial to the next level. The cross is a symbol of death. Jesus literally died on the cross. He spoke figuratively of the cross for us to bear. We died to our old selves and our past lives of sin when we became Christians. That death is followed up by a daily life of sacrifice and obedience to the Lord. This aspect of our faith in Christ is not easy but requires commitment and perseverance on a daily basis.

To follow Jesus is to live our life by his example and obey his Word. We follow him in a life of selfless love. He denied himself and took up his cross to die for our sins. He asks us to follow him in a lifestyle of self-denial, obedience, sacrifice, and death to our old ways of life.

On the third day after Jesus died on the cross, he rose from the dead. He ascended to heaven, and he is coming back. We who follow Christ in death also follow him in resurrection life. We can rise above our life of sin here on earth, and we will rise up to be with him in heaven forever!

Dear Jesus, help me today to deny myself, to pick up my cross daily, and to follow you. In Jesus' name, amen.

March 29

Enduring Suffering

"Therefore, since Christ suffered in his body, arm yourselves also with the same attitude, because whoever suffers in the body is done with sin." 1 Peter 4:1

Jesus endured suffering for our sake. He was brutally beaten and hung on a cross to die. His death was torturous, agonizing, and painful. Jesus did nothing to deserve the pain and punishment he endured. He did it for us. He suffered to save us from the punishment that our sins deserve. When we experience suffering and pain in our own lives, we remember that our Lord also knows what it is like to suffer. He understands pain and he can draw close to us in our times of pain. Jesus is an example to us in many ways, including his experience with suffering.

Our commitment to follow Christ may cause us to experience suffering in this life. When we die to our old selves, there may be pain in the process of letting go of beliefs, attitudes, relationships, and habits that do not conform with Christ. We have allowed some of our sinful behaviors and beliefs to be so ingrained in us that it feels painful to end it all. We may feel like our insides are being ripped apart. This type of suffering in the process of dying to our sin is good for us although it does not feel pleasant at the time. This type of suffering is what leads us to be done with sin. When we follow Christ in his suffering for the sake of sin, he comforts us, and then he leads us in resurrection power in new life, rising victoriously over sin.

Dear Jesus, I thank you for the suffering you endured for my sin. I pray that you will draw close to me and help me in my time of suffering. Help me to go through whatever suffering it takes for me to be done with sin. In your name, amen.

March 30

I Want to Know Christ

"I want to know Christ—yes, to know the power of his resurrection and participation in his sufferings, becoming like him in his death, and so, somehow, attaining to the resurrection from the dead." Philippians 3:10–11

"To know Christ" is the enduring aim of the Christian faith. We begin by believing in Jesus, that he, the eternal God, became a man and lived a sinless life here on earth. We believe that he died on the cross to save us from the penalty of our sins and that he rose from the dead, ascended to heaven, and is now seated at the right hand of the throne of God. We have asked Jesus' forgiveness through the blood he shed for us on the cross. We have accepted him as our Lord and Savior. We have a personal relationship with him. We want to know him more as we grow in our relationship with Jesus.

Without the suffering and death, there can be no resurrection. When we accept Christ, we experience a spiritual death to our old sinful lives. The suffering we experience is the discomfort and sacrifice it takes for us to let go of our past and surrender our lives to Christ. When we do suffer pain and hardship in this life, we can draw close to Jesus, because we know that he has experienced suffering when he did no wrong. When we do follow Jesus in this suffering and death to our sinful nature, we also follow him in resurrection life, freedom and power over sin here in this present life, and also eternal life with Jesus in heaven.

Dear Jesus, I want to know you—yes, to know the power of your resurrection and participation in your sufferings, becoming like you in your death, and so, somehow, attaining to the resurrection from the dead. In your name I pray, amen.

March 31

The Suffering Servant

"But he was pierced for our transgressions, he was crushed for our iniquities; the punishment that brought us peace was on him, and by his wounds we are healed."
Isaiah 53:5

The prophet Isaiah wrote these words regarding Jesus approximately 700 years before Christ was born. Isaiah presents Jesus the Messiah as the suffering servant. This passage describes the vicarious atonement that was accomplished on the cross. Jesus' suffering and death on the cross was vicarious because he did it for us. He was pierced for our transgressions. We sinned and deserved the punishment, but he, who was fully human and also fully God, took the punishment in our place. Atonement refers to the repair of wrongdoing. In the Old Testament, the sacrifices of animals covered the sins of the people. The New Testament concept of atonement through Jesus goes beyond covering over the sins of the Israelites to taking away the sins of the world. Our sin causes division and hostility between ourselves and God. When Jesus took our punishment upon himself, it satisfied the justice of God and he brought peace to atone for the hostility between us and God because of our sin. Our relationship with God was hurt, and Jesus brought forgiveness and healing through his suffering and death on the cross. Sin separated us from God. What Jesus did on the cross made us "at one" with God in a right relationship with him. Jesus brought us *"at–one–ment"* with God. In addition to the atonement Christ accomplished through his death, he rose victoriously over death to bring us eternal life with him in heaven.

Jesus, I worship you and I thank you that you were pierced for my transgressions, you were crushed for my iniquities, and the punishment that brought me peace was on you, and by your stripes, I am healed. In your name, amen.

91

April 1

Help with the Cross

"As the soldiers led him away, they seized Simon from Cyrene, who was on his way in from the country, and put the cross on him and made him carry it behind Jesus."
Luke 23:26

Jesus was flogged and brutally beaten before he was taken to be crucified. Historians report that the flogging was likely done with a whip made with strands of leather containing pieces of lead and bone fragments. Each flogging would have torn Jesus' flesh open. His back was probably ripped apart, leaving open wounds. He was also beaten over the head with a staff. Jesus was likely a healthy man in his early thirties. He had been raised as a carpenter and was probably a fit and rugged man. But none of us would have been able to carry that cross after a beating like he endured. He could probably barely walk, let alone carry a cross. Jesus could have used his divine power to easily carry the cross. But Jesus needed to handle this in his humanity as a man. He was our representative, taking the punishment we deserved. The soldiers knew that Jesus was not able to carry that cross. They made Simon of Cyrene carry the cross, walking behind Jesus on the path to Golgotha where he would be crucified. Jesus needed help.

Likewise, there are days when we all need help from others. Jesus knows our weaknesses and he knows we cannot do the things he calls us to do without God's help and help from others. We do not need to be afraid or ashamed to ask for help. We are not supposed to do life alone. When we feel like we cannot go on, we can ask God for help. He will always help us and put people in our lives to help us as well.

Dear Jesus, thank you for your help and the help of others you put in my life. I cannot do anything without you.
In your name, amen.

April 2

Crucified with Christ

"I have been crucified with Christ and I no longer live, but Christ lives in me. The life I now live in the body, I live by faith in the Son of God, who loved me and gave himself for me."
Galatians 2:20

Our old life has been crucified with Christ on the cross. Our past, with its sinful ways, is dead and buried. Our life of sin was nailed to the cross when we asked Jesus for forgiveness through his shed blood and accepted him as our Lord and Savior. We do not go back to our old life because it is dead. We have only a new life before us.

Just as Jesus rose from the dead, we also rose from our sinful lives with a new life in Christ. The Lord does not just give us a makeover. He gives us a new life. We experience spiritual regeneration. We are born again by the power of the Holy Spirit. We are made new. We have a new heart and a new mind. The new life that God has given us is not our own. It is his life in us. The nature of our sinful life was that we did things our own way. We put ourselves first. With our new life in Christ, we put God first and do things his way.

Jesus sacrificed his life to give us a new life. He did this out of love. We now live in a love relationship with Jesus. This love relationship is the key to our identity in Christ. This relationship is based on faith in Jesus. This gives our lives a purpose to follow. We have greater peace and satisfaction in our new life in Christ than we could ever find in our past life of sin.

Dear Heavenly Father, I thank you that I have been crucified with Christ, and I no longer live, but Christ lives in me. The life I now live in the body, I live by faith in the Son of God, who loved me and gave himself for me. Help me to live this life according to your will. In Jesus' name, amen.

April 3

You Are His Joy

"...fixing our eyes on Jesus, the pioneer and perfecter of faith. For the joy set before him he endured the cross, scorning its shame, and sat down at the right hand of the throne of God."
Hebrews 12:2

Jesus went through unthinkable abuse, torture, and pain from the time he was arrested. He was stripped, beaten, spit upon, whipped, insulted, and mocked. He was nailed to a cross where he suffered an agonizing death. Jesus was able to endure that cross and scorn its shame because of the joy set before him. We are that joy.

He did it out of love. Jesus loves us so much that he laid down his life so that we can be forgiven for our sins, set free, and have eternal life with him. We were enslaved to our sins and condemned to death with no hope without Jesus. He saved us by shedding his blood on the cross. The joy set before Jesus was the victory he experienced when he rose from the dead, ascended to heaven, and redeemed the sins of the world. Jesus did this for us. It was for our salvation and our eternity with him.

We also share that joy to endure because of our future hope for eternity with him. We too can have joy and strength during trials and difficulties because we know that they are temporary and that we will have ultimate victory in heaven with Jesus forever. After all, he gave his life for us on the cross. Let us fix our eyes on Jesus. He is the joy set before us that gives us strength to endure.

Dear Jesus, today I fix my eyes on you. You are the pioneer and perfecter of my faith. Jesus, you are the joy set before me. I thank you for forgiveness, freedom, and eternal life.
In your name, amen.

April 4

The Sin of the World on His Shoulders

"My God, my God, why have you forsaken me?..."
Psalm 22:1

Jesus shouted these words from Psalm 22 while he was on the cross. He shouted them in Aramaic, and those who heard him did not understand what he was saying. Not only did they not understand his words, but they were completely ignorant of what those words meant and also blind to the tremendous miraculous spiritual event that was taking place at that moment. They didn't get it.

Psalm 22 is rich in Messianic prophecy. This psalm predicts some of the very details that were taking place through the crucifixion of Jesus, including the insults of the crowd, the piercing of his hands and feet, and even the casting of lots for his clothing. By quoting Psalm 22, Jesus pointed to prophecy about his death and verified that this event was God's plan and purpose.

There is a spiritual meaning to the words Jesus said. Jesus was 100% God and also 100% man. He died on the cross as a representative of humankind to take the penalty and punishment of our sins on himself. Jesus had to take the sin of the world on his shoulders on the cross. The very nature of sin is that it causes separation from God. At that moment, in his humanity, for the first time in his human life, Jesus would have experienced separation from God. By doing so, Jesus made the way for forgiveness for all of us. By rising from the dead, he also made the way for eternal life for all of us.

Dear Jesus, thank you for the forgiveness of sins through your shed blood, and for taking my sins on your shoulders on the cross. In your name, amen.

April 5

Forgiven

"Jesus said, 'Father, forgive them, for they do not know what they are doing.'..." Luke 23:34

Jesus was securing forgiveness for the sins of the world through his death on the cross by taking on that suffering and death in our place as the punishment for our sins. Because of what Jesus did on the cross, we are forgiven for our sins and set free from the penalty of our sins. What Jesus did 2,000 years ago still counts for us today. Anyone who asks Jesus for forgiveness is forgiven by the blood he shed on the cross.

While he hung on the cross, Jesus prayed for the forgiveness of the very people who crucified him. We all can be included in that prayer because he was there on the cross for our sins as well. Jesus was engaged in his role as the great intercessor and the one mediator between God and man. Jesus was praying to the Father on our behalf. This is something our Risen Lord Jesus continues to do for us. He speaks favorably to the Father on our behalf. He prayerfully intercedes for God's grace and mercy for our lives.

Jesus sets an example for us by praying for the forgiveness of those who crucified him. We struggle with forgiving people who have offended us or hurt us. The offenses we have experienced are most likely mild compared to what Jesus endured. We need to follow his example and pray for God's forgiveness for those who have offended or hurt us. We need to forgive others the same way God has forgiven us. Our Savior did it. We can do it as well, with God's help.

Dear Jesus, thank you for your forgiveness on the cross, help me to forgive others in the same way you have forgiven me. In your name, amen.

April 6

It's Never Too Late

"Then he said, 'Jesus, remember me when you come into your kingdom.' Jesus answered him, 'Truly I tell you, today you will be with me in paradise.'" Luke 23:42–43

Jesus was hung on a cross between two thieves who were also crucified. One of those thieves mocked Jesus. The other asked Jesus for mercy. That thief who asked for mercy went to be with Jesus in paradise that day. That second thief shows us that, as long as someone is alive, it is never too late to accept Christ and to be with him forever in heaven. There have been many people who have accepted Christ at an elderly age or on their deathbeds. Those folks are forgiven and going to heaven, just like the person who went to church and served the Lord their entire life. The thief on the cross also shows us the simplicity of the gospel. It does not matter how long a person lived in sin, how severe or intense that sin was, or whether they ever believed in God. All they have to do is ask Jesus for forgiveness of their sins. When we ask Jesus for forgiveness and accept him as Lord and Savior, we are forgiven, saved, and going to heaven. It is that simple. God is a loving, forgiving God, who longs for us to turn to him. The thief on the cross displays the love and power of God to save people's lives. Jesus is so loving and merciful. He was ministering to others and bringing people to heaven with him right up until his dying breath. God help us when we feel like we are having a bad day and it discourages us from doing what God has called us to do. Here is Jesus dying a brutal death and yet ministering to those around him. May we be able to reflect the love and mercy of Jesus even when we are going through difficult times.

Dear Jesus, thank you for your mercy that does not turn anyone away who comes to you. Help me to be a reflection of your love and mercy to the hurting world around me.
In your name, amen.

April 7

Full Access

"The curtain of the temple was torn in two from top to bottom."
Mark 15:38

The curtain in the nearby temple in Jerusalem was torn from top to bottom right after Jesus died on the cross. The fact that it was torn from top to bottom signifies that this was an act of God coming from heaven to earth that day. Heaven came down when Jesus died on the cross. This curtain separated what was called the Holy Place from the Most Holy Place in the temple. The Most Holy Place was the dwelling place of the Ark of the Covenant, which represented the presence of the Lord to the Jewish people. The only person allowed in the Most Holy Place was the High Priest, and that was only once a year to make a sacrifice for the sins of the people. The torn curtain represented the end of the Old Covenant and the beginning of the New Covenant that God was instituting through the sacrificed blood of Jesus. The Old Covenant ended when Jesus died on the cross as a sacrifice for all humanity once and for all. No longer was there a need for a High Priest to make sacrifices for the sins of the people. The priest no longer needed to represent the people in the Lord's presence. Jesus' death and resurrection opened the way for all people to have access to the presence of the Lord and eternal life in heaven. The torn curtain also represented the removal of obstacles between us and the Lord. Our sin separated us from God but Jesus took away the barrier of our sin when he died on the cross for us. Now there is nothing to hold us back or interfere with us being in a right relationship with God because of what Jesus did for us on the cross.

Dear Heavenly Father, thank you for the miracle of the torn curtain in the temple that showed the power of Jesus' atoning death on the cross, allowing us access to your presence and eternal life. In Jesus' name, amen.

April 8

He Is Risen Indeed!

"Early on the first day of the week, while it was still dark, Mary Magdalene went to the tomb and saw that the stone had been removed from the entrance." John 20:1

Early that Sunday morning Mary found that the large stone placed at the entrance of the tomb where Jesus had been buried was rolled away and the tomb was empty. Jesus' disciples were grieving his death, but at this discovery, their grief turned to joy because Jesus had risen from the dead! He is alive! Easter is a celebration of the resurrection of Jesus Christ. We celebrate Jesus' resurrection in the United States on the first Sunday after the first full moon after the spring equinox each year. This celebration is a high point in our church calendar. The resurrection of Jesus is a high point in the Bible. The Old Testament leads up to the birth of Jesus the Messiah in the New Testament, and the Gospel narratives lead up to Jesus' death and resurrection.

The resurrection of Jesus brought the opportunity for salvation and eternal life for all humanity for all time! When Jesus was dead it appeared that Satan had defeated him. This is far from true! Jesus had to suffer and die to take the penalty and punishment for our sins. His resurrection proves his victorious power over sin, evil, and Satan for all of us! There are many miracles recorded in the Bible, but the death and resurrection of Jesus Christ is the greatest supernatural event of all time. We can be saved from the penalty of our sins and all be part of the kingdom of God. Whoever believes in Jesus will not perish but have everlasting life.

Dear Heavenly Father, I thank you for giving your Son, Jesus, to die on the cross for my sin. I thank you for raising him from the dead so that I can have eternal life.
In Jesus' name, amen.

April 9

The Hope of the Resurrection

"And I will put enmity between you and the woman, and between your offspring and hers; he will crush your head, and you will strike his heel." Genesis 3:15

Adam and Eve were tempted by the serpent and they disobeyed God. This was the original sin and captures the account of the fall of man. Sin brought a curse to humankind as well as to the serpent, who was Satan. The Lord's curse to the serpent was a fatal one. This was the occasion for the first promise of Jesus, the Messiah. Smack dab in the middle of the fall of man was the message of the hope of the resurrection.

The enmity between Eve's offspring and the serpent represents the spiritual battle between good and evil that we continue to face today. The culmination of that battle was fought by Jesus, who was the offspring of Eve, born by a woman, yet conceived by the power of God. Satan "bruised Jesus' heel" through the suffering and death Jesus endured on the cross to pay for the penalty of sin for all humankind. Jesus crushed Satan's head when he rose from the dead. Jesus displayed ultimate power over Satan by rising from the dead and ascending to heaven. Although sin and evil caused the painful suffering and death of Christ, the battle was won victoriously for eternity by Christ. We have the promised hope of the resurrection because Jesus died on the cross for our sins and rose from the dead. He led the way for us to rise victoriously over sin in this life and have eternal life with him in heaven. As we face the spiritual battles in life today, we know the battle has already been won because of our hope of the resurrection through Jesus Christ.

Dear Lord, I thank you that in the face of sin, you provide the promise and the hope of the resurrection. I thank you that the battle has been won by Jesus, our risen Lord! In Jesus' name, amen.

100

April 10

My Redeemer Lives

"I know that my redeemer lives, and that in the end he will stand on the earth." Job 19:25

The book of Job is said to be the earliest written book of the Bible. Yet in this Old Testament text, we have a beautiful prophetic picture of Jesus, our risen Savior. These words of hope and faith come from Job, who was in the middle of a dark trial. Job had lost everything but he still had hope and faith in God, even while suffering tragic loss. Amid his darkest trial, Job had the faith to say that he knew his redeemer lives.

Jesus is our redeemer because he bought us back out of our slavery to sin. He purchased our freedom with the blood he shed on the cross. Salvation from the power and penalty of sin is a gift to us, yet there was a price to pay. Jesus paid it all on the cross when he died for us. He took our penalty so that we might live. After three days, Jesus rose from the dead. He has ascended to heaven. Jesus is alive, seated at the right hand of the throne of God. Jesus not only paid the price for our redemption, he overcame death and led the way for us to have eternal life with him.

We too, like Job, can have the strength of faith and hope no matter what difficulty we face. No matter what trials we face today we know that they are temporary because we will be with Jesus forever. No matter what trials come our way, we have the faith and hope to say, "I know that my redeemer lives!"

Dear Heavenly Father, no matter what difficulties or trials I face today, I know that my redeemer lives and Jesus Christ, my living savior, gives me strength and hope for today.
In Jesus' name, amen.

April 11

First Importance

"For what I received I passed on to you as of first importance: that Christ died for our sins according to the Scriptures, that he was buried, that he was raised on the third day according to the Scriptures" 1 Corinthians 15:3–4

Jesus Christ died for our sins, he was buried, and he rose from the dead on the third day. Paul writes that this is the message he passed on as first importance. This message is the gospel in a nutshell. The gospel, or the good news, is that Jesus took the penalty of our sins so that we are free from condemnation. The good news is that God loves us so much that he made this sacrifice so that we may live. The good news is that when we accept Jesus as Lord, we are forgiven of our sins. The good news is that we can live free from the bondage of sin. The good news is that Jesus demonstrated the power to overcome death by rising victoriously from the dead. The good news is that we will follow Christ in His resurrection and that we will have eternal life with him in heaven!

Today this gospel message needs to remain as of first importance for us. This is the key message of our Christian faith. This must be what we continue to pass on as of first importance as Paul did. Someone shared the gospel with us and by this gospel, we are saved. Many more people need to experience salvation through the gospel of Jesus Christ. We need to continue to make it clear that this gospel message is of first importance.

Dear Heavenly Father, thank you that Jesus died for my sins and that he rose from the dead. Help me, Lord, to pass on this good news as of first importance to those who need your salvation. In Jesus' name, amen.

April 12

Resurrection Power

"I pray that you will know how great His power is for those who have put their trust in him. It is the same power that raised Christ from the dead." Ephesians 1:19–20

When we have asked Jesus to forgive us of our sins and have accepted him as our Lord and Savior, the Holy Spirit resides inside of us. The Lord is present in our hearts through his Holy Spirit. The Holy Spirit is the source of God's power in our lives. The same power that raised Christ from the dead is available to us. That is a lot of power! That is resurrection power! Jesus took the penalty of the sin of the world on his shoulders through his death on the cross. Think of the weight of that burden. All of the hatred and evil in the world was on him. All of that sin could not defeat the power of God for Jesus to overcome and rise victoriously from the dead. That same power is available to us. We are only one person dealing with the struggle of our own sin and pain, but we have the power of God available to us to overcome the sin of the world! God has given us the power to overcome the evil and sin in our lives. The victory has already been won by Jesus through his resurrection from the dead. Our victory does not come without struggle or pain. It is often a process of learning and growing. It is a process of overcoming and getting stronger with God's help that leads to the ultimate victory of complete freedom and power in the immediate presence of our Lord Jesus in our eternal life in heaven. We can be encouraged and empowered in our fight against sin and evil in our lives as Christians. We can walk in resurrection power!

Dear Heavenly Father, I have put my trust in you. I pray that I will know how great your power is. It is the same power that raised Christ from the dead. Lord, I need your power in my life today. In Jesus' name, amen.

April 13

Jesus Is Our Resurrection

"Jesus said to her, 'I am the resurrection and the life. The one who believes in me will live, even though they die; and whoever lives by believing in me will never die. Do you believe this?'"
John 11:25–26

Resurrection means rising from the dead. Jesus rose from the dead for all of us who believe in him. He is our resurrection and our life because he led the way for us to have life after death. We follow Jesus in death to our sinful life. We also follow him in resurrection life after death. Jesus is the source of our resurrection, our eternal life. Jesus is resurrection personified for us. We have resurrection life through our relationship with Jesus.

Jesus is our new life. Our new life in Christ begins when we accept him as our Lord and Savior and it goes on for eternity with him. Our resurrection life begins with freedom from the bondage of sin here on earth. We will have life after death with Jesus. Our eternal life will not be in these bodies on earth but in new spiritual bodies in heaven. We have eternal life because Jesus died and rose from the dead for us. He is our life! Jesus is our hope when we are dismayed. He is our strength when we are weak. He is our truth when we are confused. He is our peace when we are upset. No matter what trials or difficulties we face, we know that they are just temporary. We know that we have Jesus so we have eternal life. Jesus is our resurrection and life!

Dear Jesus, I worship you because you are my resurrection and life. I have eternal life because of you; you are my life!
In Jesus' name, amen.

April 14

Our Living Hope

"Praise be to the God and Father of our Lord Jesus Christ! In his great mercy he has given us new birth into a living hope through the resurrection of Jesus Christ from the dead"
1 Peter 1:3

We did not get the punishment our sins deserved because of God's great mercy. Jesus took that punishment for us through his death on the cross. When Jesus rose from the dead, he brought us new birth into a living hope. We follow Jesus in his death by dying to our old sinful selves through the forgiveness of our sins by the blood he shed for us. We follow Jesus in his resurrection by being born again spiritually, rising above the sinful life of our past into a living hope that goes beyond our life in this world to eternal life in heaven. We have the presence of the resurrected Jesus inside of us through the Holy Spirit for that living hope. Our hope never dies. We may have experienced hopelessness in our past because of our sin but we are hopeless no more. In this life, there are still trials and tribulations, hurt and heartache, spiritual battles and the presence of evil, yet no matter what happens or no matter what the devil throws at us, we have a living hope that the battle has already been won through the resurrection of Jesus and we will always rise victorious! That living hope is a strength inside of us that does not go away. It gives us the faith to know that we are not alone and that God is walking with us through whatever trial we are facing. The living hope we have from God gives us the perseverance to press on and not give up. The ultimate fulfillment of our living hope will be in our eternal life with God in the presence of our living Savior, Jesus Christ. Jesus is our living hope!

Dear Heavenly Father, I praise you for new birth into a living hope through the resurrection of Jesus from the dead. In Jesus' name, amen.

April 15

God and Country

"Then Jesus said to them, 'Give back to Caesar what is Caesar's and to God what is God's.' And they were amazed at him."
Mark 12:17

April 15 is the date that taxes are due every year in the United States. Jesus responded affirmatively when he was asked about paying taxes to Caesar. As Christians, we should pay our taxes and follow the laws of the land. This is one of the ways we do our duty as citizens to our country. We can be a Christian witness and positive influence in our community. We are called to be salt and light. We have the opportunity to vote and we also can be praying for our government leaders. We can have a voice through our activity in local government. Our participation in government and politics reflects our Christian values.

Jesus was asked about the taxes only because the Pharisees were trying to trap Jesus by his words regarding the politics of their time. Jesus responded so wisely to avoid the trap of getting caught up in politics. We also can avoid the trap of getting caught up in politics to the point that it overshadows our relationship with the Lord or we allow our politics to cause division in the body of Christ. In Jesus' response about taxes, he distinguished between what is God's and what is Caesar's. Jesus rose above politics. His kingdom is not of this world. We are citizens of the kingdom of heaven. The solutions to the problems in our world today will not be solved through politics. The world needs Jesus. Let's pray for our leaders and keep Jesus first!

Dear Heavenly Father, I thank you for our country. I pray for our leaders in local, state, and national government. Have mercy on our land. May your will be done on earth as it is in heaven. Lord, I pray about my involvement in the community and local government. Use me according to your will.
In Jesus' name, amen.

April 16

Restored by the Lord

"I will repay you for the years the locusts have eaten..."
Joel 2:25

We may look back and see a lot of damage in our lives caused by our sins. We may have years that we wasted because we were caught up in the emptiness of our sinful lifestyle. It can be sad and discouraging to look back and see it all. It can cause us to feel hopeless about our future becoming any different from the pattern of destruction established in our past. But we do not lose heart! The Lord is a God of restoration! He restores and repairs the damage of our past. He can put the broken pieces of our lives back together. We are on a wonderful journey of renewal and restoration with Jesus! That's what he is all about. Jesus gives us a new life that overcomes the destructive patterns of sin in our past. Now when we look back, we can see difficulties and trials that have been overcome with God's help. We see rebuilding and mending of brokenness in our lives and relationships. We see patterns of victory rather than patterns of defeat. The Lord's restoration will bring us the life that we always wanted but could never achieve on our own. We are not alone anymore. Our hope is not in ourselves, but it is in the Lord. He is doing something new in our lives. There is a miraculous restoration taking place in our lives. We are restored to our right mind, we are restored to a life of dignity and respect, we are restored with a clean conscience, we are restored in our relationships, we are restored as productive citizens, and we are restored to having hope for the future. We are restored by the unfailing, unending love of God that will never go away and will lead us to eternal life.

Dear Heavenly Father, I thank you that you have restored what the locusts of sin and my past have eaten. I thank you for the restoration in my life through Jesus my Lord!
In Jesus' name, amen.

April 17

The Melody of the Spirit

"'But now bring me a harpist.' While the harpist was playing, the hand of the LORD came on Elisha."
2 Kings 3:15

The kings of Judah, Israel, and Edom went to the prophet Elisha to inquire of the Lord as to whether they should go to battle against Moab. When Elisha wanted to hear a word from the Lord, he asked for a harpist to play some music. While the harpist was playing, the hand of the Lord came upon Elisha and gave him a vision and an answer to share with the kings. This incident is an example of how the Lord uses music to usher in the ministry of the Holy Spirit. Music has a spiritual element to it that the Holy Spirit can use to reach our spirits. The Holy Spirit can use music to help us disconnect from the pressing influence of our immediate natural environment and help us detach from mental and emotional strongholds we experience such as worry, frustration, anxiety, fear, and inadequacy to connect with the Lord's presence. God can use worship music to lift us up spiritually so that we rise above our worries, our problems, and our bad moods! God is in our midst and we rely on him. We can let go and let God move through his Holy Spirit in our lives. The Holy Spirit can use worship music to release us from our natural mindset and become open to the moving of the Holy Spirit and the realm of spiritual possibilities that we will not find in our logic or rationale. When we are struggling with our thoughts, emotions, or spiritual dryness, we can listen to godly music along with our prayers, to help us be open to the Holy Spirit in our hearts.

Dear Holy Spirit, I thank you for how you move in my heart through worship and spiritual music. Have your way in my life today. Help me to be sensitive to your presence and your guidance. In Jesus' name, amen.

April 18

With All Your Heart

*"Whatever you do, work at it with all your heart, as working
for the Lord, not for human masters"*
Colossians 3:23

God deserves our very best! Jesus saved our lives and brought us eternal life by dying on the cross and rising from the dead. The life we live is God's life; he gave it to us. Our life is an expression of worship to the Lord. Whatever we do, we can do it in a way to give glory to the Lord! We need to have a spirit of excellence in everything we do as if we were doing it for the Lord himself. Even if we do not care for our job, or we do not like our boss, we should still have a spirit of excellence as unto the Lord because everything we do is ultimately unto him. He cares about the details of our lives and he is Lord over every area of our lives. We seek to please the Lord with our lives, not our boss, not our neighbors, but God. At the end of the day, it is knowing that we are pleasing God that will provide fulfillment and satisfaction to our souls. The acceptance of people is fickle. One day they like us, the next day they don't. God is not like that. He loves us with an everlasting love. When people know that we are Christians, they will watch us and see what we do. When we put all of our hearts into what we do, and strive for a spirit of excellence, we provide an opportunity to be a Christian witness and give God the glory. We always do our best unto the Lord. He deserves nothing less.

*Dear Heavenly Father, I commit myself to have a spirit of
excellence in everything I do. Whatever I do, I will work at it with
all of my heart, as working for the Lord, not for other people.
In Jesus' name, amen.*

April 19

Standing on the Rock

"I waited patiently for the Lord; he turned to me and heard my cry. He lifted me out of the slimy pit, out of the mud and mire; he set my feet on a rock and gave me a firm place to stand."
Psalm 40:1–2

It is right for us to look at our old life before Christ as the slimy pit and the mud and mire. We were so dirty and immersed in our sin! We were such a mess! The pit was so slimy that we could not get out of it on our own. Whenever we tried to climb out, we just slid back in. That was our story until the Lord heard our cries and lifted us out of the slimy pit of our sin by his love. We recall how the Lord miraculously saved us from our troubles and delivered us. No more sliding back into the pit! He has the power to lift us out for good. We are not doing this on our own. He sets our feet on a rock and gives us a firm place to stand. The Lord is our rock. We can stand on him. When we surrender our lives totally to the Lord, we are standing on solid ground. He is trustworthy. Our hope and our faith are in him. If he was not a miracle-working God, we would still be in the slimy pit of sin. But we are saved and delivered. The hand of the Lord is on our lives. We need the Lord just as much today as when we first cried out to him. He continues to hear our cries and he has the power to answer them! Just as he has brought us this far, he will continue to be there, to answer prayer, to lift us, and to provide a firm place for us to stand. God is faithful. He is our rock! Nothing is too difficult for God!

Dear Lord, I thank you that you waited patiently for me! You turned to me and heard my cry. You set my feet on a rock and gave me a firm place to stand. I love you and I thank you that you are still lifting me. In Jesus' name, amen.

April 20

An Anatomy of Iniquity

"When I saw in the plunder a beautiful robe from Babylonia, two hundred shekels of silver and a bar of gold weighing fifty shekels, I coveted them and took them. They are hidden in the ground inside my tent, with the silver underneath."
Joshua 7:21

In this verse, Achan confesses that he *saw* the items, he *coveted* them, he *took* them, and he *hid* them. These four experiences provide an overview of how sin runs its course. When Achan saw the plunder, he was tempted. This is the threshold to sin. Seeing, or thinking about something is not sinful, it is what we do next that matters. Achan coveted the items. This changed the thoughts from temptation to sinful thinking by dwelling on them. Our sin is conceived and developed in our thoughts first. Even if it is for a second, we think about it before we do it. The third stage is the action stage. He took them. This is the stage where the sin is committed by action. The fourth stage is that he hid them. We often try to cover up and hide our sins. We may feel bad about it, but we still try to hide it. Our shame keeps it locked inside. Thank God that just as the sin progressed, it can be reversed through confession, repentance, the Lord's forgiveness, and his deliverance. With God's help, we can stop the cycle of sin before it develops. The Lord can turn our lives around even when we have been fully immersed in the cycle of sin. The Lord can help us stop the cycle at any time, at any stage. The Lord can forgive us and turn our lives around. We can be free from the bondage of sin through Jesus Christ.

Dear Jesus, thank you for setting me free and breaking the cycle of sin in my life. Help me to stay free by stopping the cycle before it starts. In your name, amen.

April 21

Stepping into God's Dream

"Joseph had a dream, and when he told it to his brothers, they hated him all the more." Genesis 37:5

God can make our dreams come true. The dreams that God has for us are undoubtedly beyond our wildest dreams. The Lord often has us on a journey toward our dreams, a journey that does not take place overnight.

Joseph was a dreamer who stepped into God's dreams for his life. Joseph's journey to God's dream for his life had many setbacks. When Joseph shared his dreams, he was opposed by his family. His brothers threw him into a pit and sold him as a slave. Things started going better for Joseph when he worked for a man named Potiphar. He was later falsely accused by Potiphar's wife and thrown into prison. While he was in prison, he was with a man who served as the king's cupbearer. Joseph predicted that the cupbearer would be restored to his position. Joseph told the cupbearer to remember him and help Joseph when the cupbearer got out of prison. When the cupbearer got out of prison, he forgot all about Joseph for two years. Finally, the cupbearer remembered Joseph. Joseph was released from prison and ended up being second in command over all of Egypt. The dream came true! Joseph went through some really hard times on the journey to his dream. We will go through difficulties as well and, like Joseph, we can hold on to the dreams God has given us! Nothing is impossible with God!

Lord, I thank you for the dreams that you have for my life. Help me to be patient and wait on you as you make those dreams come true. In Jesus' name, amen.

April 22

The Battle in Our Minds

"We demolish arguments and every pretension that sets itself up against the knowledge of God, and we take captive every thought to make it obedient to Christ." 2 Corinthians 10:5

The Word of God and the Spirit of God work hand in hand to help us win the battle in our minds. The truth in the Word of God will help us to think right, to act right, and to live right. Lies and destructive ideas in our minds lead to hurt, destruction, and misery. God's Word will help us to think and live healthily. If we just let our thoughts run wild, we will live wild! We have thoughts and ideas that are based on feelings, fears, or falsehoods. Those thoughts can turn into belief systems and we make unhealthy decisions because we have unhealthy beliefs. When we learn the Word of God and allow the Word to become part of our belief system, we can make healthy choices based on the principles for health, happiness, and fulfillment set forth by our Creator. When we know the truth in the Word of God, we can recognize lies and falsehoods when they come up in our thinking and we can cast those thoughts down, rather than let them grow and affect our beliefs, our choices, and our lifestyles. The Holy Spirit helps us with this. He is the Spirit of Truth. He helps us understand and remember the truth in God's Word. The Holy Spirit helps us to overcome lies and ungodly thoughts and to have victory over them rather than our ungodly thoughts having control over us. With God's help, we can demolish our old unhealthy belief systems and replace them with holy and healthy beliefs based on the Word of God.

Dear Lord, help me today to demolish arguments and every pretension that sets itself up against the knowledge of God and to take captive every thought to make it obedient to Christ. In Jesus' name, amen.

April 23

Keep God First

"The seed that fell among thorns stands for those who hear, but as they go on their way they are choked by life's worries, riches and pleasures, and they do not mature." Luke 8:14

In the Parable of the Sower, Jesus taught that a farmer scattered seeds in four different types of soil. Some fell along the path, some fell among rocks, some fell among thorns, and some fell on good soil. Jesus went on to explain that the soil is our hearts, and the seed is the Word of God. The seeds that fell among the thorns are those who hear, but as they go on their way they are choked by life's worries, riches, and pleasures and they do not mature. We have to be careful to guard our relationship with the Lord from being choked out by the demands of life. We have jobs, bills to pay, family members to care for, kids to take to soccer practice, medical issues, hobbies, entertainment, and more. Those activities may be necessary parts of life. However, if we are not careful, we can take on so many different activities that they begin to overtake our lives to the point that we are not cultivating our relationship with the Lord. We stop going to church, we stop reading the Bible, we stop praying. The Lord wants us to have a joyful, balanced life. We need to make our relationship with the Lord a priority or else it can be overcome by life's demands and interests. When we continue to put God first in our lives, he will continue to bless our lives to fulfill his purpose for us. We need to be able to recognize activities or interests that are interfering with our spiritual lives and say "No" to those things that will choke out our time with the Lord. We can't do anything without God, so let's remember to always keep him first, and he will help us with everything else. Guard the precious gift of our relationship with God.

Dear Heavenly Father, help me to not allow my relationship with you to get choked out by life's worries, riches, and pleasures. In Jesus' name, amen.

April 24

He Is Divine, We Are the Branches

"Remain in me, as I also remain in you. No branch can bear fruit by itself; it must remain in the vine. Neither can you bear fruit unless you remain in me." John 15:4

Jesus describes himself as the true vine. Just as the branch receives life and nourishment from its connection to the vine, we receive life through our connection in our personal relationship with Jesus Christ.

Jesus described a mutual indwelling when he said that we remain in him and he remains in us. To remain in him is to be still in his presence without the distractions of the world and the cravings of our flesh pulling us away from the spiritual fullness of his presence. Certainly, this is intentional in undisturbed, enduring, and earnest seasons of prayer. Yet we can maintain the spirit of remaining in his presence, abiding in him throughout the day, as we go to work or school or spend time with friends or family. We remain in him when we are mindful of his will for us and we are aware of his love for us at all times. We reflect and meditate on his Word and we are conscientious of our relationship with him and how our relationship with him is impacted by our actions and our thoughts. His presence with us at all times impacts our choices, our behavior, our thoughts, and our emotions. We maintain constant contact and awareness of his presence wherever we are and whatever we are doing. We are "in him" and he is "in us." This is a vivacious connection that offers a flow of spiritual strength, love, and wisdom that we just do not have on our own without Christ. Without Christ, we can do nothing, but with Christ, we can do all things because we remain, we abide, we dwell, in him.

Dear Jesus, you are the vine, and I am the branch. I cannot bear fruit by myself. Help me to remain in you.
In your name, amen.

April 25

Delight In the Lord

"Take delight in the LORD, and he will give you the desires of your heart." Psalm 37:4

To take delight in the Lord is to immerse ourselves in his presence. There is beauty in the presence of the Lord! God's love is so rich and powerful that it changes our lives. We see ourselves differently when we can grasp how much God loves us. When we delight ourselves in the Lord, he satisfies the yearnings and longings of our souls. When we delight in a loving relationship with God, he responds by giving us the desires of our hearts. He is so good to us and generous with us. God can truly make our dreams come true, even more than we could have imagined. He does this in his way and in his time. It is a misconception to view the Lord as a "Santa Clause" figure; as if when we pray, we just jump onto his lap and tell him what we want. No, our focus should be on the delighting, not on the desires. When we are in the Lord's presence, our focus is not on "I want this, and I want that," our focus is "I want you, Lord!" We focus on loving and pleasing him first, and the fulfillment of our desires is a blessing that flows from our relationship with our Heavenly Father. The main point is not getting our desires fulfilled; it's loving him! When we do experience love and fulfillment in our relationship with the Lord, he changes the desires of our hearts. Our desires become his desires. Then he truly does bless us in ways that we can never have imagined. He is so good to us. The blessings of God are so good and we thank him for giving us the desires of our hearts. Whether we are being blessed or facing a season of difficulty, our greatest joy is delighting in the Lord!

Dear Lord, I take delight in you. I love you and need you more than anyone or anything in my life! You are my greatest desire! I thank you for filling the longings and desires of my heart. In Jesus' name, amen.

April 26

A New Heart

"I will give you a new heart and put a new spirit in you; I will remove from you your heart of stone and give you a heart of flesh." Ezekiel 36:26

When we become Christians, the Lord gives us a new heart. He removes our heart of stone and gives us a heart of flesh. We had a heart of stone because our hearts became hardened. The Lord created us to have a relationship with him and to have him in our hearts. When we grew up without the Lord in our hearts, we had to figure things out on our own. We survived, but our hearts became hardened along the way. We were hurt, but we did the best we could to move forward. We did things our own way. When our hearts become hard, we do not want to listen to other people or God. We become used to doing things our own way. When we finally turn to God, he takes that hardened heart out and gives us a new heart. God does not give our hardened hearts a makeover; he totally changes us from the inside out. He gives us a heart of flesh, a heart that is able to receive and give love. When our hearts were hardened, we did not allow ourselves to feel painful feelings. Our hearts were hard from scars of pain that were never healed. Now that we have a heart of flesh, we can experience our feelings. Perhaps we cry like we have not cried in years. We deal with the pain that we held in our hardened hearts for a long time. Experiencing that hurt is not pleasant, but we are not alone. We have the presence of the Holy Spirit in us to bring comfort, love, and strength. God loves us through our moments of pain. He heals our hearts so that we can engage in love with him, others, and ourselves.

Dear Heavenly Father, I thank you that you gave me a new heart and put a new spirit in me. You removed my heart of stone and gave me a heart of flesh. I love you, Lord. I give my heart to you. In Jesus' name, amen.

117

April 27

Total Surrender

"Therefore, I urge you, brothers and sisters, in view of God's mercy, to offer your bodies as a living sacrifice, holy and pleasing to God—this is your true and proper worship."
Romans 12:1

The Lord has shown us his great mercy by forgiving our sins. God loves us so much that he sent his Son, Jesus, to take the penalty of our sins on his shoulders so that we can be free. Jesus loves us so much that he died for us so that we may be forgiven.

Our response to this great expression of love and mercy is to turn our lives over to the Lord. Jesus died for us so that we can live for him. To offer our bodies as a living sacrifice means to live our life in total surrender to the Lord. We are devoted to him and his purpose and will for our lives. We give up trying to do things our way and now we do things God's way. We are turning over control of our lives to the Lord. We get out of the driver's seat and let him drive. We take on a lifestyle of obedience to the Word of God. We now seek to please the Lord first rather than ourselves. We live in total surrender to Jesus. This is the way we worship God the most, by living our life for him.

Dear Lord, today I offer my life as a living sacrifice. I turn over my will and my ways to you. Your will, not mine, be done. Help me to live in total surrender to you today.
In Jesus' name, amen.

April 28

Little by Little

"The LORD your God will drive out those nations before you, little by little. You will not be allowed to eliminate them all at once, or the wild animals will multiply around you."
Deuteronomy 7:22

God's plan was for the Israelites to take over the Promised Land a little at a time. That way while they were taking the time to get established in one area of the land, the rest of the land remained inhabited and the inhabitants were keeping the number of wild animals down as well as maintaining the farmland so as the Israelites moved into a new area, the land would be best ready for them to move in and get settled. God's plan for the Israelites was for them to take their time and do it right. This is often a wise strategy for accomplishing any task and it is also common for the Lord to accomplish his will concerning us little by little. We want to get things done right away; God likes to take his time! In this example, the Lord provided a good reason why he wanted possession of the Promised Land to occur little by little. The Lord does not always bless us with the reason for his timing. We need to trust him in that process and slow down to his pace so that we do not miss anything he is trying to teach us or do in us. We will grow in the Lord, accomplish his will, and take possession of all that he has in store for us little by little. Enjoy the journey with him. Celebrate small victories and small steps in progress. Every day we are growing in the Lord and accomplishing his will for our lives little by little.

Dear Heavenly Father, thank you for progress little by little. Help me to slow down and trust you and trust your timing. My focus is not on completing a goal or receiving a blessing, my focus is on you. In Jesus' name, amen.

April 29

Quick to Listen

"My dear brothers and sisters, take note of this: Everyone should be quick to listen, slow to speak and slow to become angry, because human anger does not produce the righteousness that God desires." James 1:19–20

Our anger can get out of control and take us to a place where we do not want to be. God can help us to overcome anger that leads us to lose control. The Holy Spirit works inside of us to overcome the power of anger over us. The Lord is stronger than our anger. We can submit our anger to the power of God. James provides some practical advice on what we can do to allow God to bring victory over sinful anger. Anger is like a fire that burns inside us, then moves outside of us as it is expressed through our words and actions. The Lord can help us put the fire out. We need to stop adding fuel to the fire of our anger. When we keep venting, yelling, arguing, and talking, we are adding fuel to the fire. We become locked into a mindset that escalates our anger. James tells us to be quiet and listen! Stopping ourselves from speaking is one step toward putting the fire out. Listening is like adding water instead of fuel to the fire. Listening can bring in other ideas and points of view including the consequences of destructive anger and the will of God to best handle this situation. We can listen to wise counsel. We can listen to the other person's side of the story. We can listen to the Word of God and the guidance of the Holy Spirit. This will help us to regroup and process our anger in a healthy way rather than allowing it to hurt ourselves and others. With God's help, we can have control over anger rather than anger controlling us. We can start by being quiet and listening!

Dear Heavenly Father, I submit my anger to you. Help me to be quick to listen, slow to speak, and slow to become angry. Help me to handle my anger in the righteous way that you desire. In Jesus' name, amen.

April 30

The Lord Is My Victory

"Moses built an altar and called it The LORD is my Banner."
Exodus 17:15

Moses built this altar in commemoration of the victory the Israelite army had over the Amalekites. A banner was used to go before an army in battle. When we are under God's banner, he gives us victory. When the army led by Joshua was fighting the Amalekites, Moses was on the top of a hill, raising his hands to the Lord. As long as Moses held up his hands, the Israelites were winning the battle. Whenever he lowered his hands, the Amalekites were winning. This is an example of how intercessory prayer works. Moses was on top of the hill making the connection with God on behalf of Joshua and the army who were fighting the battle down below. This is also a powerful display of the spiritual dynamic that takes place in our own lives. Moses lifting his hands was symbolic of a spiritual connection with the Lord. When we are in a right relationship with the Lord, he brings us victory. The battle is the Lord's. Victory comes from him. Jesus already won the victory for us when he defeated Satan by rising from the dead.

When Moses raised his hands up to the Lord, his arms started getting tired. Moses had his two friends, Aaron and Hur come along his right and left sides and hold his arms up until the victory was won. In the same way, we can become weary when we are in a spiritual battle. Like Moses, we need people to come alongside us and give us help and encouragement. We need to reach out to others and let them in on our lives and our battles because we do get tired and the Lord will use others to give us strength. We are not supposed to do this alone! Thank God that he is our victory!

Dear Lord, I thank you that you are my victory. I thank you for the people you put in my life to help me when I am losing strength. In Jesus' name, amen.

May 1

Heal Our Land

"If my people, who are called by my name, will humble themselves and pray and seek my face and turn from their wicked ways, then I will hear from heaven, and I will forgive their sin and will heal their land." 2 Chronicles 7:14

The National Day of Prayer is observed in the United States on the first Thursday of May. We are blessed to live in a country that protects the freedom of prayer and honors the place of prayer in our lives and our society. With that being said, our country needs prayer! There is a great degree of violence, injustice, abuse, perversion, and evil in our land. There are people in our country who are alone, impoverished, wounded, and addicted. Our society is hurting. People need the Lord! Our prayers make a difference for the hand of God to move in our own lives and the lives of those around us. There is power when we come together to pray as God's people who are called by his name as Christians. When we turn to the Lord to pray, we humble ourselves by declaring our need for him. We admit that we all have sinned and fallen short of the glory of God. We humbly receive his forgiveness and reverently honor him with lives of obedience to his Word. We turn from ungodliness and sinful ways and instead turn to him. We pray that others will join us and turn from ungodliness to seek the Lord. God desires all people to turn to him. He loves the world so much that he gave his Son, Jesus, to save us from our sins. The Lord promises to hear and answer our prayers. God is almighty and powerful. He has the power to bring healing to our land. God answers prayer!

Dear Heavenly Father, I thank you that when we humble ourselves and pray and seek your face and turn from our wicked ways, then you will hear from heaven and you will forgive our sin and heal our land. In Jesus' name, amen.

May 2

Spiritual Warfare

"For our struggle is not against flesh and blood, but against the rulers, against the authorities, against the powers of this dark world and against the spiritual forces of evil in the heavenly realms." Ephesians 6:12

When we pay attention to everything going on around us, we see that there is undoubtedly a presence of evil in the world today. The devil is real. There is a war taking place in the spiritual realm. When we are fighting with each other, we are feeding into the hands of the devil. We need to see beyond the natural personal conflict and recognize the spiritual war that is taking place. Other people are not our true enemies; Satan and the spirit of evil is our true enemy. We can overcome the influences of evil that we contend with through the power of God in our lives. The power of God is greater than the power of the devil and any evil forces. Jesus has already won the victory over Satan when he died for our sins and rose from the dead. We have the power of God in us through the Holy Spirit. The Lord grants us victory in spiritual warfare when we rely on him and his power to defeat the enemy. The truth of God's Word can overcome the lies of the enemy. The love of God can overcome the ruthless attempts of the enemy to cause division among us. God is giving us power and victory in spiritual warfare today. We can be aware of the source of the presence of evil in our lives and stand firm in the power and love of God to live in victory over evil today.

Dear Heavenly Father, you are mighty and powerful. Thank you for your victory over spiritual warfare in my life today. In Jesus' name, amen.

May 3

The Lord Is My Shepherd

"The LORD is my shepherd, I lack nothing. He makes me lie down in green pastures, he leads me beside quiet waters, he refreshes my soul...." Psalm 23:1–3

Just as a shepherd cares for his flock, the Lord cares for us. We lack nothing because the Lord is our provider. He knows our needs and he gives us everything we need. We have peace, satisfaction, and fulfillment when we trust in the Lord to meet all of our needs. We do not have to worry or fret about the things we need because we know the Lord loves us and provides for us. Green pastures and still waters describe the inner peace and beauty we experience when we trust in the Lord. We can relax and rest in his presence. A shepherd protects his flock from the wolves and any other harm or danger. Similarly, God also watches over us and protects us so that we can live in peace and safety. He guides us to new pastures. When we trust him to lead us, he shows us his plan and purpose for our lives. The Lord will take us to places we never dreamed we could go. He knows the way and will guide us and lead us according to his will. He cares for us too much to let us wander off on our own. He knows that we will encounter harm or danger if we do. He keeps us together with his flock and helps us stay where we are supposed to stay and go where we are supposed to go. He knows what's ideal for us. We do best when we trust in him and enjoy safe pastures. He restores our souls. He refreshes our lives from the inside out. We experience peace, fulfillment, security, and love because of the Lord. He is our Good Shepherd.

Dear Lord, you are my shepherd, I shall not want. You make me lie down in green pastures. You lead me beside still waters. You restore my soul. In Jesus' name, amen.

May 4

God Is Able to Keep Us from Falling

"To him who is able to keep you from stumbling and to present you before his glorious presence without fault and with great joy—to the only God our Savior be glory, majesty, power and authority, through Jesus Christ our Lord, before all ages, now and forevermore! Amen." Jude 1:24–25

God lifted us out of our sins and gave us a firm place to stand. He set us on a path of righteousness. He gave us a new life and a new purpose. He is not only a saving God; he is a keeping God! We do not have to go back to our old life anymore. There is no turning back. God put our past behind us and our sins are forgiven through the blood of Jesus. The Lord is able to keep us on the path of righteousness and victory that we are on. He will keep us from stumbling and falling. The Lord loves us so much that his love lifts us to a place that we have never been before. We don't fall because we are loved by God. The Lord gave us his Holy Spirit to reside inside of us to give us strength, encouragement, and perseverance to keep us from falling. The Lord gave us his Word to keep us from falling. The Word of God is a lamp to our feet and a light to our path. The Word keeps us going in the right direction and on track with the Lord. The Lord also puts other believers in our lives to keep us from falling. Today they may encourage us. Tomorrow, we may encourage them. That's the way Christ-centered friendships work. We help keep each other from falling. God has us in his strong hands. He will never leave us nor forsake us. He has angels watching over us because he loves us so much. We have security in the Lord. He is our rock and our fortress; he is our strength. God is able to keep us from falling!

Dear Heavenly Father, I thank you that you are able to keep me from falling through Jesus Christ my Lord.
In Jesus' name, amen.

May 5

But for the Grace of God

"You should not gloat over your brother in the day of his misfortune, nor rejoice over the people of Judah in the day of their destruction, nor boast so much in the day of their trouble."
Obadiah 1:12

The Lord rebukes the nation Edom for being prideful and gloating over Judah's defeat and hardships. We need to be aware that gloating over another person's downfall is not what God desires. Even if that person was our enemy, we should not delight in another person's hardship. When someone has hurt us, a part of us feels that they should be paid back for what they did. But we are called to forgive and love our enemies. To delight in another's downfall is not what God desires. The Lord wants us to bless those who curse us and pray for those who have offended us. The Lord wants us to be kind and reflect his love. The Lord does not want us to take pleasure in other people's pain. To gloat when others fail is a prideful attitude. We need to remember that pride goes before destruction. We are not in a position to feel prideful when others fall, because if it were not for the grace of God in our own lives, we would be falling as well. With the Lord's help, we need to be humble and compassionate toward all people, wanting God's best for them and leaving it to the Lord to judge. As followers of Jesus, God will always watch over us to bring justice to our causes and judgment on those who do us wrong. We do not need to seek vengeance, lash back at people who have offended us, or take pleasure in their suffering. We pray God's best for them and entrust them into the Lord's hands.

Dear Lord, help me to refrain from ungodly responses to others on their day of misfortune. Use me as a channel of your love and your grace. In Jesus' name, amen.

May 6

The Discipline of Stillness

"He says, 'Be still, and know that I am God; I will be exalted among the nations, I will be exalted in the earth.'"
Psalm 46:10

The practice of stillness is a spiritual discipline that the Lord can help us develop in our relationship with him. Stillness will help us to rest and refresh in the presence of the Lord. When we are faced with challenges or difficulties, we may react by trying to fix things or trying to make them better. Then we find that our efforts just made things worse. We are like that car stuck in the mud. We step on the gas to get out but just dig ourselves deeper. Sometimes the best thing to do is to just be still. When we become still, we can trust the Lord, rather than thinking that we have to fix things on our own. Stillness will help us have a deeper personal relationship with the Lord. When we are constantly moving, we cannot truly focus on the Lord or the things of God. Stillness involves being physically still and not moving. It also involves our environment. We need to be in a quiet atmosphere without noise or distraction. We need to put away all electronic devices and be fully focused. Stillness also involves an internal experience. We are thinking, planning, and worrying about so many things. We allow our emotions to rise up inside us and overpower the influence of the Spirit of God. With God's help, we can quiet our thoughts and emotions and allow the Holy Spirit to be the dominant presence and our strongest internal influence. When we truly quiet ourselves, we are in a better place to listen to the Lord and hear the gentle whisper of his Holy Spirit inside of us. The Lord can help us learn to be still before him.

Dear Lord, help me to be still and know that you are God.
In Jesus' name, amen.

May 7

God Is Good All the Time

"Give thanks to the LORD, for he is good. His love endures forever."
Psalm 136:1

We can thank God every day for his goodness and his love. When we do, we are worshipping him for who he is. God is good! The goodness of God is his moral excellence. There is no shadow of evil in him. He is righteous, positive, desirable, and superior. He is of the highest honor and greatest benefit. He is generous and loving. He is complete, thorough, and perfect. God is loyal, faithful, reliable, and dependable. We can count on him. God is trustworthy and enduring; he is gracious, patient, kind, and forgiving. He is favorable, satisfying, and propitious! He is upright, bountiful, pleasant, enjoyable, and delightful. God is benevolent, virtuous, advantageous, and valuable. God is good!

God's love endures forever. His love never quits. He never gives up. He never turns his back on us. He will never leave us nor forsake us. His love never runs out. He doesn't get fed up and leave. He does not change his commitment to love us. His love is a covenant love. It is a bond that cannot be broken. He knows everything about us and still loves us! He loves us even more for that! God's love is unconditional, there are no strings attached. His love is eternal, he loves us so much he prepared a place in heaven for us and he longs to spend all of eternity with us. God loves us so much that he gave his only Son, Jesus, to die on the cross to save us from our sins and to rise from the dead to lead us in eternal life!

Dear Lord, I give you thanks today and every day, for you are good! Your love endures forever! In Jesus' name, amen.

May 8

A Mother's Prayers

"A Canaanite woman from that vicinity came to him, crying out, 'Lord, Son of David, have mercy on me! My daughter is demon-possessed and suffering terribly.'...Then Jesus said to her, 'Woman, you have great faith! Your request is granted.' And her daughter was healed at that moment."
Matthew 15:22, 28

Mother's Day is celebrated as a national holiday in the United States on the second Sunday of May. This is a day to celebrate and honor our mothers. The Canaanite woman is an example of the power of a mother's prayer. A mother has a unique love for her children. This is a comforting, nurturing love. A mother has great compassion for her children. A mother's love also has great strength. This is a love that perseveres and will fight resistance if it has to. The strength of a mother's love empowers a mother's prayers, which will never give up. The Canaanite woman persisted in her passionate prayer for her daughter to Jesus. Jesus commended her great faith and granted her request. Thank God for a mother's prayers! A mother's persistence and passion in prayer for her children is an example to all of us of how we should be praying for the people the Lord puts in our lives. God can do the impossible. Let's put our faith into action with powerful, persistent, and passionate prayers.

Dear Lord, I thank you for the passion, persistence, and power that you provide when I pray for others. I thank you that you hear my prayers. You are an awesome God! Nothing is too difficult for you! In Jesus' name, amen.

May 9

Right Relationship

"If we confess our sins, he is faithful and just and will forgive us our sins and purify us from all unrighteousness."
1 John 1:9

When we accept Jesus as Lord and ask forgiveness for our sins, we are cleansed and forgiven by the blood that Jesus shed, once and for all! We are forgiven unto salvation. We are saved and going to heaven when we accept Christ and receive his forgiveness. We do not have to carry the guilt and shame of our sins anymore. We receive deliverance from the power of sin over our lives and we are free from the bondage of sin. The Lord transforms us and makes us new. As we live and grow as Christians, we continue to contend with our sinful nature. We make mistakes. We have failures. We still deal with sin in our lives. We don't just keep sinning without addressing it before the Lord. We continue to confess our sin when it occurs and the Lord applies his forgiveness. This is not forgiveness unto salvation; that has already been done when we became Christians. This is forgiveness unto a right relationship with the Lord. Our righteousness as Christians is not our moral perfection, it is Christ's. We need to be in a right relationship with him. When we have agreed with God that we sinned, we can get back on track with his help without the unrighteousness of sin between us. When we own up to our sins before the Lord, he forgives us and helps us to overcome them. When we have integrity and authenticity before the Lord about our struggle with sin, he cleanses us from the unrighteousness that sin brings into our hearts as well as our relationship with him. We are in a right relationship with the Lord because of his grace, his love, and his forgiveness!

Dear Heavenly Father, I thank you that when I confess my sins, you are faithful and just to forgive my sins and cleanse me from all unrighteousness. In Jesus' name, amen.

May 10

Put Off / Put On

"You were taught, with regard to your former way of life, to put off your old self, which is being corrupted by its deceitful desires; to be made new in the attitude of your minds; and to put on the new self, created to be like God in true righteousness and holiness." Ephesians 4:22–24

Paul identifies three experiences that occur in the process of change: put off the old self, be made new in the attitude of your minds, and put on the new self. Each of these is important for solid change.

When we put off the old self, we are getting rid of sinful habits. We recognize those behaviors that are disobedient to the Word of God, and we stop them with God's help. This is an obvious step, but it is not enough in itself.

When we are made new in the attitude of our minds, we are changing the way we think. To change the way we act, we need to change the way we think. Through the power of the Holy Spirit, the Lord renews the attitude of our minds. The Lord uses his Word to renew our thoughts and replace ungodly beliefs with beliefs based on the truth of the Word of God.

When we put on the new self, we are practicing godly behaviors to replace our old sinful behaviors. The Lord is developing new character qualities in our lives that overcome the destructive patterns of our past. He is conforming us to his image. Thank God for changing us and making us new!

Dear Lord, I pray that you help me to put off the old self, which is being corrupted by deceitful desires, to be made new in the attitude of my mind, and to put on the new self, created to be like you, Lord, in true righteousness and holiness. In Jesus' name, amen.

May 11

Don't Give Up

"Let us not become weary in doing good, for at the proper time we will reap a harvest if we do not give up."
Galatians 6:9

Serving the Lord and doing good is not always easy. Sometimes it's just plain hard work. We can become weary in our spiritual disciplines; getting up early to pray and read our Bibles, and participating in church and Bible study. We may get discouraged when we are trying to do good but not seeing results. We may not be receiving encouragement or assistance from anybody else. Sometimes it feels like the only thing we get from others is a hard time! Although we are tired and doing good is not easy, giving up is not an option. We mustn't quit. We are not going backward; only forward. Perseverance will pay off. The blessing is around the corner. We do not need the immediate gratification of giving up when we know that the Lord is with us and that he will provide for what we need. We may feel like we can't go on, but the truth is, we can because the Lord is with us. Ours is a journey of faith. We walk by faith in God, not by sight. We believe in him and do the right thing even when there are no thanks or immediate results. We know that we will reap a harvest at the proper time if we do not give up. We are encouraged by the Lord when we know that we are doing what he wants us to do. We are fulfilled and satisfied to know that we are pleasing him. The Lord gives us strength and encouragement in those times of weariness and discouragement. We need to keep doing what God has called us to do. The results are up to him. Don't give up and watch the Lord come through with results and a harvest that is bigger and better than we can imagine. Our trust and our hope are in him!

Dear Heavenly Father, help me to not become weary in doing good, I trust you that at the proper time, I will reap a harvest if I do not give up. In Jesus' name, amen.

May 12

The Virtuous Person

*"Charm is deceptive, and beauty is fleeting; but a woman who
fears the Lord is to be praised."*
Proverbs 31:30

The last chapter of the book of Proverbs presents a tribute
to the woman of noble character. This passage highlights the
value of godly character and provides examples of how that
character is exhibited in a lifestyle. The virtuous woman is described as hardworking, industrious, stable, caring, wise, prudent, skillful, generous, strong, trustworthy, and noble. These
are qualities that are not limited to women who fear the Lord.
These are important qualities for men of God as well. For
those who are single and hope to be married and have a family someday, these are qualities that are valuable in the spouse
that God brings to our life. These are also the qualities that
God is developing in our own lives. Being a person of noble
character is more important than how we look, what kind of
clothes we wear, or what kind of car we drive. Godly character
is inner beauty, which far outweighs the value of outward appearance. We need to be careful about getting caught up in
outward appearances because appearances are far less important than character. How we look on the outside is not as
important as who we are on the inside. A person's true beauty
is not measured by outward appearance but by their inner
qualities. As Christians, we live a productive life that honors
the Lord and is a blessing to our family and others around us.
We are a blessing, not a burden. Our productive and virtuous
lifestyle is a witness to the excellence and virtue of our Lord.
He deserves our best!

*Dear Heavenly Father, I pray that you will help me to be a person
of noble character. May the virtues of your Spirit be evident in
my lifestyle. In Jesus' name, amen.*

May 13

Safe and Secure

"Whoever dwells in the shelter of the Most High will rest in the shadow of the Almighty. I will say of the LORD, 'He is my refuge and my fortress, my God, in whom I trust.'"
Psalm 91:1–2

When we are in a personal relationship with the Lord, he holds us close and watches over us. He protects us from harm and danger. He protects us from evil. We are safe in his mighty hands. When life has so much craziness and chaos, we can find peace and rest in his presence. We can be refreshed and renewed in the presence of the Lord instead of being constantly drained and worn down by the pressures and stresses of the world. We have this safety and security when we dwell in the shelter of his presence. This means that we are abiding and remaining in his presence, not just popping in once and a while for a quick visit. We remain close to the Lord. He is our shelter and refuge. We do not go out on our own. We abide and dwell in the Lord's presence through a lifestyle of devotion and obedience to him. When we disobey the Lord, it is as if we are stepping out from his covering, we are leaving the shelter and safety of his presence and making ourselves vulnerable to the forces of evil without the blessing of his covering to watch over us. Disobedience and sin always cause separation between ourselves and the Lord. That is the last thing we want. Our trust in the Lord keeps us close to him and we live out our trust by living in obedience to his Word. We remain and abide in his presence where there is peace and rest. When we abide in him, the Lord protects us and watches over us. We are safe and secure in the Lord.

Most High God, I choose to dwell and rest in your presence. You are my refuge and my fortress, you are my God, in whom I trust. In Jesus' name, amen.

May 14

God Is Our Strength

"My flesh and my heart may fail, but God is the strength of my heart and my portion forever."
Psalm 73:26

There is only so much we can do in our own strength. We try our best, but we become tired. We have weaknesses, we make mistakes. Some problems and issues we face seem too difficult for us. We cannot face these challenges on our own. We need help. The Lord is our help and our strength. The Lord will call us to do things that we cannot possibly do in our own strength. He wants us to depend on him to strengthen us and help us accomplish what he calls us to do. We may deal with struggles like addiction. We want to quit, yet we just cannot seem to do it in our own strength. The Lord gives us the strength to overcome addiction and other life-controlling problems. The Lord is stronger than any drug or problem! He has the power to set us free. We are weak, but he is strong. He is mighty and powerful. When we have a personal relationship with Jesus Christ, we are plugged into the source of our power. Nothing is impossible with God when we rely on him. We receive strength from the Spirit of God, the Word of God, and the people of God. The Holy Spirit gives us inner spiritual strength that we do not have on our own. When we are weary and discouraged, God's Word can lift us and build us up. The Lord also places other Christians in our lives to encourage us with his love when we have a hard time receiving it on our own. Although our own strength fails, the Lord helps us to carry on because he is our strength.

Dear Lord, my flesh and my heart may fail, but you are the strength of my heart and my portion forever.
In Jesus' name, amen.

May 15

Open Up

"He asked them, 'What are you discussing together as you walk along?'..." Luke 24:17

The very day Jesus rose from the dead, he made an appearance to two of his followers who were walking to a nearby village called Emmaus, about seven miles from Jerusalem. He kept his identity hidden from them, gently walked up to them, and asked what they were talking about. As unusual as this seems for the magnitude of that day's event, this encounter is a reflection of the way Jesus interacts with us in our day-to-day lives. Jesus walks with us on our journey of life. Where we go, he goes. He is always present with us. Just as Jesus gently asked the men what they were discussing, he gently asks us what is going on with us. He wants to know what is on our hearts and minds. Jesus wants to be involved and connected in every aspect of our lives. We can talk with Jesus like we talk with a friend, taking a walk. As Jesus walked with these two men, he proceeded to open up to them and share things with them about himself and his Word. In the same way, when we focus on our relationship with Jesus, he shares his love with us. He gives us understanding and insight into himself and his Word. Let's not make the mistake of rushing through our busy days without slowing down to connect with Jesus. He is with us. He wants us to open up to him and he wants to share with us as well.

Dear Jesus, I thank you that you are always present and that you walk through this journey of life with me. I love you and I love spending time with you. I open up my life to you. I want to be closer to you. In Jesus' name, amen.

May 16

On Wings like Eagles

"Even youths grow tired and weary, and young men stumble and fall; but those who hope in the LORD will renew their strength. They will soar on wings like eagles; they will run and not grow weary, they will walk and not be faint."
Isaiah 40:30–31

Life can become wearisome. We all get tired at times. The Lord helps us by providing rest and strength. We are not alone and we are not limited to our own strength. There is a spiritual rest and refreshing that comes from the Lord. The Lord helps us to have perseverance to accomplish his will and purpose for our lives. We can wear ourselves out when we keep pushing ourselves. The Lord wants us to have a balance in our lives that includes healthy rest and time with him. An example of the Lord's standard of rest is the practice of the Sabbath in the Old Testament. This was a day that was set apart for rest. The principle of having a day of rest and time with the Lord carries over to the New Testament. Physical rest is good for us, but there is also a spiritual refreshing that takes place when we spend time in the Lord's presence with prayer, Bible study, worship, and fellowship with other believers. When we cast our cares to the Lord and put our hope and trust in him, he lifts our burdens and provides spiritual refreshing. When we wait on the Lord rather than relying on our own strength, he enables us to rise above discouragement and soar with his grace and perseverance. Our hope is in the Lord!

Dear Lord, I wait on you and place my hope in you. I pray that you renew my strength that I may soar on wings like eagles and that I will run and not be weary, and I will walk and not faint. In Jesus' name, amen.

May 17

A Quiet Place

"Then, because so many people were coming and going that they did not even have a chance to eat, he said to them, 'Come with me by yourselves to a quiet place and get some rest.'"
Mark 6:31

It was so busy that the apostles did not have time to eat. In the middle of all that activity, Jesus called them away with him to a quiet place to get some rest. Jesus also invites us to come away with him by ourselves to a quiet place to get some rest. When there is a lot of stress and activity, it is even more important that we get away with the Lord and have some quiet time with him. We may feel like we are too busy to pray, but the truth is that we are too busy not to pray! Throughout the Gospels, we read that Jesus would go away by himself to solitary places and spend time in prayer. If this was Jesus' practice, how much more do we need to do the same? The irony is that although we at times feel like we are too busy to spend time with the Lord, he is never too busy to spend time with us! Jesus loves us so much and he desires to have us spend time in his presence. What a privilege for us to have that access to our Lord and Savior. When we spend time alone with Jesus, we are developing our relationship with him through prayer. Like all relationships, we grow closer by spending more time together. Jesus invites us to a quiet place. We need to get away from the noise and activity when we are in prayer. The Lord will help us to be in a quiet place on our insides as well as in our environment so that we are truly focused on him with all of our minds, all of our hearts, and all of our souls. There is rest in his presence.

Dear Jesus, I thank you today for your invitation to come with you by myself to a quiet place and get some rest.
In your name, amen.

May 18

Plant Gardens

"This is what the LORD Almighty, the God of Israel, says to all those I carried into exile from Jerusalem to Babylon: 'Build houses and settle down; plant gardens and eat what they produce.'" Jeremiah 29:4–5

Jeremiah was writing to the Israelites who were carried away as captives to Babylon. Jeremiah knew that the Lord allowed Babylon to overtake Jerusalem as chastisement for Israel's disobedience to the Lord. Jeremiah knew that captivity was the Lord's discipline. He is instructing the captives to accept this season of discipline rather than resist it. Jeremiah instructs the captives to make the best of the situation; to build houses and settle down, to plant gardens and eat what they produce. Our initial reaction when faced with difficult circumstances may be to get out of the situation. There may be difficult circumstances that the Lord wants us to accept rather than resist or get out of. This may include discipline from the Lord, although every time we are facing difficulty does not mean we are being disciplined. The Christian life is not a life free from difficulty, pain, or sorrow. Rather than asking ourselves, "How can I get out of this situation?" we should be asking, "Lord what do you want to accomplish through this? What can I learn through this? In what way do I need to grow or change?" The Lord's purposes and our sanctification are more important to the Lord than our comfort. We can't get out of a situation every time we are uncomfortable or we don't like it. The Lord may want us to accept the situation and go through it with his help rather than trying to run away. Sometimes we need to bloom where we are planted.

Dear Heavenly Father, help me to accept difficult realities rather than try to escape them. Help me to turn to you instead of running away. Have your way in my life. I trust you. In Jesus' name, amen.

May 19

A Life Transformed

"I appeal to you for my son Onesimus, who became my son while I was in chains. Formerly he was useless to you, but now he has become useful both to you and to me."
Philemon 1:10–11

Onesimus was a slave who worked for a man named Philemon. Onesimus stole from Philemon and ran away. In his travels, Onesimus met the apostle Paul. Paul took Onesimus under his wing. Onesimus stayed with Paul and helped him. Onesimus went from being a thief and a runaway slave to a laborer for the gospel of Jesus Christ and a spiritual son of the apostle Paul. Onesimus' life was changed by the power of the gospel of Jesus Christ. After some time, Paul encouraged Onesimus to make things right and return to Philemon. Paul sent Onesimus back to Philemon along with a letter encouraging Philemon to forgive Onesimus and take him back. The Lord uses other believers in the lives of those whom he is transforming. Paul reached out to Onesimus and accepted him. Paul took on the role of mentor and spiritual father. There was a time in Paul's journey with the Lord that he needed to be encouraged. Then the Lord used him to mentor and encourage others. As Christians, we participate in the miraculous ministry of transformation that God does in people's lives by showing others grace and forgiveness and by practicing the ministry of reconciliation. We can give people the benefit of the doubt and offer them another chance in the same way the Lord extended grace and mercy to us when we needed it. We are all participating in the journey of God's transformation, in our own lives and the lives of others. Glory to God for a transformed life!

Dear Lord, I thank you that you transformed my life. I pray that you will use me to share love and encouragement with others whom you are transforming as well. In Jesus' name, amen.

May 20

Bridging the Gap

"'For my thoughts are not your thoughts, neither are your ways my ways,' declares the LORD. 'As the heavens are higher than the earth, so are my ways higher than your ways and my thoughts than your thoughts.'" Isaiah 55:8–9

We were isolated from the Lord in our sins. Jesus brought forgiveness for our sins through his shed blood and his death on the cross. He brought us new life through his resurrection from the dead. God reconciled us to himself through Christ. Where there was separation and disconnection, now there is relationship and connection. The Holy Spirit comes inside of us so that we have a connection with the Lord through his presence. We draw closer to the Lord in our relationship with him. However, even as Christians, we are limited by our natural mindset and inclinations. There is still a difference that exists between our thoughts and God's thoughts; between our ways and his ways. The Lord can continue to decrease that distance and bridge that gap between us. He can help us to have thoughts more like his thoughts and ways more like his ways. The Lord has provided his thoughts to us through the Bible. His Word presents a revelation of who he is and how he wants us to live. When we read and meditate on the Word of God, it will help us to think more like God thinks. When we apply the Word of God to our lives through obedience, it helps our ways to be more like his ways. The Holy Spirit also continues to renew our hearts and our minds. This is a process that begins when we become Christians and will continue to take place until we are in the Lord's presence in heaven. With the Lord's help, we can bridge the gap between us every day.

Dear Lord, I pray for your help today that my thoughts will be more like your thoughts, and that my ways will be more like your ways. In Jesus' name, amen.

May 21

For Such a Time as This

"...And who knows but that you have come to your royal position for such a time as this?" Esther 4:14

The book of Esther is a beautiful story in the Old Testament of how a poor Jewish girl became queen of Persia, and how she was able to save the Jewish people from a plan to annihilate them. Esther had hidden her Jewish background from the king. She was going to have to take the risk of losing her own life to reveal her identity as a Jew to save her people. When Esther was faced with the dilemma of taking this risk, her cousin Mordecai challenged her with the statement, "And who knows but that you have come to your royal position for such a time as this?" This challenging statement implies the reality that the Lord orchestrates events to happen at a certain time to fulfill his plans and purposes. God works in mysterious ways. What seems like random chance events may be the divine providence of the Lord working according to his timing to accomplish his purpose. What appears to us as coincidence may be in fact "God incidents." We need to be aware of the timing of God to accomplish his will. God may use surprise encounters to get our attention. We need to be sensitive to the Lord's timing and be willing and flexible to surrender our own plans and agenda to accomplish his will in his time. We also may experience disappointment regarding something we had hoped for. We may need to consider that it was not the Lord's time. We need to trust in the Lord for his will to be accomplished in his time. God's timing is perfect.

Dear Heavenly Father, help me to be aware of your will and your timing in my life today. May your perfect will be accomplished in my life for such a time as this. In Jesus' name, amen.

May 22

Amazing Grace

"For it is by grace you have been saved, through faith—and this is not from yourselves, it is the gift of God—not by works, so that no one can boast." Ephesians 2:8-9

We are saved from the penalty of our sins because of God's great love for us. We are cleansed from the guilt and shame of our sins because of God's merciful forgiveness. Our eternal destiny is changed from condemnation to eternal life through the sacrificial death of Jesus on the cross. Even the saving faith we have in Christ to ask for his forgiveness was given to us as a gift of God. All of these awesome experiences are gifts from God. They were given to us by God's unmerited favor. We did not have to change our lives first to be saved. There is nothing we can do to earn the gifts of God's love, grace, forgiveness, and salvation. Our part is to receive. We respond to the grace of God with thanksgiving in our hearts because of the great gifts he has given us. We respond to his grace with humility knowing that we did nothing to deserve this. We remember where we came from and we know that we need the Lord's grace in our lives as much today as we ever did. The only thing we can boast about is the goodness and grace of God! We respond to God's generous grace by sharing that same grace with others. We cannot judge or look down on others because we are only here by the grace of God ourselves. We can be channels of God's grace by sharing the good gifts of God that we have received with others who are also in need of God's love, forgiveness, and grace.

Dear Heavenly Father, I thank you that it is by your grace that I am saved, through faith, and this not of myself, it is the gift of God, not by works, so that I cannot boast. I thank you for your amazing grace. Help me to share it with others today. In Jesus' name, amen.

May 23

He Has Shown Us

"He has shown you, O mortal, what is good. And what does the LORD require of you? To act justly and to love mercy and to walk humbly with your God." Micah 6:8

The prophet Micah provides an example of three standards the Lord has given us to live by. God requires us to act justly, to love mercy, and to walk humbly with our God.

We act justly when we do good to those who need it when it is in our power to act. We treat all people with fairness, dignity, and respect. We maintain integrity in our decisions and interactions with others. We do not take advantage of other people or use them for our personal gain. Rather than exploit those who are weaker or less privileged than ourselves, we should be helping them.

Mercy is an outstanding quality of God. To show mercy is to come alongside others with compassion rather than judgment. Mercy brings forgiveness and kindness rather than harshness and criticism. Mercy withholds punishment even when we believe it is deserved. Mercy is shown out of grace, love, and compassion.

We walk humbly with our God when we put him and others above ourselves. We seek his will and his glory over our own. We serve the Lord and others over ourselves. We do not seek credit or glory for ourselves. We just want to please the Lord and experience life in a personal relationship with him. We trust in the Lord and know that when we humble ourselves in the sight of the Lord, he will lift us up.

*Dear Heavenly Father, thank you for showing me what is good and what you require of me: to act justly, to love mercy, and to walk humbly with you, my Lord, and my God.
In Jesus' name, amen.*

May 24

The Bitter Root

"See to it that no one falls short of the grace of God and that no bitter root grows up to cause trouble and defile many."
Hebrews 12:15

A person who holds on to negative feelings such as hurt, anger, or disappointment becomes bitter. It is one thing to experience these emotions at the time the incident occurs. It is another to hold on to those negative feelings and allow them to grow inside of us. An example of this is a person who was hurt by another person years ago and is still mad about it. Unforgiveness becomes resentment and resentment becomes bitterness. Bitterness is like a wound that got infected. It is like a poison inside of us that we carry around. That bitterness inside of us causes our hearts to become hardened. The solution to bitterness is forgiveness. To forgive is to release the person who offended us from the debt we feel they owe us. It is when we take our hurts or disappointments to the Lord that he can heal our hearts. When we hold on to hurt, resentment, anger, or disappointment, it festers inside of us. It causes us to become unhappy and negative. The bitterness influences our ability to live in freedom with love, joy, and gratitude. Love keeps no record of wrongs. To be free from bitterness we need to take our hurts to the Lord in prayer and ask him to forgive those who hurt us. We need to let it go rather than hold on to the offense. In those times when it comes back to our minds we go back to the Lord and pray some more rather than picking it up again. When we forgive and pray, the Lord will take the bitter root away.

Dear Lord, help me to forgive and let go of anger, hurt, disappointment, and resentment. Heal my heart and help me from becoming bitter. In Jesus' name, amen.

May 25

Do What Is Right

*"If you do what is right, will you not be accepted? But if you do
not do what is right, sin is crouching at your door; it desires to
have you, but you must rule over it."*
Genesis 4:7

The choices we make lead to results, either good or bad.
We experience success when we choose to follow the Lord's
way in obedience to his Word. When we choose to be disobedient, we leave the path of success and walk on the path of destruction. Sin is described as crouching at the door. We have
a choice of which door we go through. When we begin to do
things our own way, we are allowing sin to get a foothold. This
sin can worsen and cause destruction and hurt in our lives. We
can stop this hurt before it starts by making the right choices
with God's help. Sin wants to take over our lives and control
us, but God can help us to rule over sin. When we surrender
our lives and our wills to the Lord, he keeps us free from the
bondage of sin. We prevent sin from ruling over us when we
obey the Word of God. We take the time to pray about our
feelings, our thoughts, and our decisions. We are in constant
contact with the Lord through our relationship with him. The
Holy Spirit will guide us so that we can walk securely on the
path of freedom. When we are doing what God wants us to
do, we do not even open the door where sin lurks. In those
times of temptation, the Lord helps us to recognize the enticement and trappings of sin so that we can prevent becoming
entangled in sin and walk in the freedom and victory of God.

*Dear Lord, I surrender my will to you. Show me your ways, and
give me the grace to walk in obedience to your Word. Help me to
live in victory over sin today. In Jesus' name, amen.*

May 26

Remember and Give Thanks

"I thank my God every time I remember you."
Philippians 1:3

Memorial Day is a national holiday in the United States designated to honor the men and women in our armed forces who have lost their lives fighting for our country. This is a day of mourning for their loss. It is a day to remember our fallen soldiers and give thanks for their commitment to our country for which they made the greatest sacrifice. We need to honor them and remember that the freedoms that we enjoy in our country were fought for and secured at the cost of many lives. We thank God for our fallen soldiers who lost their lives fighting for our freedom. They paid the price with their lives for the freedom that we enjoy today.

Jesus Christ gave his life so that we may be free from the burden of sin. Jesus paid the price for our freedom from sin by shedding his blood and dying on the cross so that we may be free from the power and the penalty of sin. Jesus suffered the torturous and painful death on the cross to take the penalty of our sins for us so that we may be forgiven and have eternal life. This salvation is a free gift to us. Jesus paid the price. We enjoy the benefit of his atoning death with freedom from the power and penalty of sin. As we enjoy the freedom that Jesus purchased for us with his life, we should thank God and remember the sacrifice that Jesus made for us. We honor the Lord with our lives in devotion to Jesus.

Dear Heavenly Father, this Memorial Day we remember those who gave their lives for our country. We thank you for them and for the freedoms that we have in our nation. We also thank you for the freedom that we have through Jesus Christ. May my life be a reflection of the gratitude and honor for the price that was paid. In Jesus' name, amen.

May 27

No Turning Back

"Whenever the Lord raised up a judge for them, he was with the judge and saved them out of the hands of their enemies as long as the judge lived; for the Lord relented because of their groaning under those who oppressed and afflicted them."
Judges 2:18

Once the Israelites got settled in the Promised Land, they stopped serving the Lord and began to worship other gods. As a chastisement for their disobedience, the Lord would allow outside armies to overtake Israel and rule over them. The Israelites suffered under oppression and then called on the name of the Lord to rescue them. Then the Lord would raise up a judge to lead them in victory over their oppressors. Once they attained freedom, they would stop serving the Lord again and worship other gods. Tragically, this pattern repeated itself for several hundred years as recorded in the book of Judges.

We need to be careful not to allow a similar pattern to develop in our own lives. The Lord wants us to live in consistent freedom and a constant and stable relationship with him. We do not have to live life like a roller coaster! We can have long-term victorious success in our relationship with the Lord by continuing to devote ourselves to him and not allowing the comfort of success to cause us to lose our passion for the Lord. We need to call out to the Lord in the good times as well as the difficult times. When we keep that solid relationship with the Lord and a lifestyle of obedience to him, we do not have to go back into that cycle of disobedience and oppression anymore. With God's help, there is no turning back!

Dear Lord, I thank you that you are my deliverer and you are my steadfast victory. My hope and my trust are in you.
In Jesus' name, amen.

May 28

Faithful Protection

"But the Lord is faithful, and he will strengthen and protect you from the evil one." 2 Thessalonians 3:3

The Christian life has many battles. We are in a spiritual war against the devil and the forces of evil. That warfare may come in the form of hardships and challenges. We face trials and tribulations in our lives. We have faith and encouragement even when we are going through a spiritual battle because God is faithful. We rely on God. He is our victory. He has already defeated the devil when Jesus died to save us from the penalty of our sins and then rose from the dead to lead us in resurrection life and victory over the enemy with the promise of eternal life. We can trust and rely on the faithfulness of God. We know that the Lord has more power than the devil. We have nothing to be afraid of because God is watching over us. God's resources for our victory are both internal and external. His strength is internal and his protection is external. The internal strength God provides for us is the presence of the Holy Spirit. This very presence of God inside of us is greater than the strength of the enemy. Although it is not comfortable to be in a battle, we do not give up. We know that we have the strength of the Lord inside of us to persevere and we do not lose faith. God's external protection comes through his sovereignty. God is the supreme power over the devil and all forces of evil. The Lord can push the devil back anytime he wants. The Lord also puts a guard over us to protect us from evil. He uses his angels to watch over us to fight for us over spiritual forces. We are on the winning side with the Lord! We may be in a fight, but with God, we always win!

Dear Heavenly Father, you are faithful! Thank you for your strength and protection from the evil one. You are my victory! In Jesus' name, amen.

May 29

No Condemnation

"Therefore there is now no condemnation for those who are in Christ Jesus." Romans 8:1

To be condemned is to be denounced or to be declared as evil or wrong. To be condemned is to be pronounced guilty and sentenced to death. There was a condemnation that came from our sinful state. We deserved to be punished for our sins. However, we are free from condemnation through Jesus Christ. Jesus took the punishment our sins deserved through his death on the cross. Jesus shed his blood for the forgiveness of our sins. Now that we are in a position of freedom from condemnation, we need to carry that mindset toward ourselves and others. We may tend to feel guilty when we are faced with the reality of our failures and sins. We may tend to beat ourselves up for our mistakes and feel like we are not worthy or that we will never succeed or change. We also may be critical of other people and want to hold their sins and mistakes against them. These attitudes go against the grace of God. Condemnation is one of the tactics of the devil and goes against the grace and forgiveness of our Lord Jesus Christ. When we have harsh, critical, or unforgiving thoughts toward ourselves or others, we are contradicting the redeeming work of Christ on the cross. If Jesus died to bring forgiveness and grace, why would we bring condemnation back to the picture? We need to recognize those condemning thoughts and attitudes and cast them down. With God's help, we can embrace the forgiveness and grace of God and turn it to others and ourselves.

Dear Heavenly Father, I thank you that there is now no condemnation at all for those who are in Christ Jesus. Help me to embrace your forgiveness and grace and turn it to myself and others today. In Jesus' name, amen.

May 30

By His Spirit

"...'Not by might nor by power, but by my Spirit,' says the
LORD Almighty." Zechariah 4:6

Our success as Christians is not found in our natural abilities. We may be good-looking, intelligent, or physically fit. We may have wealth or social influence. All those things do not matter without God. Our success comes from the Lord, not from ourselves. We rely on him. We do not have to do things in our own strength. We all have shortcomings and weaknesses. God does not leave us on our own to accomplish all that he has called us to do. The Lord has given us his Holy Spirit as a source of strength and power in our lives. Whether it is overcoming addiction, forgiving those who hurt us, loving the unlovable, or enduring hardship, we have the power of the Holy Spirit to go through these experiences with God's help. We do not run away, we don't give up, we do not avoid challenges, but with the Lord's help, we go through them. The Holy Spirit empowers us through the Word of God. The Spirit leads us into all truth and gives us an understanding of God's Word. The Holy Spirit brings back to remembrance the Word of God and helps us to know God's Word and apply it to our lives. The Holy Spirit gives us the grace to follow through and obey the Word of God even when it is difficult for us. The Holy Spirit gives us strength to overcome temptation. The Holy Spirit gives us perseverance so that we do not give up. The Holy Spirit guides us as we make decisions. The Holy Spirit brings conviction of our sins to help us get back on track in a right relationship with the Lord. God can bring us victory by the power of his Holy Spirit working in our lives.

Dear Heavenly Father, my victory is not by my might, nor by my
power, but by your Spirit. In Jesus' name, amen.

May 31

For the Glory of God

"...whatever you do, do it all for the glory of God."
1 Corinthians 10:31

The Westminster Shorter Catechism states that "Man's chief end is to glorify God and to enjoy him forever." To glorify God is our greatest purpose. Giving God glory is a way to worship him. We worship him and glorify his name with our words, our shouts of praise, and our songs of praise and worship. We bring glory to God when we acknowledge him for the great things he has done. We credit God when great things happen because we know that all good things come from his hand. We give honor to God publicly for achievements and accomplishments because we know that we can do nothing without him. When we honor God and give him credit, it is a witness to other people about the goodness and the glory of God. Others can experience God's love and salvation when we give him glory and share how great he is. We also bring glory to God through our behavior and lifestyle. When other people know we are Christians, they watch our lives and see how we behave. When we live a righteous life and do good things, it gives God glory. We glorify God when God's light shines through us to other people. Since glorifying God is our chief end, that should be a guideline for everything we do. Before we make a decision, we should ask, "Will this bring glory to God?" If so, then we should do it, if not, then why would we do that? Everything we do and everything we say can bring glory to God. Let's find a way to bring glory to God today!

Dear Heavenly Father, whatever I do, help me to bring glory to you and your name. I thank you for all of the good things in my life and I give you all the glory! In Jesus' name, amen.

June 1

A Prayer of Repentance

*"Have mercy on me, O God, according to your unfailing love;
according to your great compassion blot out my transgressions."*
Psalm 51:1

Psalm 51 is a model prayer of repentance. This psalm, written by David, is attributed to the time in David's life when he was confronted by the prophet Nathan for committing adultery with Bathsheba and having her husband Uriah killed in an attempt to cover up his adultery. In this prayer, David wholeheartedly confessed his sin. He laid all of his cards on the table before the Lord rather than continuing to try to keep a secret sin. At this point, David was humble and broken, taking full responsibility with no excuses, blaming, or minimizing. He was not confessing in an attempt to get out of trouble; a repentant heart accepts the consequences of sin. David had an attitude of acceptance toward God's judgment. David was focusing on change, praying to God for a clean heart and a right spirit.

David calls on God's mercy, unfailing love, and great compassion. It is the power of God that gives repentance its effectiveness. God's kindness leads us to repentance. God has so much love, mercy, and compassion, that he gave his Son, Jesus, to die on the cross for our sins. It is through the blood of Jesus that our sins are forgiven and, as David prayed, our transgressions are blotted out. God forgives, restores us, and helps us live a new life in victory over the sins that bring us down. When we go to God with a repentant heart, he forgives us and changes us. Because of God's great love and God's power to restore, even after committing adultery and murder, David is known as a man after God's own heart. A repentant heart is a heart after God.

*Have mercy on me, O God, according to your unfailing love;
according to your great compassion blot out my transgressions.
In Jesus' name, amen.*

June 2

The Outpouring of the Holy Spirit

"When the day of Pentecost came, they were all together in one place. Suddenly a sound like the blowing of a violent wind came from heaven and filled the whole house where they were sitting."
Acts 2:1–2

The day of Pentecost mentioned in the New Testament is a holiday established in the Old Testament known as Shavuot (Hebrew for "weeks"), also known as the Feast of Weeks because it was held seven weeks after the Passover. It is also known as the Feast of the Harvest because it celebrates the first fruits of the wheat harvest. The New Testament uses the Greek word transliterated "Pentecost" which means "fiftieth day" because it was held fifty days after the Passover. It was on the day of Pentecost that the Lord poured his Holy Spirit out on the believers who were gathered in Jerusalem, an event that had been previously prophesied in the Old Testament. When Jesus was with his disciples, he promised them that the Father would send the Holy Spirit. After Jesus rose from the dead, he repeated his promise and instructed them to wait in Jerusalem until the Holy Spirit came upon them. When the Holy Spirit came on the disciples on the Day of Pentecost, Peter preached about Jesus to the crowds that were gathered in Jerusalem for the Feast of Pentecost. Three thousand people who heard Peter's message that day joined the disciples in following Jesus Christ. This event is known as the birthday of the Christian Church. This Old Testament harvest of the first fruits was fulfilled with the first fruits of the Holy Spirit on the church. The Christian Church around the world now recognizes "Pentecost Sunday" fifty days after Easter. We have the Holy Spirit to empower us to live the Christian life and to do the Lord's work until he returns.

Dear Heavenly Father, I thank you for pouring out your Holy Spirit on your church and my life. I pray for a fresh outpouring of your Holy Spirit in my life today. In Jesus' name, amen.

June 3

God Sings over You

"The LORD your God is with you, the Mighty Warrior who saves. He will take great delight in you; in his love he will no longer rebuke you, but will rejoice over you with singing."
Zephaniah 3:17

We are never alone. God is always with us. His Spirit is in us. He will never leave us nor forsake us. When we feel alone, all we have to do is call on his name. He will give us the strength to stand when we feel like we cannot go on. God is the Mighty Warrior who saves. When we are in a battle, God gives us victory. God fights our battles for us. We just need to trust him by faith and not give up or give in to the enemy. The Lord saved us from harm, difficulty, and danger in the past. He will do the same again. God is faithful and will continue to be the God who saves us when we need him. God fights for us because of his great love. He delights in us. We are so important to him that he will do anything to help us. God loves us so much that he sent his Son, Jesus, to die on the cross for our sins. Jesus sacrificed his life to save us because of his love. God is not trying to criticize us or put us down, he desires to love us. He surrounds us with his love and rejoices over us with singing. He has so much hope and love for us that even during trials he sings songs of love and redemption over us. We can embrace his love and his song by faith to walk through trials and battles with faith, hope, and victory. We are not alone.

Dear Heavenly Father, I thank you that you are always with me. You are the Mighty Warrior who saves. Thank you for taking delight in me and loving me. I love you, Lord, and I take delight in you. Thank you for rejoicing over me with singing. I sing praises to your name. In Jesus' name, amen.

155

June 4

This Is Love

"And this is love: that we walk in obedience to his commands. As you have heard from the beginning, his command is that you walk in love." 2 John 1:6

Love and obedience go hand in hand. To love God is to obey him. Our obedience is the way we show our love to God. God's priorities are for us to love him and love each other. God wants us to enjoy life in a right relationship with him as well as with each other. Our obedience is not about adhering to strict rules of what to do and what not to do. It is about our relationship with the Lord. God wants the best for us. He wants to have a thriving love relationship with us. His Word informs us how to do that. God's best for us is laid out in the Bible. When we live according to God's Word, we can live life to its fullest. When we disobey the Word of the Lord, we are falling short of God's plan and will for us. Disobedience and sin separate us from the Lord. Our love for God is what motivates and strengthens us to walk in obedience to him. We love God so much that we do not want to do anything to hurt him or our relationship with him. When we disobey, we not only hurt our relationship with the Lord, but we hurt ourselves. God's Word is there to guide us to live a successful and fulfilled life. Our love for God is expressed through our lifestyle. We enjoy a right relationship with the Lord when we live a lifestyle of obedience to his Word. This is love.

Dear Lord, I thank you for your love and I love you, Lord. Help me to walk in love and obedience to you and your Word today. In Jesus' name, amen.

June 5

God Devises Ways

"Like water spilled on the ground, which cannot be recovered, so we must die. But that is not what God desires; rather, he devises ways so that a banished person does not remain banished from him." 2 Samuel 14:14

God devises ways so that people who are separated from him can be in a right relationship with him. God so loved the world, that he sent his Son, Jesus, to save us from our sin. Jesus, the eternal God, took on the form of a man so that he would die on the cross to save us from the penalty of our sins. Jesus made a way for everyone to come to God in a right relationship with him. Jesus came to seek and save those who were lost. He is our Good Shepherd who leaves the ninety-nine sheep to go and find the one who is lost. There is no one beyond Christ's redemption. He can reach anyone with his love, no matter how far down the path of sin and destruction that person has gone. God still devises ways to bring lost and backslidden people to him. God orchestrates divine appointments so that Christian witnesses share his love and the gospel message at the right time at the right place to those who are separated from him. God can draw people to him with a display of his power and love such as a miraculous healing, or miraculously surviving a dangerous situation. The Lord can also use difficulties to get people's attention such as an arrest, broken relationships, or getting fired. The way of the transgressor is hard. A person who is separated from the Lord may just get sick and tired of being sick and tired. That is when the Lord will reach out to them with his love.

Dear Heavenly Father, I thank you that you devise ways so that a lost or backslidden person can receive your love and salvation. Use me, Lord, to pray for them, and to share your love and your truth. In Jesus' name, amen.

June 6

It's about Relationship

"'But like a woman unfaithful to her husband, so you, Israel, have been unfaithful to me,' declares the LORD."
Jeremiah 3:20

Throughout the Old Testament, the Lord refers to idol worship as spiritual unfaithfulness and adultery. God's people who worshipped other gods committed spiritual adultery when they were unfaithful in their loyalty and commitment to their relationship with God. This concept should impact our perspective of sin and disobedience. We can develop an attitude of permissiveness when we view God's laws as a list of rules and the Lord as a policeman or a judge who watches over us. Rather than have this behavioral view of the Lord and our obedience, we need to have a relational view of the Lord and our obedience or disobedience. God has an intimate covenant relationship with us, and our faithfulness in that love relationship is reflected by our obedience to the Word of God. When we disobey the Lord, it is not just that we break a rule, but that we affect our love relationship with the Lord. When we disobey God, we hurt him and our relationship with him.

Our love relationship with the Lord is our strength to refrain from disobedience and live in obedience and a right relationship with God. When we experience the love of God, we do not need to turn away from him to have our needs met anywhere else. The enticement of sin loses its appeal when compared to the love of God. We do not have to strain our way through obedience in our own feeble strength, but when we bask in the love of God, we will not need to disobey. We love God so much that we do not want to hurt him or our relationship with him.

Dear Heavenly Father, thank you for your love that has changed my life! I love you so much God, let me live in your love today in a right relationship with you and in obedience to your Word. In Jesus' name, amen.

June 7

A Willing Heart

*"'I am the Lord's servant,' Mary answered. 'May your word
to me be fulfilled.' Then the angel left her."*
Luke 1:38

The angel Gabriel visited Mary to inform her that she was
going to have a child through the power of God. Mary's response is an excellent example of a willing heart before the
Lord. Mary was a virgin yet she was informed that she was
going to have a baby. She showed her faith in God by receiving and accepting that reality even though she could not completely understand how this could happen. We cannot always
understand the Lord's ways and purposes. We have questions,
uncertainties, and insecurities. We accept and trust God's will
by faith.

Mary displayed humility by stating that she was the Lord's
servant. Humility is an attitude of submission and willingness
to do whatever God wants us to do. We lay aside our plans
and ideas to accept God's plans and desire for his will to be
done rather than trying to impose our will on the Lord. We
practice humility when we submit ourselves to the Lord and
his will for our lives.

Mary displayed an attitude of obedience by stating that
she wanted the word spoken by the angel to be fulfilled. We
also display an attitude of obedience when we seek the Word
of God to be fulfilled in our lives. We are willing to do whatever
the Word of God tells us to do. We seek direction from the
Word rather than the leading of our own desires and ambi-
tions. We are committed to adhering to the Word even when
it is difficult or uncomfortable for us. We can follow Mary's
example of a willing heart by practicing faith, humility, and
obedience today.

*Dear Heavenly Father, I am the Lord's servant, may your Word to
me be fulfilled in my life today. In Jesus' name, amen.*

June 8

A Glimpse of Heaven

"'He will wipe every tear from their eyes. There will be no more death' or mourning or crying or pain, for the old order of things has passed away." Revelation 21:4

In the book of Revelation, John has a vision of the New Jerusalem, coming down from heaven. The Bible states that in the future, heaven and earth, as we know it will pass away. There will be a new heaven and a new earth for eternity. Jesus will be with us and we will be with him forever. This description of the New Jerusalem provides a glimpse of what our eternal life will be like with Jesus in heaven. All of us who have asked Jesus for forgiveness of our sins and have received him as our Lord and Savior have received his salvation from eternal death and we have received the gift of eternal life in Christ Jesus our Lord. The greatest part of this eternal reward is to be present with Jesus forever. The description of the Lord himself wiping every tear from our eyes shows the love and tenderness that God has for us right now. Although that time has not come, his love is here for us today. He has sympathy and tender mercies for the pain we feel today. He is present with us today through his Holy Spirit and he wants to draw close to us and love us when we are hurting. This love he has for us will be ultimately fulfilled when we are in heaven and truly in his presence. There will be no more death or mourning or crying or pain. We will have eternal rest and comfort in the presence of the Lord. The life we live on earth is temporary. Our eternal home is in heaven. Meanwhile, we are ambassadors of heaven, sharing God's love and this hope of eternal life with those who do not know him.

Dear Heavenly Father, I thank you for the promise of eternal life. Your promise of heaven gives me strength and hope today. In Jesus' name, amen.

June 9

Remember Where You Came From

"Brothers and sisters, think of what you were when you were called. Not many of you were wise by human standards; not many were influential; not many were of noble birth. But God chose the foolish things of the world to shame the wise; God chose the weak things of the world to shame the strong."
1 Corinthians 1:26–27

When we remember where we came from, we will always be grateful. God has been so good to us! He gave us love when we had no love. He gave us hope when we had no hope. Jesus gave us forgiveness of our sins through his death on the cross. We have a new life because of him. He has restored our lives and our relationships. Our hearts are filled with gratitude and we thank him and praise him every day!

When we remember where we came from, we will always be humble. It is by the grace of God that we are saved. We did nothing to deserve the goodness of God in our lives. Every good thing in our lives is from the grace of God. We can do nothing without him. We need God in our lives as much today as we did the first day we cried out to him. We can take no credit for any good that is in our lives, all glory and honor to God!

When we remember where we came from, we will always show mercy and grace to others. Those of us who have been forgiven much will love much. We share the same mercy and grace that was given to us. Now that we are rescued, we need to be mindful of those who are hurting among us. We show love to God by sharing his love with others.

Dear Lord, when I remember where you brought me from, I am so grateful. I give you thanks and praise. Help me to share your mercy and grace with others. In Jesus' name, amen.

161

June 10

Workers in His Harvest

"He told them, 'The harvest is plentiful, but the workers are few. Ask the Lord of the harvest, therefore, to send out workers into his harvest field.'" Luke 10:2

Jesus is not talking about a harvest of wheat, corn, or barley. He is talking about a harvest of souls. There remains a harvest of souls in the world today. Humanity is God's harvest field. People are lost and hurting who do not know the love of God. God is the Lord of the harvest. As a farmer plants seeds to bring in a harvest, the Lord created humankind to follow him and to have eternal life in heaven with him. The Lord desires for all people to receive his love and to turn to him in faith. For God so loved the world that he gave his son Jesus that whoever believes in him shall not perish but have everlasting life. Jesus calls us to pray for workers to go out into God's harvest field and help bring in the harvest. Our prayers are powerful and effective as they come alongside the will of God to draw men and women to him. We pray for those who are lost, that the Lord will work in their lives to bring them to a saving faith in Jesus.

We are all called to serve as workers in God's harvest. The Lord did not call us out of our sin for us to sit back in our comfort and enjoy the blessings of his salvation and eternal life without doing our part to help those who are lost and also need Jesus. We all have a place to serve in the body of Christ and in God's harvest field to bring in the harvest of souls.

Dear Heavenly Father, you are the Lord of the harvest of souls. Use me as a worker in your harvest to share your love and the gospel of Jesus with those who are lost. I pray that you would raise up more workers for the harvest for your glory. In Jesus' name, amen.

June 11

Faith over Feelings

"Why, my soul, are you downcast? Why so disturbed within me? Put your hope in God, for I will yet praise him, my Savior and my God." Psalm 42:5

David confronts his soul and asks: "Why are you downcast?" He challenged himself, saying, "Put your hope in God." He chose to praise the Lord. We can challenge ourselves when our emotions begin to take over and negatively control us. With God's help, we can control our emotions rather than allowing our emotions to control us. We can decide to praise the Lord even when we are upset about something. We are human. All of our emotions are God-given. Our emotions do not just go away, but we can prevent our emotions from controlling us. This does not mean that we deny or suppress our feelings; we express and process our emotions in healthy ways. We can express our feelings to the Lord in prayer. Our emotions are not the rulers of our lives. We do not do everything we feel like doing. We can choose to submit our emotions to the Lord and put our faith in him. We can allow the Word of God and the Spirit of God to be a greater influence in our lives than our feelings. We choose to adhere to the Word of God even though our feelings are strong. This is not easy. This does not happen suddenly or instantly. This is a discipline that will develop as we grow in our relationship with the Lord. God is greater than our emotions. He can help us experience our emotions in a healthy way. Our emotions will always affect our choices, but with God's help, our feelings do not rule over our lives.

Dear Heavenly Father, you are the Lord of my emotions. Use your Word and your Spirit to guide me when my feelings are strong. In Jesus' name, amen.

163

June 12

Discipline with Love

"My son, do not despise the Lord's discipline, and do not resent his rebuke, because the Lord disciplines those he loves, as a father the son he delights in." Proverbs 3:11–12

One of the ways our Heavenly Father shows his love to us is by disciplining us. God gives us discipline like a loving father who disciplines his children. He does it out of love. The Lord disciplines us to help us learn and grow to make right choices. The immediate lesson designed in discipline is that negative choices and behavior bring negative consequences. Discomfort can be a teacher because we hopefully learn to not do that again! We learn new things when we can connect consequences with choices. We practice prudence when our thinking becomes consequential and we think things through rather than acting impulsively and seeking immediate gratification, thus causing negative consequences for ourselves. Discipline is unpleasant. We do not like it. Our first reaction may be to try to get out of it. However, if we embrace discipline and get everything out of it that we are supposed to, it will help us to grow and to be stronger and wiser. We may be challenged by the concept of a father lovingly giving discipline because we did not have that growing up. Perhaps discipline was done out of anger and was abusive. Perhaps we were not disciplined at all. This concept of a loving father may be new to us. God does not discipline us out of anger or in an abusive way. God gives his discipline with love. He is there with us to walk through the season of discipline. He wants to help us to learn from the discipline and to grow to be men and women of God.

*Dear Heavenly Father, help me to not despise your discipline or resent your rebuke. Help me to trust that you discipline those you love, as a father who delights in his children.
In Jesus' name, amen.*

June 13

Respect All People

"Do to others as you would have them do to you."
Luke 6:31

A simple working definition of respect is to treat other people the way we would like to be treated. All people deserve to be treated with respect. It does not matter who they are, if we like them or not, where they are from, whether they are Christians are not, or whether we agree with their lifestyle or not. When we show respect, we reflect the love of God. All people deserve this dignity because they were created by our Father God. Jesus died on the cross for all people. When we do not show respect to others, we miss the mark with the Lord. There is no excuse for showing disrespect. As Christians we are called to live a life becoming of the name of Christ and respect for all people is an important standard for us to display. We expect other people to have respect for us and our values. The best way for us to get respect from others is to show them respect. Respect is not demanded, it is a gift, or it is earned. We use our own values as a guideline for showing respect to others. We treat others the way we like to be treated and we do not do things to others that we do not like people doing to us. In today's culture, respect is becoming a lost quality. People can be rude and selfish. The light of God's love can shine through us with this simple practice of showing others respect.

Dear Lord, help me today to do unto others as I would have
them do unto me. In Jesus' name, amen.

June 14

Setting Healthy Boundaries

*"A hot-tempered person must pay the penalty; rescue
them, and you will have to do it again."*
Proverbs 19:19

If we rescue someone from the consequences of their behavior, we will have to do it again and again. The person will
never learn to stop when we keep rescuing them from consequences. They learn the opposite—that it is OK for them
to do wrong. They learn that when they do wrong, they will
get away with it, so it is okay. This practice of rescuing others
from the consequences of their choices is called "enabling."
This is an unhealthy habit that hurts others and ourselves.
The sad misconception is that we think we are helping them
by shielding them from the consequences of their behavior.
When we enable a person with a life-controlling problem such
as drug addiction, we are helping them to worsen their addiction and in today's dangerous culture, we could be contribut-
ing to their death. Enabling is not a healthy way to show love.
Love sets boundaries. We don't do it out of anger or spite.
We are helping the other person and ourselves to live with
healthy boundaries. An example of setting boundaries could
be telling the person you will help them this one time, but also
telling them how to prevent this from happening again and
that you will not help them a second time. Once we communicate a boundary, it is important to stick to it. With God's help,
we can set healthy boundaries in our lives to help others and
protect ourselves.

*Dear Heavenly Father, give me the wisdom and strength in my
life to set and keep healthy boundaries. In Jesus' name, amen.*

June 15

Honor Your Father and Your Mother

*"Honor your father and your mother, so that you may live long
in the land the Lord your God is giving you."*
Exodus 20:12

In the United States, Father's Day is celebrated on the third Sunday of June. This is a day to honor our fathers and to thank them for their love in our lives. To honor our father and mother is one of the Ten Commandments. The apostle Paul points out that this is the first commandment with a promise, that we will have a long life. This reflects the importance that honoring our parents is to the Lord. When we become adults, we are not under the cover of our parents as we were when we were children. We do not obey them like we needed to do when we were children. However, we can always honor our parents, no matter how old we are. That is what the Lord wants us to do. We honor our parents when we show gratitude to them because we would not be here without them. We honor our parents through our lifestyle. Our life reflects our values and it reflects our parents as well. We honor our parents when we respect their values and their wishes even when we are adults. We honor our parents and the Lord by forgiving our parents for their faults. We also show honor to our parents by respecting and honoring their friends and family. We show honor to our parents by maintaining a relationship with them, even when we are busy or out of touch or have differences with them. This Father's Day, if we are out of touch with our fathers, we can reach out to them out of our love for the Lord. It is great to celebrate Father's Day by buying that card, or planning that dinner, but more than that, we can live a life that honors our parents and the Lord.

*Dear Heavenly Father, I thank you for my parents who gave me
life. Show me how I can honor my parents today.
In Jesus' name, amen.*

June 16

The Power of Prayer

"...The prayer of a righteous person is powerful and effective."
James 5:16

God answers prayer. When we pray, we are connecting with the power of God to move in our own lives and the lives of others. We pray petitions for our own needs, we make intercessory prayers for the needs of others. Whatever we pray, we pray with faith and confidence. Our confidence is not in our faith or our prayers, it is in the Lord. God is faithful to hear and answer our prayers. God is almighty and powerful and able to answer those prayers. Our prayers are powerful and effective because God is powerful and effective! We do not have power, God does. We are righteous through the righteousness of Jesus Christ. We have a personal relationship with Jesus, and we do not allow sin to come between us and the Lord. When we have been convicted of sin in our lives or our hearts, we confess that sin in prayer and ask for the Lord's forgiveness. The Lord cleanses us of unrighteousness so that we may continue to cultivate that right relationship with him. The powerfulness and effectiveness of our prayers do not mean we just pray once. We need to be persistent in our prayers and not give up. When there is not an immediate response to our prayers, it does not mean God has not heard, or that he will not answer. To the praying Christian, a delay in response means, "keep praying." God is faithful to answer our prayers in his time. He calls us to be faithful in prayer. Our prayers are our connection with the Lord in our spiritual relationship with him. He wants us to spend time in his presence in prayer. When we pray, we engage in the supernatural power of God to move in our lives. When we pray, we have faith that miracles will happen!

Dear Lord, I thank you that the prayers of a righteous person are powerful and effective. Help me to be faithful in prayer.
In Jesus' name, amen.

June 17

Face Everything and Reach

"For the Spirit God gave us does not make us timid, but gives us power, love and self-discipline."
2 Timothy 1:7

God has not given us a spirit of fear. Fear shrinks back with timidity. Our fears can hold us back from accomplishing God's best plans for our lives. There are rational and healthy fears that prevent us from doing dangerous things. On the other hand, there are fears and insecurities we may have that stop us from taking healthy and positive steps to grow and accomplish the Lord's purpose for our lives. These insecurities lead to a timidity that restrains us from growing and causes stagnation in our lives. We should not allow baseless fears to constrain us from growing and doing what the Lord wants us to do. The Lord has given us his Holy Spirit inside of us to help us overcome our fears that hold us back.

The Holy Spirit imparts the Lord's love to us in such a way that he dispels our fears. God's love comforts us in a way that casts out disabling fear. God's Spirit also provides power for us to step out with courage and confidence with faith because we know that God is greater than our fears. The Holy Spirit also enables us to have a sound mind. Fears cause us to be confused and apprehensive but the Spirit of Truth gives us clarity of mind and equips us with the Word of God to think in a positive way to move forward.

Dear Heavenly Father, I thank you for your Holy Spirit that gives me power, love, and a sound mind to overcome fears that hold me back. In Jesus' name, amen.

June 18

Growing Fruit

"But the fruit of the Spirit is love, joy, peace, forbearance, kindness, goodness, faithfulness, gentleness, and self-control. Against such things there is no law."
Galatians 5:22–23

Just as a healthy fruit tree will produce good and abundant fruit, the Holy Spirit will produce these qualities in our lives as Christians. These qualities develop in our lives because the Holy Spirit resides inside of us. The Holy Spirit impacts our spirit in such a way that he changes the way we think, feel, and act. We can overcome our old ways of thinking and acting because of the transforming ministry of the Holy Spirit inside of us to produce the fruit of these nine qualities that Paul lists. These qualities are in contrast to the works of the flesh, those negative inclinations to act in sinful and hurtful ways. The influence of the Holy Spirit is greater than the inclinations of the flesh no matter how long we have allowed the flesh to have influence and control over our lives. The development of these qualities in our lives is evidence of the Holy Spirit working inside of us. We will notice a change. Others will notice a change as these qualities become more evident as we grow in the Lord. We cooperate with the Holy Spirit as he is developing his fruit in our lives. We identify these qualities as fruit that God desires and do our part to be intentional about developing them and getting rid of the opposite qualities such as selfishness, complaining, confusion, unfaithfulness, impatience, rudeness, and lack of self-control. As we grow close to the Lord in our personal relationship with him, the Holy Spirit produces this good fruit in our lives.

Dear Heavenly Father, thank you that the fruit of your Spirit in my life is love, joy, peace, forbearance, kindness, goodness, faithfulness, gentleness, and self-control. I pray that the Holy Spirit will continue to grow this fruit in my life today. In Jesus' name, amen.

June 19

In the Potter's Hands

*"Yet you, Lord, are our Father. We are the clay, you are the
potter; we are all the work of your hand."*
Isaiah 64:8

As a potter forms a lump of clay into pottery, the Lord
molds us and makes us become the men and women of God
that he wants us to be. His gentle and strong hands will lovingly form us to make changes in our attitudes, feelings, beliefs,
and behavior. As the clay is soft and supple in the hands of the
potter, we need to be submissive, accepting, and surrendered
to the Lord as he is working in our lives to make us more like
Jesus. If there is hardness in the clay, the potter cannot mold
those hard parts. We also cannot have hardness, stubborn-
ness, resistance, or defiance in our hearts toward the changes
that the Lord wants to make in us. The hands of the Potter
shaping us may at times feel uncomfortable. We were accus-
tomed to the way we were. Change brings discomfort. We do
not like it when the hands of the Lord are shaping us and making us different. We may feel like we are being harassed or
violated and want to resist or defend ourselves. This is when
we need to trust the Lord and allow him to shape us and mold
us even though it feels uncomfortable and we do not understand exactly what he is doing. The Lord may use circumstances, conflict, or trials to accomplish the shaping in our lives that
he desires. During those times of challenge and difficulty, we
pray, "Lord, how are you using this situation to bring change
in my life?" Then we trust him and submit ourselves to him as
clay in the hands of the Potter.

Dear Lord, you are my Father. I am the clay, you are the Potter;
I am the work of your hand. Mold me and make me to be the
person you want me to be. In Jesus' name, amen.

June 20

Truth in Love

"Instead, speaking the truth in love, we will grow to become in every respect the mature body of him who is the head, that is, Christ." Ephesians 4:15

We speak the truth in love. The truth needs to be told and heard. Falsehoods and misconceptions lead to delusional thinking and then to wrong decisions. Lies are tactics of the devil. When we believe the lie, we become deceived and misled. The Lord gave us his Word as the truth for us to live by. The Bible provides a foundation of right thinking for us to build the right beliefs and to make the right decisions. We need the truth of God's Word in our own lives, and we can share the truth of God's Word with others. When we do share God's Word with others, we need to speak the truth in love. We do not use the Word of God to beat people up. We do not speak the truth to judge or criticize others. We do not speak to others in a way that would embarrass or shame them. We speak the truth in love. The most important truth we need to share is that God loves that person. The way we talk to others will express that truth. When we have love, the truth in our message comes across as a positive support to build up, not to tear down. God's Word edifies others, which means it gives them strength and encouragement. The truth offers hope, not condemnation. When we are speaking God's truth into someone's life, we need to do it with love. They may not agree with what we are saying but they will be assured that we care about them.

Dear Lord, help me today to speak the truth in love.
In Jesus' name, amen.

June 21

Reverence for God

"But I, by your great love, can come into your house; in reverence I bow down toward your holy temple." Psalm 5:7

We show reverence to God by approaching him with honor, respect, and awe. He is the Creator of the universe. God is the most powerful force in the universe. Jesus is the King of Kings and the Lord of Lords. The attitude of reverence is described in the Bible as the "fear of the Lord." We have a fear of the Lord, not because he is bad or evil; God is good and loving. The fear we have is a sense of his greatness, his holiness, and his power while also knowing that he has great love for us and that we also love him. We can have an intimate love relationship with the Lord; yet we do not approach God as if he is a pal, a chum, or a "homie." He is a mighty God, our Creator, who loves us very much. We lose a sense of reverence that God deserves when we become too familiar and casual toward the things of God. We need to take the Lord and the things of God seriously. Some of the ways we show reverence to God are: when we acknowledge the sacredness of his presence, his Word, and his church; when we worship the Lord for his holiness and his greatness; when we are quiet with a holy hush before the Lord in awe and honor of his presence; through our devotion to church attendance, prayer, and Bible reading; and we do not take the Lord's name in vain. We live a life of obedience that honors God and we practice holiness by separating ourselves from ungodliness out of reverence for our relationship with the Lord.

Dear Heavenly Father, I love you and give you honor and glory. You are mighty and holy. I humbly bow down and worship you with reverence. Help me to show my reverence for you by the way I live today. In Jesus' name, amen.

173

June 22

Worshipping Jesus

"You are worthy, our Lord and God, to receive glory and honor and power, for you created all things, and by your will they were created and have their being." Revelation 4:11

In the book of Revelation, the apostle John has a vision of heaven and of Jesus, sitting on the throne. Jesus is being worshipped by angelic beings and by the elders day and night. The elders fall before the throne and lay their crowns before Jesus and worship him. The worship of the living creatures and the elders also provides an example to us of worshipping Jesus. Falling before Jesus showed their submission to him. When we kneel in prayer before the Lord, we take on a posture of humility, surrender, and reverence for our mighty and holy King Jesus who sits on his throne. The elders lay their crowns before the throne. In this way, they gave any honor they had back to Jesus. Any honor or recognition we receive should also go to Jesus. He deserves all the glory and honor and praise. The words of their praise start with "You are worthy, our Lord and God...." This is the foundation of worship; it is "worth-ship," we are declaring how worthy the Lord is to us. This worship acknowledges the eternal nature of the Lord and his power to create all things. This worship also acknowledges that we were created by God's will. The Lord has a will and a purpose for each of our lives. The Bible shows us that it is God's will that we should worship Jesus and give him all the glory.

You are worthy, our Lord and God, to receive glory and honor and power, for you created all things, and by your will they were created and have their being. In Jesus' name, amen.

June 23

Dealing With Anger

"'In your anger do not sin': Do not let the sun go down while you are still angry, and do not give the devil a foothold."
Ephesians 4:26–27

Anger is a God-given emotion and is not sinful in and of itself. How we react to our anger can become sinful and harmful to others and ourselves. Two extremes of sinful anger are "clamming up" and "blowing up." The person who blows up is quick-tempered and reacts impulsively to anger. This person may yell and curse or become physically aggressive by slamming doors, throwing things, or even assaulting people. The person who clams up holds that anger in and becomes unforgiving and bitter. Some people turn to drugs or alcohol as an attempt to soothe or suppress their bottled-up anger. Others experience a time bomb phenomenon where they can hold on to that anger for so long, then one day they blow up in a rage.

Becoming a Christian does not make all our anger go away. With God's help, we can have victory over sinful and harmful anger. Managing our anger is a learning process. Our first response can be to talk it out in prayer with God and also with a neutral trusted individual. Talking it out can help process anger. An important key to letting go of anger is forgiveness. When we forgive, we are letting go of the offense and not holding on to it anymore. With God's help, we can control our anger rather than allowing our anger to control us.

Dear Lord, I pray for your help with my anger today. Help me find a healthy way to express my anger. Help me to forgive those with whom I am angry as you have forgiven me.
In Jesus' name, amen.

June 24

Beyond Our Wildest Dreams

"Now to him who is able to do immeasurably more than all we ask or imagine, according to his power that is at work within us, to him be glory in the church and in Christ Jesus throughout all generations, for ever and ever! Amen."
Ephesians 3:20–21

When we are faced with a challenging situation in which we think there is no way out, God can make a way where there seems to be no way. He impacts our world with his supernatural power to do things that we could not have imagined. It is because of God's great love that he does care about our lives and will watch over us and help us in ways that we could not comprehend. We pray for our plans, our heart's desires, and our future. The Lord may have even bigger and better plans than we had in mind. God can make things happen that are beyond our wildest dreams. For this reason, we need to trust him and allow him to bring about his great plans in his way in his time. The Lord's awesome plans may not take place as fast as we hoped for. We wait on him, trusting in his power, his love, and his faithfulness to accomplish his will according to his power. Our impatience or lack of faith in him could cause us to make hasty decisions and interfere with the Lord's great plan which is unfolding in his time. The Lord's faithfulness and awesome ability to do great things is a source of comfort to us when we feel like we are overwhelmed with problems too big for us. Our problems are not too big for God; God is able!

Dear Heavenly Father, you are able to do immeasurably more than all I ask or imagine, according to your power that is at work within me, to you be glory in the church and in Christ Jesus throughout all generations, for ever and ever!
In Jesus' name, amen.

June 25

God Turns Things Around

"You intended to harm me, but God intended it for good to accomplish what is now being done, the saving of many lives."
Genesis 50:20

Joseph was sold into slavery by his brothers. Through the passing of years and a series of events, Joseph ended up being second-in-command in all of Egypt. When a famine came across the land, Joseph's brothers traveled to Egypt looking for grain. When Joseph encountered them, he used his position to help them and to bring his family to Egypt where they could settle and survive the famine. After their father Jacob died, the brothers were afraid that Joseph would seek revenge for what they did to him years earlier. Joseph wisely and graciously responded that although they meant to harm him, God turned that situation around and made something good out of it. The Lord can work in our lives in the same way. We may have experienced hurtful and harmful situations in our lives. Those situations may have originated through intentional and hurtful acts of someone else, by our own poor choices, by circumstances beyond our control, or even by the influence of evil. Although our Christian life may include these difficult experiences, the Lord can redeem the harm that has occurred and turn it around for good. The Lord can bring good out of something terrible. When we turn to him and trust him for his help, God can turn things around. This does not always mean he removes the hardship we are facing, but he walks with us through it and he finds ways to use the situation for our good and his glory.

Dear Heavenly Father, I thank you that when I am faced with circumstances intended to harm me, that you can turn things around for my good and your glory. In Jesus' name, amen.

June 26

God's Supreme Power

"...'LORD, the God of our ancestors, are you not the God who is in heaven? You rule over all the kingdoms of the nations. Power and might are in your hand, and no one can withstand you.'"
2 Chronicles 20:6

The supreme power of God is described as the sovereignty of God. God is supreme over time as we understand it; God has no beginning and no end. He is eternal; he always was and always will be. God created all things in heaven and on earth. There is no power or authority on earth or in the universe that is greater than God's power. Rulers and leaders have authority on earth, but God has authority over all leaders. God has the authority to raise one leader up and set another leader down. God has authority over evil and the devil. Jesus defeated the devil by dying on the cross to take the penalty for our sins and rising from the dead to overcome the power of death, hell, and the grave for all of us who follow Christ. We acknowledge the sovereignty of God when we submit our will and our lives to the lordship of Jesus Christ. We know that our lives are in his hands and that he is in ultimate control and rules over all things. We entrust our lives to the Lord and his authority. Our faith is in the Lord's power to accomplish his will and purposes according to his mighty power. We trust the Lord with our lives because of his mighty power and his sovereign rule and reign over all things in heaven and earth.

Dear Lord, you are the God of heaven. You rule over all the kingdoms of the nations. Power and might are in your hand, and no one can withstand you. In Jesus' name, amen.

June 27

The Ministry of Interruption

"Very early in the morning, while it was still dark, Jesus got up, left the house and went off to a solitary place, where he prayed. Simon and his companions went to look for him, and when they found him, they exclaimed: 'Everyone is looking for you!'"
Mark 1:35–37

Jesus got away in the morning to a quiet place to pray. Peter and the disciples found Jesus and interrupted his prayer time to tell him that everyone was looking for him. Jesus replied, "Let us go somewhere else—to the nearby villages—so I can preach there also." Jesus did not say, "Leave me alone! Can't you see that I'm praying right now?" Jesus accepted the interruption rather than resisting it. The Gospel narratives describe many miraculous encounters that people had with Jesus. Just about all of these encounters were interruptions. Jesus did not make appointments with these folks; they just came up to him while he was doing something else or on his way somewhere else. We can be more like Jesus by embracing interruptions to take the opportunity to make time for the people that the Lord puts in our path. We can honor the Lord and other people by laying our schedule and agenda on the side and giving people 100% of our attention even when they have interrupted us. We can ask God what he wants us to accomplish throughout our day rather than imposing our plans and schedule on God, and being so busy and inflexible that we do not have time to share God's love, a kind act, or a prayer with someone that the Lord puts in our path.

Dear Heavenly Father, I submit myself and this new day to you today. Help me to accomplish whatever you want me to accomplish. Help me to be open to the ministry of interruption. In Jesus' name, amen.

June 28

A New Thing

"See, I am doing a new thing! Now it springs up; do you not perceive it? I am making a way in the wilderness and streams in the wasteland." Isaiah 43:19

God is still doing new things! God continues to save people for eternal life and work miracles in lives around us every day. God wants to do new things in our own lives. We can make the mistake of getting used to things going a certain way that we are not as open to seeing the new things that God is doing. The Lord asks: "Do you not perceive it?" God wants to know if we are paying attention to him and if we truly see and understand that he wants to do something new. This may be something totally unexpected that we had not even thought about before. This may be an area of our own lives that the Lord wants to improve or change. The Lord will continue to change us until we are in his presence in eternity. The Lord may be doing something new in our circle of family or friends or in the influence of our vocation or ministry. We make a mistake when we have the attitude that we have always done things a certain way so that is the best way to carry on. Times change and the best way to do some things also changes. The Lord will lead us to do things in new ways if we let him. It could be that it is the Lord's timing for a major change in our lives, like moving or changing jobs or getting involved in a new ministry that we never thought about before. God does new things. We need to be open to allow him to do new things in our lives.

Dear Heavenly Father, help me to perceive the new things that you are doing in me and around me. In Jesus' name, amen.

June 29

Tough Times Make Us Stronger

"Consider it pure joy, my brothers and sisters, whenever you face trials of many kinds, because you know that the testing of your faith produces perseverance. Let perseverance finish its work so that you may be mature and complete, not lacking anything."
James 1:2–4

James challenges us to consider it pure joy when faced with trials of many kinds. He encourages us to look at the positive side—that going through tough times makes us stronger in Christ. Trials test our faith because they hit us so hard that we are more likely to take our eyes off Jesus. It is during difficult times that our faith goes into action. We turn to the Lord for help with the faith that he has given us. We trust in the Lord by faith rather than focusing on the difficult circumstances we are facing. Our faith in Jesus Christ is a source of strength when we are going through a trial. Just as a weightlifter develops stronger muscles when he adds more weight, we develop spiritual muscles when we trust God through difficult times. Perseverance is the ability to continue to move forward and not give up. When we are close to the Lord and believe and trust in him, we will not give up. While we are growing in faith and developing perseverance, the Lord is helping us to become mature and complete. The Lord is helping us to become the men and women of God that he knows we can be. It is not pleasant, but with God's help, tough times make us stronger.

Dear Heavenly Father, help me to consider it pure joy whenever I face trials of many kinds because I know that the testing of my faith produces perseverance. Let perseverance finish its work so that I may be mature and complete, not lacking anything.
In Jesus' name, amen.

181

June 30

God Is Close When We Hurt

"The LORD is close to the brokenhearted and saves those who are crushed in spirit." Psalm 34:18

It is a painful experience to go through a deep emotional hurt. The loss of a loved one, betrayed trust, offensive words or actions, and rejection are some of the experiences we have that cause us to feel brokenhearted. Hurtful actions go deeper when they come from someone who is close to us; someone that we trusted. This kind of hurt can have a great impact on us. It can cause us to shut down and lose interest in all things. It may even affect our faith. It can cause us to be filled with anger and rage. Deep hurts may be a factor in a person's addiction to drugs or alcohol. Hurtful experiences do occur, even when we are Christians, but we do not have to go through them alone. The Lord draws close to us when we are brokenhearted. God loves us so much that he wants to be closer to us when we are hurting. He has great compassion for us. He does not want us to be in pain, but to be comforted and to know how much he loves us. God loves us so much that he sent his Son, Jesus, to live as a human; to be close with us, to be "God with us." Jesus died on the cross to save us from the penalty of our sins. When Jesus rose from the dead and ascended into heaven, the Lord sent his Holy Spirit to be with us, to be in us. The Lord also gave us his Word as a source of his love and comfort. When we are brokenhearted, God is there with us every step of the way as he brings healing to our hurts and puts the pieces of our broken hearts together.

Dear Lord, thank you that you draw close to me when I am brokenhearted and that you save me when I am crushed in spirit. In Jesus' name, amen.

July 1

On the Side of Grace

*"Jesus straightened up and asked her, 'Woman, where are they?
Has no one condemned you?' 'No one, sir,' she said. 'Then neither
do I condemn you,' Jesus declared. 'Go now and leave your life
of sin.'" John 8:10–11*

A woman was brought to Jesus. She had been allegedly caught in the act of adultery. The religious leaders, wanting to trap Jesus, informed him that the law said she should be stoned to death. They wanted Jesus to say what should be done with her. Jesus wisely responded, "Let any one of you who is without sin be the first to throw a stone at her." The woman's accusers walked away. Jesus did not judge the woman according to the law. He said, "Go now and leave your life of sin." Jesus did not say that what the woman had done was okay. Grace is not overlooking sin or minimizing the seriousness of sin. It is not enabling a person by supporting their bad choices. Grace is not throwing rules or consequences out the window, but rules and consequences can be seasoned with grace. Grace recognizes that everyone is on a journey and each person has a different pace. Grace leaves room for flexibility rather than maintaining strict rigidity. It is giving someone another chance rather than exercising dogmatic intolerance toward the person. We can show grace by continuing a relationship with boundaries rather than pushing someone away with harsh judgment. Giving grace is extending favor that is not deserved. We are all recipients of God's grace. We can share grace with others the same way the Lord has given us grace. Jesus showed grace. We can be more like Jesus in this way. If we are going to err, it is better to err on the side of grace.

*Dear Lord, I thank you for your amazing grace in my life. Help
me to show your amazing grace to others.
In Jesus' name, amen.*

July 2

Like a Little Child

"Truly I tell you, anyone who will not receive the kingdom of God like a little child will never enter it." Mark 10:15

Jesus states that we need to enter the kingdom of heaven like a little child. Jesus was not referring to immaturity but to endearing qualities that children have that set an example for us as adults. He wants us to be childlike, not childish!

The first childlike quality for us to have in our relationship with God is faith. Our experiences in life may have affected us in a way that we have doubts and cynicism in our outlook on life and our relationship with God. To practice a childlike faith is to trust and surrender to God without reservation.

A second childlike quality is humility. Children can experience the Lord with reverence, awe, respect, and honor. As we grow older, we may develop pride in such a way that it interferes with our relationship with God. We think we do not need help and that we can do things our way. When we have childlike humility, we do not think so highly of ourselves and we can submit and surrender to our mighty God.

A third childlike quality is dependence. As a child depends on his or her parents to take care of daily needs, we need to have that same attitude toward God. We need the Lord's love, strength, and guidance to live a successful life as Christians. Rather than developing self-sufficiency and thinking we can do this on our own, we need to maintain that child-like quality of dependence on the Lord.

Dear Heavenly Father, help me to come to you with childlike faith, humility, and dependence on you. I love you and I need you in my life. In Jesus' name, amen.

July 3

Our Blessed Hope

"For the grace of God has appeared that offers salvation to all people. It teaches us to say 'No' to ungodliness and worldly passions, and to live self-controlled, upright and godly lives in this present age, while we wait for the blessed hope—the appearing of the glory of our great God and Savior, Jesus Christ"
Titus 2:11–13

That same grace by which we were saved can teach us to say "No" to ungodliness and worldly passions. When we consider how good God has been to us, we will not want to jeopardize his grace or take it for granted. When we consider the great salvation that the Lord accomplished in our lives, it causes us to grow closer to him, and to avoid going back to the world and sin. When we experience the love of God through Jesus Christ, it teaches us that the fleeting pleasure of sin, ungodliness, and worldly passions are mere facades of the bondage and despair of sin and evil. Paul describes the goodness of God's grace as temporary while we wait for the Blessed Hope—the return of Jesus Christ, our Lord and Savior. Jesus is coming back! Our life on earth is temporary. Our true joy and fulfillment of the grace of God and his love will be in the presence of Jesus for eternity. Jesus will return in the same physical way that his disciples saw him ascend to heaven. No one knows when Jesus will return. The return of the Lord is imminent, it can happen anytime. When Jesus returns, he will come as the bridegroom to be with us, his bride, his church who believes in him and is waiting for his return. Jesus is our Blessed Hope.

Dear Heavenly Father, I thank you for your grace that offers salvation to all people and teaches us to say "No" to ungodliness and worldly passions and to live self-controlled, upright, and godly lives in this present age, while we wait for our blessed hope—the appearing of the glory of our great God and Savior, Jesus Christ. In Jesus' name, amen.

July 4

Jesus Frees Us

"So if the Son sets you free, you will be free indeed."
John 8:36

Today in the United States we celebrate Independence Day. The celebration of Independence Day commemorates the freedom our country fought for in the Revolutionary War. The blood of many soldiers was shed for the freedom of our nation from the rule of Great Britain. In like manner, the blood of Jesus Christ was shed so that all people everywhere may be free from the tyranny of the devil.

Jesus frees us from the penalty of sin. All of us have sinned against God and become subject to his judgment. The penalty for sin is eternal death. When Jesus died on the cross, he took the penalty we deserved for our sins on his shoulders so that we could be free. When we ask Jesus to forgive us of our sins and accept him as our Lord and Savior, he forgives us and sets us free. His death on the cross became the satisfaction of the judgment we deserved. Freedom from the penalty of sin means that we will have eternal life in heaven.

Jesus frees us from the power of sin. Sinful desires can grow into sinful behaviors. Sinful behaviors grow into sinful habits. Sin is a cruel master. Unforgiveness can grow into hatred. Lust can grow into adultery. Experimentation with drugs can grow into addiction. When Jesus is Lord of our lives sin is no longer our master and does not have that power over our lives anymore. The Holy Spirit gives us power over sin in our lives. We can have a life free from the penalty and the power of sin because Jesus frees us!

Dear Heavenly Father, I thank you that whom the Son sets free is free indeed. Help me to live in your freedom from sin today. In Jesus' name, amen.

July 5

No Compromise

"But Daniel resolved not to defile himself with the royal food and wine, and he asked the chief official for permission not to defile himself this way." Daniel 1:8

When the king of Babylon defeated Jerusalem, he carried away the inhabitants as captives. He chose several young men to be trained to serve him in Babylon. While the king was having these young noblemen trained in his palace, he directed for them to be provided with wine and rich food to eat. Daniel resolved not to eat the king's delicacies because the food violated Old Testament dietary laws. Daniel sets an excellent example of doing the right thing regardless of the circumstances. When things go wrong and we feel defeated, our faith can be challenged and this could be the scenario where we begin to compromise and lower our standards of holiness and dedication to the Lord. Daniel resolved to not allow any compromise even though he was facing difficult times. Once we compromise by justifying a "little sin" in our lives, it is likely that that little sin will grow into a big sin. We can prevent this from happening by allowing no compromise in our lives. As we study the Bible, the Lord provides guidelines for us to live by to stay on solid ground and in a right relationship with him. We live by the Word of God and we hide God's Word in our heart so that we might not sin against the Lord. The Holy Spirit inside of us also helps us to avoid compromise by working on our conscience, providing conviction of sin, and helping us do the right thing. We need to be sensitive to the conviction of the Holy Spirit. With God's help, we can resolve to make the right choices and not allow compromise or sin to grow in our lives.

Dear Heavenly Father, help me to resolve to reject compromise and sin in my life today. I resolve to follow you in obedience to your Word. In Jesus' name, amen.

July 6

No More Shame

"Do not be afraid; you will not be put to shame. Do not fear disgrace; you will not be humiliated. You will forget the shame of your youth..." Isaiah 54:4

Experiences from our past may have caused the development of shame that has a long-lasting effect on our self-worth and self-image. Feelings of disgrace, embarrassment, and unworthiness are so strong that we feel that we are unworthy of success and we feel that we do not deserve to be loved by other people or even by the Lord. Toxic, debilitating shame is different from guilt. Guilt says, "You have done something bad" or "What you did is not good enough." Shame says, "You are bad; you are not good enough." These feelings and beliefs are based on lies. They may have developed through traumatic or hurtful experiences. Shame may have developed through failures, mistakes, or sins from our past. Jesus died on the cross to forgive us of our sins. The blood of Jesus can cleanse us of our sins and the feelings of guilt and shame that we have held on to for so long. The Lord loves us so much. He does not see us through our past sins or who we were or what we did in the past. The Lord wants us to know freedom from shame in our personal relationship with Jesus Christ. This is a process that may take time and prayer. The stronghold of shame can be removed and healed through the love of God, the power of the Holy Spirit, and the truth of God's Word ministering to our souls.

Dear Heavenly Father, heal my heart from the hurt of shame. Cleanse my mind from the lies of shame. Help me to see myself the way you see me and love myself the way you love me. Deliver me from shame and fill me with your love.
In Jesus' name, amen.

July 7

God Can Break the Pattern

"In those days people will no longer say, 'The parents have eaten sour grapes, and the children's teeth are set on edge.' Instead, everyone will die for their own sin; whoever eats sour grapes—their own teeth will be set on edge."
Jeremiah 31:29–30

The influence of our family of origin can be positive or negative. Positive values such as respect, politeness, a strong work ethic, and faith in God may have been taught and modeled by our parents. Negative characteristics and patterns can also be developed through the influence of our family of origin. Destructive anger, abuse, divorce, and addiction are some examples of negative patterns of behavior that can be passed down from one generation to the next. As adult Christians, we are responsible for our own beliefs, choices, and behavior. We cannot blame our parents or our upbringing for our choices and behavior today. We can distinguish the good habits from the bad habits that were passed down to us from our parents. The Lord can break the pattern of negative behavior being passed down from one generation to the next. This is often a process of the Lord's healing and deliverance from our past as we grow in him. Beliefs, characteristics, and patterns of behavior passed on from our family may run deep, but the Holy Spirit is able to heal, cleanse, and renew the deep parts of our souls and minds. We can hand a godly legacy down to the next generation.

Dear Heavenly Father, break the pattern of any negative influences from my upbringing. Purify my heart, and help me to carry on a legacy of love and faith to hand down to the next generation. In Jesus' name, amen.

July 8

Lord of the Hills and the Valleys

"...This is what the LORD says: 'Because the Arameans think the LORD is a god of the hills and not a god of the valleys, I will deliver this vast army into your hands, and you will know that I am the LORD.'" 1 Kings 20:28

Ben Hadad, ruler of Aram, rose up his army against Israel in Samaria. Under the leadership of King Ahab, Israel fought and defeated Aram. After their defeat, the king of Aram's officials advised him that the Israelites won the battle because Aram fought Israel on a hill and that the god of Israel was a god of the hills. They told the king of Aram that he should fight Israel in the valley and they would win. The Lord knew of their plans, so he sent the prophet to King Ahab to tell the king that he was the God of the hills *and* the valleys and that they would win the battle again. The Arameans made the mistake of limiting God. God cannot be limited by people, places, things, or circumstances. God is bigger than our circumstances and he is bigger than any problem we are facing. We need to take our focus off the circumstances, off of our problems, off of the hills and the valleys, and put our trust and our faith in God! God has no limits; nothing is impossible with God! God is the God of the hills and the God of the valleys; he is the God of the good times and the God of hard times. We worship God and trust him when times are good; we also worship and trust the Lord when times are rough. When we have submitted and surrendered our lives to God, he is Lord over all things in our lives.

Dear Heavenly Father, I thank you that you are the God of the hills and the God of the valleys; you are the God of the good times and you are the God of the hard times. You are bigger than my problems. Nothing is too difficult for you. My faith and trust are in you. In Jesus' name, amen.

July 9

Be Cool

*"Better a patient person than a warrior, one with self-control
than one who takes a city." Proverbs 16:32*

Patience is a virtue that enables us to wait when people
and circumstances are not moving along the way we want,
or as quickly as we would like. Patience allows us to remain
calm, cool, and collected while we are waiting. Patience is a
strength in our interpersonal relationships because other
people appreciate the gentle support that patience provides.
When we become impatient with others, it comes across like
we are not pleased with them and that we are agitated. This
could cause them to become offended or feel defensive and
this creates an atmosphere for conflict. Our impatience also
takes us to an unpleasant emotional place. When we become
impatient, we give up our peace. We become frustrated, then
annoyed, then angry. Patience is a fruit of the Spirit and an
important strength in our spiritual relationship with the Lord.
We patiently trust the Lord and wait on him in faith rather
than becoming impatient and hasty and then getting ahead
of God and doing things our own way. Sometimes patience
means letting the Lord make things happen rather than doing
them ourselves. When we become impatient, we get in the
flesh and make things happen ourselves. This is like winning
the battle but losing the war. We may end up getting what
we want, but it is more important to the Lord that we remain
patient and control our spirit than to get what we want. With
the Lord's help, we can practice patience and maintain a spirit
of peace, love, and self-control while we trust him to do things
his way in his time.

*Dear Heavenly Father, develop the quality of patience in my life.
Help me to be patient rather than be a warrior. Help me to have
self-control rather than push to get my way.
In Jesus' name, amen.*

July 10

A Worker Approved by God

"Do your best to present yourself to God as one approved, a worker who does not need to be ashamed and who correctly handles the word of truth." 2 Timothy 2:15

As with any other relationship, we do our part in our relationship with the Lord. We trust in him rather than leaning on our own understanding. We walk by faith and not by sight, trusting in the Lord as we go. We have a commitment to the Lord and the things of God that we take seriously. We walk in obedience to the Word of God. The Lord provides his Word as guidelines for us to live by. When we are doing our best to obey God and honor him with our lifestyle, our conscience is clean. We are not perfect. God is still working on us, but we do not need to be ashamed because we have been cleansed and washed by the blood of Jesus and renewed by the power of the Holy Spirit. We do our part in our collaborative relationship with the Lord to do and be our best. We read and study God's Word in our own private quiet time as well as with others and in our church. We meditate on the Word of God and hide it in our hearts. The Holy Spirit ministers to us to retain and understand the Word of God in our lives. With God's help, we correctly handle the Word of God by applying God's Word and its principles into our everyday lives. We also correctly handle God's Word when we share his truth with others. God enables us as we do our best.

*Heavenly Father, help me to do my best to present myself to you as one approved, a worker who does not need to be ashamed and who correctly handles the word of truth.
In Jesus' name, amen.*

July 11

Our God of All Comfort

"Praise be to the God and Father of our Lord Jesus Christ, the Father of compassion and the God of all comfort, who comforts us in all our troubles so that we can comfort those in any trouble with the comfort we ourselves receive from God."
2 Corinthians 1:3–4

Comfort is one of God's strengths and attributes. God is very compassionate toward us because of his great love for us. He is sensitive to our feelings and our needs. He truly loves us and cares about our hurts. God draws close to us when we are in need of comfort. He listens to our hearts when we are hurting. He is there for us with his presence. He shares comfort with us through his Word. He comforts us through his Holy Spirit inside of us. God also puts people in our lives to bring us comfort. One of the positive results of going through a difficulty or hardship and coming out the other side with God's help is that we have this experience to share with others who are going through what we went through. It is powerful to have somebody understand what you are going through because they have been through the same thing. Since we have gone through hurtful experiences, we can be more sensitive to others and empathetic toward their pain and understanding of what to do to help because we went through the same thing. We comfort others the same way God comforted us. We share comfort with others when we show compassion and express our love to them the same way God loved us when we needed comfort.

Heavenly Father, I praise you for being the Father of compassion and the God of all comfort. Thank you for comforting me when I was in trouble. Help me to comfort those in any trouble with the comfort I myself received from you. In Jesus' name, amen.

July 12

Hope in Times of Loss

"Brothers and sisters, we do not want you to be uninformed about those who sleep in death, so that you do not grieve like the rest of mankind, who have no hope. For we believe that Jesus died and rose again, and so we believe that God will bring with Jesus those who have fallen asleep in him."
1 Thessalonians 4:13–14

Grief is one of the most painful emotional experiences in life. The loss of someone we love causes deep hurt. It feels like a part of our heart has been ripped out. There are other circumstances that also can bring feelings of grief and loss such as divorce, the loss of a career, or having to move away suddenly. Grief is often accompanied by a lot of other emotions. The experience of grief and loss is sacred. People experience the journey of grief in different ways. The way a person deals with grief is personal. For believers in Christ, grief has an innate strength because of our hope in eternity through Jesus Christ. We know that this world is temporary. We have an eternity with Jesus in our future in heaven where there will be no more pain. As Christians, we are comforted to know that we are never alone. The Lord is close to us when we are grieving. His presence brings us love, comfort, and strength for this painful experience and process in our lives.

Dear Heavenly Father, I pray for your love, comfort, and strength in the experience of my own grief and for those who are on my heart. I thank you for the inner strength that comes from our hope for eternal life through Jesus Christ. In Jesus' name, amen.

July 13

Our Identity Is in Jesus Christ

"It is because of him that you are in Christ Jesus, who has become for us wisdom from God—that is, our righteousness, holiness and redemption. Therefore, as it is written: 'Let the one who boasts boast in the Lord.'" 1 Corinthians 1:30–31

The New Testament describes Christians as being "in Christ." This signifies that we have accepted Jesus as Lord, that we have a personal relationship with Jesus, and that our identity is in Jesus Christ. Paul mentions just four parts of our identity that we have in Christ: wisdom, righteousness, holiness, and redemption. We have these and other spiritual attributes because Jesus died on the cross for our sins and rose from the dead. We followed Jesus in death by dying to our old life. The life we live now, we live in him. Our identity is in Jesus. Our identity is not in where we are from or where we live now. Our Identity is not in the type of house we live in, the car we drive, or the clothes we wear. Our identity is not in our job title or how much money we make. It is not in our friends, our social circle, the team we follow, or the gang we ran with. Our identity is not even in our ethnicity, our culture, or our family relationships. Our identity is not in our past, whether good or bad. It does not matter what we have done in the past. That is not who we are anymore. Even any good qualities we have are from God and because of him. If we are going to boast, we will boast in our Lord Jesus Christ. He gave us a new life and he is our life today!

Dear Lord, thank you that by your grace I am in Christ today. My identity is in Jesus, not my past. All that I am is in Christ Jesus my Lord. In Jesus' name, amen.

July 14

No Turning Back

*"But if serving the L*ord* seems undesirable to you, then choose for yourselves this day whom you will serve, whether the gods your ancestors served beyond the Euphrates, or the gods of the Amorites, in whose land you are living. But as for me and my household, we will serve the L*ord.*" Joshua 24:15*

Joshua was the leader of the Israelites. He addressed those he led by informing them that they needed to make a choice. They could choose to follow the Lord, the One True God, or they could choose to follow the false gods of that time. He also made it clear that he and his family had chosen to follow and serve the Lord.

We all have to make a choice. God loves us so much that he gives us a choice. He waits with arms open for each of us to choose him. Joshua sets an example for us by declaring his choice and his commitment to serve the Lord. He speaks not only for himself but for his family as well. As the leader of his home, he takes responsibility that his family is committed to the Lord. To declare that commitment is to express unwavering devotion to the Lord. Committing to Christ is like shooting an arrow from a bow; there is no turning back. When we choose to follow Jesus, we follow that choice with a commitment to follow him with a lifestyle of devotion and obedience.

Dear Heavenly Father, today I make a renewed commitment to follow and serve you. As for me and my household, we will serve the Lord. May my life be an expression of my commitment to you. In Jesus' name, amen.

July 15

Do Not Believe the Lies

"...When he lies, he speaks his native language, for he is a liar and the father of lies." John 8:44

In this Scripture, Jesus is describing an attribute of the devil: he is a liar and the father of lies. It is helpful for us to remember that one of the greatest tactics the enemy uses against us is lies. We hear things and believe them without ever verifying that the things we hear are true. We make judgments and decisions based on something that is not even true. We may have even developed beliefs that were originally founded upon lies. The devil distorts the truth and misrepresents God's Word. He presents falsehoods and deception to throw us off from walking in the light of God's Truth. We need to examine our thoughts and prove whether our thinking is based on truth or lies. Just because we think something or hear it from somebody or read it on the internet does not mean it is true! We use the Word of God as the basis of truth. We can have sound judgment when we ask, "What does the Word of God say about this?" The Word of God helps us to have godly thoughts and not allow our thinking to take us off track with the Lord into lies and delusion. When we realize that the thoughts or ideas being presented are not based on truth, then we need to recognize the source: the devil is the father of all lies. With God's help, we can recognize this tactic of the enemy and combat the lies of the devil with the truth of God.

Dear Heavenly Father, help me to recognize the lies of the enemy and to live and act according to the truth in your Word. In Jesus' name, amen.

July 16

A Lover Will Cover Another

"Above all, love each other deeply, because love covers over a multitude of sins." 1 Peter 4:8

God's love is his redemptive response to sin. For God so loved the world that he gave his Son, Jesus, that whoever believes in him shall not perish but have everlasting life. Jesus died to forgive us for our sins, to save us from the penalty of our sins, and to set us free from the bondage of our sins. Our sins are not just covered by God's love, they are washed away by the blood of Jesus. God continues to love people in sin and rescue them today. We can show God's love to others who are struggling with sin. It is the love of God that can lead a person to repentance and a better way of life in God. We can reflect the love of God to people struggling with sin to help them experience the supernatural love of Jesus Christ on their own. We need to refrain from judging, criticizing, and talking about people who are caught up in sin. If we want to talk about them, we should talk to Jesus and lift them up in prayer! We can cover others with God's love by communicating acceptance and support to the person to give them hope and encouragement rather than being unloving and putting them down with judgment and condemnation. Loving a person does not mean ignoring or supporting their sin, but opening the door with love as a path to God. Our love does not take away their sins but can lead them to the love of God who can forgive them and deliver them from their sins. Let's love each other deeply and cover each other with God's love!

Dear Heavenly Father, help me to love others deeply because your love covers over a multitude of sins.
In Jesus' name, amen.

July 17

A Work in Progress

"being confident of this, that he who began a good work in you will carry it on to completion until the day of Christ Jesus."
Philippians 1:6

God started a great work in our lives when we turned to Jesus and asked him to forgive us for our sins. The Lord gave his Holy Spirit to be in us. He set us apart for heaven. He gave us a new heart and renewed the attitude of our mind. He has helped us to change and grow every day. God is still working on us! There is so much more he wants to do in our lives. He continues to conform us to the image of Jesus Christ. He continues to cleanse us, heal us, and change us. We are all a work in progress! God is not finished with us yet. None of us have achieved that place of maturity and perfection that we do not need to grow anymore! We have not "arrived" until we arrive in heaven or until Jesus comes back. Until then, God continues to carry on the good work he started in us. God is patient with us. He who created the universe in just six days is still working on us. Despite our setbacks and failures, the Lord will not give up on us. He has not brought us this far to leave us now. He is carrying on the work he started. God will show us new areas we need to grow. He is faithful to do the work in us. It was not in our own strength that we have come this far. God is doing it. We are not relying on our own strength now. We continue to rely on the love and power of God and trust in him. To God be the glory!

Dear Heavenly Father, I trust that you who began a good work in my life will carry it on to completion until the day of Jesus Christ. In Jesus' name, amen.

July 18

Run with the Vision

"Then the LORD replied: "Write down the revelation and make it plain on tablets so that a herald may run with it. For the revelation awaits an appointed time; it speaks of the end and will not prove false. Though it linger, wait for it; it will certainly come and will not delay." Habakkuk 2:2–3

Throughout the Bible, there are accounts of how the Lord used vision to bring guidance and direction to his followers as well as to provide insight for the future. The Lord may provide vision to us in our walk with him. This vision may not be vivid imagery, but spiritual insight into the Lord's will that he has put on our hearts. The Lord may grant vision of the awareness of a goal or dream. The Lord may provide assurance of his will being accomplished. We may gain spiritual understanding of what the Lord is doing and what his plans are. We may gain awareness of the limitless possibilities available through God. As Christians, we walk by faith and not by sight. The vision that God puts on our hearts may be the guidance for us to direct our path as we walk by faith. Vision from the Lord will line up with his Word and his will. The vision God has placed in our hearts may not happen right away. The Lord told Habakkuk, "Though it linger, wait for it..." It may take decades for the vision to come to fruition, but we hold on to that vision that God has given us, and we run with his vision with perseverance.

Dear Heavenly Father, I thank you for the vision that you have put on my heart. I submit my life and vision to you. Help me to run with the vision. May your will be done in your time as I trust in you. In Jesus' name, amen.

July 19

A Changed Life

"When Jesus reached the spot, he looked up and said to him, 'Zacchaeus, come down immediately. I must stay at your house today.'" Luke 19:5

When Jesus passed through Jericho, crowds of people who wanted to see him lined the street where he passed through. A man named Zacchaeus also wanted to see Jesus. Zacchaeus was a tax collector with a bad reputation. He also was short so he had difficulty seeing through the crowd. Zacchaeus ran ahead and climbed a tree so that he would have a good view when Jesus came down the road. When Jesus came to the tree that Zacchaeus had climbed, our Lord stopped and told Zacchaeus that he wanted to stay at Zacchaeus' home. Zacchaeus gladly welcomed Jesus to his home. Zacchaeus became a changed man and promised to pay back all that he had stolen. Jesus' encounter with Zacchaeus is similar to the encounter he has had with all of us. Jesus goes out of his way so that we can have a personal, life-changing encounter with him. There is no place that life can take us that the love of Jesus cannot reach us. Whether we are up in a tree, or down in a pit, Jesus wants to meet us where we are and call us out of that situation to experience a new life in him. Jesus did not criticize or judge Zacchaeus. He did not demand that Zacchaeus change his life before Jesus entered his home. He accepted Zacchaeus just the way he was and loved him. Like Zacchaeus, we can experience a supernatural and joyful change in our lives when we experience the love, kindness, and presence of our Lord and Savior Jesus Christ.

Dear Jesus, thank you for reaching out to me with your love and changing my life. I give my life to you. Have your way in my life. In your name, amen.

July 20

Sing Praises to the Lord

"Sing praises to God, sing praises; sing praises to our King, sing praises. For God is the King of all the earth; sing to him a psalm of praise." Psalm 47:6–7

Singing is good for our health. Singing exercises our lungs and helps build our respiratory system; it tones up the muscles in our diaphragm; it releases endorphins to elevate our mood; it boosts our immune system; it provides a release for anger or stress. Singing is also a vital spiritual practice. Throughout the pages of the Bible, we are instructed to worship the Lord in song. Many of the psalms were actually songs written to be sung in liturgical worship. Singing is done collectively with others in church as well as in our personal prayer time. Songs of worship are a great way to start our time of prayer with the Lord, in much the same way we sing worship songs at the beginning of our church services. Singing is an expression of our love for the Lord. We sing love songs to the Lord. Singing is also an expression of our thanks to the Lord. We sing songs of thanksgiving to express our gratitude for his many blessings and to give him all the glory for the good things in our lives. Worshipping the Lord in song is not limited to the times in our lives when we are celebrating his goodness. We can worship the Lord in the difficult times of our lives as well. God does not change. He is worthy of praise whether we are doing well or going through a hard time. Our worship during difficult times is our "song in the night" that will draw us closer to the Lord at a time when we really need him most. Our singing to the Lord is preparation for our eternal life with Jesus. We will be joining the angels and worshipping Jesus day and night. Let's worship the Lord in song today!

Dear Heavenly Father, I sing praises to your name. Thank you for putting a song on my heart. Let my life be a song of praise to you. In Jesus' name, amen.

July 21

Come Follow Me

"As Jesus walked beside the Sea of Galilee, he saw Simon and his brother Andrew casting a net into the lake, for they were fishermen. 'Come, follow me,' Jesus said, 'and I will send you out to fish for people.' At once they left their nets and followed him."
Mark 1:16–18

When Jesus calls us to follow him, he calls us out of our old life and into a new life in him. Simon and Andrew were fishermen. Jesus called them to follow him and told them he would send them to fish for people. Jesus gave them a new purpose for their lives. The Lord has a new plan and purpose for our lives as well. Simon and Andrew left their nets at once and followed him. When the Lord calls us to follow him, there may be people, places, and things that he wants us to leave at once as well. It may be relationships, hobbies, or lifestyles. Some of us are called to leave our vocation and serve the Lord full-time. The Lord may desire a person to remain in his or her vocation and be salt and light and an influence for the kingdom of God in the marketplace. It is something for each of us to pray about and seek God's will for our lives. It is a blessing to serve the Lord in ministry. When we follow Jesus and serve him there is joy and satisfaction that cannot be matched by money or material things. Whatever we leave behind for the sake of Christ is worth it.

Dear Jesus, thank you for calling me out of my old life and into a new life with you. Show me your plan and purpose for my life. Show me what I need to leave behind to follow you. In Jesus' name, amen.

July 22

The Lord Our Provider

"So Abraham called that place The LORD Will Provide. And to this day it is said, 'On the mountain of the LORD it will be provided.'"
Genesis 22:14

The Lord tested Abraham by asking him to sacrifice his son Isaac. Abraham was obedient. He took Isaac to a mountain where he built an altar. He tied up his son Isaac and laid him on the altar. Abraham raised his knife to slay Isaac but the angel of the Lord stopped him from going through with it. Abraham looked up and saw a ram nearby caught in a thicket. He got the ram and used it as a sacrifice instead of his son Isaac. Then Abram named the place "The Lord Will Provide." The Hebrew name here is translated as "Jehovah-Jireh." This compound name reveals the attribute and nature of the Lord as our provider. The context of God's provision in this story is not the Lord's ability to provide for our physical needs such as food, clothing, a home, or money. God can and does provide for all of those things out of the riches of his glory, but that is not what this story is about. The context of the Lord's provision here is one of providing a sacrifice to save Isaac from being slain on the altar. This Old Testament account and compound name of God as our provider points to the Lord's provision for our salvation through the substitutionary sacrifice of his one and only Son, Jesus, to take our place by dying on the cross to save us from the penalty of our sin. Jesus is the Lamb of God who takes away the sin of the world. God provides forgiveness, salvation, and eternal life for us through his Son, Jesus Christ, our Lord.

Dear Heavenly Father, you are Jehovah-Jireh, the Lord my provider. Thank you for providing my salvation through your Son, Jesus, my Lord. In Jesus' name, amen.

July 23

Make Me a Servant

"Now that I, your Lord and Teacher, have washed your feet, you also should wash one another's feet. I have set you an example that you should do as I have done for you." John 13:14–15

In washing his disciples' feet, Jesus set an example for us. Jesus was a master teacher and the best way to teach is always by example. Jesus taught us to love others, to forgive others, and to have a servant's attitude toward others. He did all these things by example. Washing his disciples' feet was a very humble act for Jesus to do. Jesus could have set an example of humble service by serving his disciples cold water or their lunch. But Jesus did something more personal than that. He was willing to deal with the unpleasantness and discomfort of washing dirty feet. Those feelings of discomfort and unpleasantness may come against our pride when we have opportunities to serve others. Jesus knew that this was challenging for us so he went out of his way to very specifically show us that he had a humble, servant's heart and he wants us to have a servant's heart toward the Lord and others. Ministry to the Lord is service to him and others. Jesus modeled servant leadership and showed us how to lead others and teach others while maintaining a humble heart rather than rising up with pride or arrogance and acting like we are better than other people or that positions of authority and leadership warrant harshness or disrespect. When we keep a servant's heart like Jesus did, we can truly show others the love of God.

Dear Heavenly Father, I pray that I will have a humble heart and a servant spirit. Help me to follow the example of Jesus in this way. In Jesus' name, amen.

July 24

Justified through Faith

"Therefore, since we have been justified through faith, we have peace with God through our Lord Jesus Christ,"
Romans 5:1

To be justified means that we are declared righteous. We are justified through our faith in Jesus Christ. We all have sinned and fallen short of the glory of God. Jesus came to save us from the bondage and the penalty of our sins. Jesus always was and always will be God. He emptied himself of his divinity and became a human and yet Jesus lived a sinless life. He died on the cross to save us from the penalty of our sins. Jesus took the penalty that we deserved so we could be justified. He shed his blood for the forgiveness of our sins. He credited his righteousness to us so that we are declared righteous through his righteousness.

Justification is applied to us through our faith in Jesus. When we ask Jesus to forgive us for our sins and accept Jesus as our Lord and Savior, then his atoning death and his righteousness are credited to us. We do not carry the guilt and shame of our sins anymore because the blood of Jesus washes our sins away. We do not have to fear condemnation or punishment for our sins because Jesus took that punishment for us on the cross. We also do not have to do anything to earn our forgiveness or justification. Jesus did it for us. There is nothing we can do to justify ourselves. We come to Jesus just as we are and he gives us his forgiveness and peace with God only through faith in him. We are justified by faith in Jesus.

Dear Heavenly Father, since I have been justified by faith, I have peace with you through Jesus Christ my Lord.
In Jesus' name, amen.

July 25

Growing in the Lord

"When I was a child, I talked like a child, I thought like a child, I reasoned like a child. When I became a man, I put the ways of childhood behind me." 1 Corinthians 13:11

As we grow in the Lord, he changes us from the inside out. The Holy Spirit inside of us changes how we talk, how we think, and how we reason. Our maturity in the Lord brings a deeper understanding of the Lord and his Word. We also learn to apply his Word to our daily lives. Our mind transforms from focusing on ourselves to pleasing the Lord and loving others. The Lord reveals to us childish habits in our thinking, our conversations, and our behaviors. He helps us to put childish ways behind us and to become more mature in him. Our motivations mature as we seek God's will and focus on obeying his Word. Our values change as we seek God first and make him a priority in our lives. We learn to find purpose in serving the Lord rather than simply pleasing ourselves. We learn to overcome the impulses of our desires for pleasure and immediate gratification. We develop spiritual strength to resist the temptation to sin. We develop perseverance and patience to grow through difficulties without allowing challenges to cause us to give up or act out in unhealthy ways. As we mature in Christ, we learn to receive correction. We learn to take "No" for an answer, and we remain gracious and prayerful when faced with criticism or conflict. We learn to trust the Lord and walk in faith. We continue to grow in the Lord no matter how old we are, or how long we have been Christians. As we walk with God, he will continue to show us new ways he wants to help us grow.

Dear Heavenly Father, show me what areas of my life I need to put behind me and show me new ways you want me to grow. In Jesus' name, amen.

July 26

The Depths of the Sea

"You will again have compassion on us; you will tread our sins underfoot and hurl all our iniquities into the depths of the sea."
Micah 7:19

Jesus died on the cross to bring us forgiveness for our sins. He took the penalty we deserved on his shoulders so that we might be forgiven and set free from the penalty and bondage of sin. Jesus shed his blood for the remission of our sins. Jesus not only saved us from eternal death, but he brought us eternal life through his resurrection from the dead. The prophet Micah provides a beautiful description of God's forgiveness that was fulfilled through the death and resurrection of Jesus Christ. The Lord has great compassion for us. Even when we were rebellious and defiant, God's great compassion for us caused him to show us his love through Jesus Christ. God does not hold our sins against us when we come to him and ask for forgiveness. To have our sins tread underfoot shows that God wipes out the presence and crushes the power that sin has in our lives. This illustration of God stepping on our sins shows that he gives us victory over our sins and that he can annihilate the power of sin in our lives. Then, after our sins are knocked down to the ground and stepped on, God hurls them into the depths of the sea. This illustrates the deliverance and forgiveness of sins we have through Jesus. Our sins are hurled away from us. Our past sin is no longer part of our lives when we are in Christ. Our sin does not define us anymore. Our salvation and regeneration in Christ define us as new creations. Our sins are in the depths of the sea where they are remembered no more. God's forgiveness takes our sins away.

Dear Heavenly Father, thank you for your great compassion to tread my sins underfoot and hurl my iniquities into the depths of the sea. In Jesus' name, amen.

July 27

Faith Comes From Hearing

"Consequently, faith comes from hearing the message, and the message is heard through the word about Christ."
Romans 10:17

When we became Christians, many of us accepted Jesus Christ as Lord in response to hearing the message of the gospel of Jesus Christ. However the message was shared with us, we listened and responded to that message of the gospel. It is so important that we don't stop listening to the message now! We need to listen even more as the Lord wants to bring us into a deeper relationship with him and lead and guide us into a life surrendered to him and to his will and purpose for our lives. When we attend church services, we listen to the Word of God and prayerfully consider what the Lord is saying to us to impact our lives. The importance of listening to God also carries over to our everyday lives outside of church. When we read the Word of God in our personal time of Bible reading, we can listen to what the Holy Spirit is saying to us through God's Word. When we pray, we also need to take the time to listen to the Lord. Our prayer time should not be only a one-way conversation where we do all the talking. The practice of being quiet and still before the Lord gives us an opportunity to be sensitive to the promptings of the Holy Spirit. Even throughout our busy days, the Lord may be trying to get our attention and speak to our hearts through other people, circumstances, or through his creation. Are we listening? We can draw closer to the Lord and fulfill his will and purposes in our lives when we continue to keep a posture and readiness to listen to him.

Dear Heavenly Father, help me to listen to you and to what you are saying to me through your Word. In Jesus' name, amen.

July 28

Jesus Our Jubilee

"Consecrate the fiftieth year and proclaim liberty throughout the land to all its inhabitants. It shall be a jubilee for you; each of you is to return to your family property and to your own clan."
Leviticus 25:10

In the time period of the Old Testament, The Lord instituted the practice of the Jubilee year every fifty years. The year of the Jubilee was not only an additional Sabbath year of rest for the fields, but it also required that anyone who was sold as a slave would be set free and returned to their family. The Jubilee year also canceled debts and allowed property that was sold to be redeemed by its original owner. The coming of the Jubilee year gave hope to people who were in difficult times. The provisions in the Jubilee prevented social oppression and poverty by giving people a renewed opportunity when they had become indebted or enslaved. The Jubilee year is a reflection of the mercy and justice of the Lord as civil practice in Old Testament times. The spiritual embodiment and fulfillment of the heart of the Jubilee year is found in Jesus Christ. Just as the Jubilee year was a provision of liberty, rest, redemption, and restoration, Jesus brings those experiences to all of us who call on his name today. The ultimate fulfillment of the Jubilee will be when Christ returns. Just as the Jubilee year was commemorated with the blowing of the ram's horn, the return of Jesus will be proclaimed with a trumpet call of angels. Just as that fiftieth year was a time that those who were oppressed could look forward to with hope, we will have our ultimate deliverance from all oppression when our Lord Jesus, our Blessed Hope, returns and we will be with him forever. Jesus is our Jubilee.

Dear Heavenly Father, thank you for the hope, liberty, rest, and deliverance found in my Lord and Savior, Jesus Christ.
In Jesus' name, amen.

July 29

People Who Persevere

*"As you know, we count as blessed those who have persevered.
You have heard of Job's perseverance and have seen what
the Lord finally brought about. The Lord is full of compassion
and mercy." James 5:11*

To persevere is to keep going and not give up. James informs us that Job was a person who persevered. Job was faced with tragic loss. He lost all of his livestock and his ten children died. Job was afflicted with painful sores. Despite the pain and suffering that Job experienced, he continued to worship the Lord. Job's attitude of worship gave him strength during his time of adversity. We can draw close to our Lord Jesus during our times of suffering because he too suffered. Jesus was a man of sorrows. He suffered and died on the cross to save us from the penalty of our sins. Jesus rose from the dead with victory over death and the suffering he endured. We have his resurrection power in our lives to give us strength during our times of adversity. As we turn to the Lord in prayer and trust in him, he will give us the strength to persevere, even when everything inside of us is telling us we cannot make it. We can do it with God's help. Job is not only an example of perseverance; he is also an example of one who experienced healing and restoration from God. The Lord restored Job's health and the Lord blessed the latter part of Job's life more than the first. Job had more children and saw their children to the fourth generation. Just as the Lord blessed and restored Job's life, God is full of compassion and mercy to do the same in our lives when we persevere.

*Dear Lord, grant me perseverance as I wait on you and trust
you. I need your strength and look to you to give me endurance
and not give up. In Jesus' name, amen.*

July 30

Mighty for God

"David left Gath and escaped to the cave of Adullam. When his brothers and his father's household heard about it, they went down to him there. All those who were in distress or in debt or discontented gathered around him, and he became their commander. About four hundred men were with him."
1 Samuel 22:1–2

This was a difficult time in David's life. He was running from King Saul in fear for his life and ended up hiding in a cave. His family joined him there, then other people also joined him in the cave. Those who were in distress, in debt, or discontented gathered around him. Now this was a group of people who all were not doing well, hiding out in a cave together. It was this rag-tag group of misfits that became the army of Israel, including King David and his mighty men who achieved great exploits and conquered the enemies of Israel. The Lord took this group of down-and-out people and used them to become a mighty army. The Lord is doing the same in our lives and in his church today. Many of us came to the Lord for refuge at a difficult time in our lives. When we gather together in our churches in the name of Jesus, he turns our lives around and God is now making us into mighty men and women for God. God is raising up an army to serve him, to overcome evil in our communities, and to advance the kingdom of God by sharing the love of God and the gospel of Jesus Christ. We can be mighty for God.

Lord, thank you that when I seek refuge in you, that you are raising me up to be mighty for you and to serve in the army of God. In Jesus' name, amen.

July 31

Shine for Jesus

"You are the light of the world. A town built on a hill cannot be hidden." Matthew 5:14

Jesus is the light of the world. When we have Jesus in our hearts, we become the light of the world. God's presence is his light. His light is love, power, purity, and truth. We have God's light in us. God has sent his Holy Spirit to be inside of us. His Spirit is the light of God in us. God does not want us to keep him to ourselves. The love, purity, and goodness of God contrast the darkness and despair of evil and sin. We were in darkness in our sins at one time, but the Lord has called us out of the darkness and into his marvelous light. There is light in the Word of God. Our minds were corrupted by the darkness of sinful thinking, The Word of God brings light with truth so that we can walk in the light of the will and purposes of God. All of this light that God has given us needs to be shared with others, God's light emanates through us so that his light touches other people's lives through our lives. We share the light of God when we share God's love with others. We share the light of God when we share God's Word and the gospel of Jesus Christ with others. Our lives shine God's light when we do good deeds and live in purity and integrity. The goodness of God shines through us in contrast to the darkness of the world around us. We glorify the Lord when we share his light and his love with others.

Dear Heavenly Father, thank you for the light of your Holy Spirit inside of me. May your love and your truth shine through me to touch other people today. In Jesus' name, amen.

August 1

The Hope of Glory

"'The glory of this present house will be greater than the glory of the former house,' says the Lord Almighty. 'And in this place I will grant peace,' declares the Lord Almighty."
Haggai 2:9

The prophet Haggai was ministering to the people in Jerusalem during the temple reconstruction. But at this time, the people were procrastinating on the work of rebuilding the temple. One of the issues that delayed the work was that people remembered the glory of Solomon's temple and they were discouraged that they would not be able to rebuild the new temple to be as beautiful and glorious as the former one. The Lord spoke through Haggai to say that the *desired of all nations* would come and that God's glory would fill the temple. The people who remembered Solomon's temple were sad about losing the beautiful gold-covered ornate features of the building, but the presence and the glory of God is more glorious than silver or gold or any beautiful architecture. The Lord does not want us to allow our discouragement over our losses or our focus on material things to interfere with the work he has for us at present and the future hope of glory and peace he has in store for us. Just as Haggai encouraged the people with the promise that the new temple will be more glorious than the former one, we also have the promise of the return of Jesus Christ and our eternal life with him, which far exceeds any glory or beauty that we can experience on earth. Let's get to the business of doing what the Lord wants us to do today as we work toward the glory of his kingdom.

Dear Heavenly Father, as I serve you today, I am eternally minded because of the hope of your glory through Jesus Christ. In Jesus' name, amen.

August 2

Patient Promise

"The Lord is not slow in keeping his promise, as some understand slowness. Instead, he is patient with you, not wanting anyone to perish, but everyone to come to repentance."
2 Peter 3:9

Jesus is coming back. No one knows the day or the hour when that will take place. Peter addresses scoffers who questioned the promise of the second coming of Jesus. Peter points out that it is not that the Lord is slow in keeping his promise. God has not forgotten. He has not changed his mind and decided that Jesus will not come after all. God is not limited by anything or anyone to fulfill his promise for the return of Christ. The reason that God is holding off on the return of Jesus is his patience. The Lord is waiting for more people to accept Jesus Christ as Lord. The Lord is building his kingdom until the Day of the Lord that Jesus returns in glory. God wants everybody to repent and be forgiven through the blood of Jesus Christ and have everlasting life with him. This shows the love and compassion that God has for all people. There is no one beyond Christ's redemption. God has so generously and lovingly sacrificed his Son for us while we were still sinners so that we may have eternal life. God is so lovingly patient that he is waiting for others to come to him. The Lord is patiently waiting to return while we fulfill the Great Commission to go into all the world and make disciples. We do not know when Jesus will return. We can share his love with others so that his will for all people to come to repentance will be fulfilled.

Dear Lord, thank you for your patience and your love that you do not want anyone to perish, but everyone to come to repentance. I pray for the salvation of those who are lost. I pray that you will use me to share your love and the hope of the gospel of Jesus Christ, my precious Lord. In Jesus' name, amen.

August 3

Do Your Best and Trust God for the Rest

"Be strong, and let us fight bravely for our people and the cities of our God. The LORD will do what is good in his sight."
1 Chronicles 19:13

During the reign of King David, the Ammonite army came out against Israel in battle. The king of Ammon hired Aramean soldiers to fight Israel as well. Joab, the captain of Israel's army saw that they were going to be attacked on both sides. Joab decided to split up the army and go to battle in two different directions. Joab would lead the charge against the Arameans, and he sent his brother Abishai to lead the rest of Israel's soldiers to fight Ammon. Joab told Abishai and the troops to do their best to fight for their people and that the Lord would do what was good in his sight. Israel won the battle on both sides.

Joab's instruction to his brother captures a spiritual principle. We do our best and trust the Lord for the rest. When we serve the Lord, he deserves our best. A spirit of excellence is an expression of worship to the Lord. We give the Lord one hundred percent of our effort and we give him all the glory. As much as it is vital for us to do our best with excellence, our efforts are in vain without the Lord's help and blessing. Our faith is not in our own efforts, but in the power of the Lord as we trust in him. When we feel our best efforts are futile, we move forward with faith in God, trusting him and knowing that we are not alone. The point where our efforts to do what God wants us to do fall short is where the grace and power of God enable us to accomplish his will.

Dear Heavenly Father, help me to do my best with whatever you want me to do today. My trust and faith are in you for success. In Jesus' name, amen.

August 4

Set Apart for God

"May God himself, the God of peace, sanctify you through and through. May your whole spirit, soul and body be kept blameless at the coming of our Lord Jesus Christ." 1 Thessalonians 5:23

To be sanctified is to be set apart for God. Sanctification takes place when we accept Jesus as Lord and receive his forgiveness for our sins. We are sanctified by the blood of Jesus that was shed for the remission of our sins. This is an immediate and positional sanctification that takes place at our conversion. We are forgiven and set apart by God for heaven. We have the Holy Spirit inside of us and we are now set apart from our sinful past and set apart for the Lord. After we become Christians, the Lord continues to do a spiritual work inside of us. There is an ongoing and progressive sanctification that takes place in our lives as Christians. We have been sanctified and we are being sanctified. The Holy Spirit continues to cleanse our hearts and renew the attitude of our minds. The Spirit of God and the Word of God work together as the Lord sanctifies us by his truth. The Lord continues to show us new attitudes and areas of our lives that he wants to change. We surrender ourselves fully to the Lord as he does a deeper work in us. We respond to the sanctifying work of the Holy Spirit by submitting to the Lord in those areas that he is changing and letting go of thoughts, feelings, and behaviors that do not please him. God is still working in us and will continue to sanctify us through and through until we are in his presence in eternity.

Dear Lord, thank you for setting me apart through the blood of Jesus Christ and the power of the Holy Spirit. Continue to sanctify me through and through. In Jesus' name, amen.

217

August 5

God's Got Your Back

"'Because he loves me,' says the LORD, 'I will rescue him; I will protect him, for he acknowledges my name.'" Psalm 91:14

Our mighty God watches over us and promises to rescue and protect us. After declaring the security and protection to be found in the Lord, the psalmist takes on the role of prophetic oracle by speaking from the Lord's voice in this part of the psalm and gives the Lord's response and assurance of his love and protection. There may be difficult times that we wonder if God is there, or if he hears our prayers. The Lord provides his assurance that he cherishes our love and that he hears our prayers. He responds to our prayers when we acknowledge his name. The Lord responds to our love with his love and protection. Our faith relationship with God started because of his great love for us. When we receive that love and love him back, he loves us even more. Our relationship with the Lord can grow as we love him, trust him, and put our faith in him. The love of God is unconditional, but there is a blessing in having a deeper, fuller relationship with the Lord. His strong and mighty power to protect is just one of the ways God shows his love back to us. The Lord is with us in difficult times. God has the power to save. He is our rescuer and our protector. Who knows what harm or danger we would have experienced if not for God's loving protection? We can pray for the Lord's protection over our own lives and our loved ones. We have faith and confidence in God's love and his power to rescue us and protect us.

Dear Lord, I love you and I acknowledge your name in every area of my life. I pray for your protection for my life and my family according to your great love and power.
In Jesus' name, amen.

August 6

Our God of Miracles

"Jesus looked at them and said, 'With man this is impossible, but not with God; all things are possible with God.'" Mark 10:27

God has miraculous supernatural power to do all things. The miracles of God are displayed throughout the narrative of the Bible. In the Old Testament God parted the Red Sea; he brought water from a rock; he made the sun "stand still." In the New Testament Jesus changed water into wine, he made a paralyzed man walk, he made the blind man see, and he rose Lazarus from the dead. God is a God of miracles! Nothing is too hard for him. We may feel like we are facing an impossible situation, but nothing is impossible with God!

The greatest miracle of all times is that Jesus saved us from our sin by dying on the cross in our place. Jesus took the penalty that we deserved through his suffering, his shed blood, and his death on the cross. The blood of Jesus brings remission of sin for all humankind. Jesus rose from the dead and defeated death, hell, and the grave. He led the way for us in resurrection power to rise above our sinful past and to have eternal life with Jesus in his presence. That great miracle of salvation occurs when we ask Jesus to forgive us of our sins and accept him as our Lord and Savior. We have received the great miracle of salvation in our own lives. There are others who still need to receive Christ. If the Lord saved us, then he can save them too. We continue to pray for the miracle of salvation to take place in the lives of those who have not yet accepted Christ. Nothing is impossible with God.

Dear Lord, you are the God of miracles. All things are possible with you. I pray for your miraculous will to continue in my own life. I pray for the miracle of salvation for those on my heart who have not received you. In Jesus' name, amen.

August 7

The Lord's Searchlight

"Search me, God, and know my heart; test me and know my anxious thoughts. See if there is any offensive way in me, and lead me in the way everlasting." Psalm 139:23–24

When we pray, we can ask the Lord to search our hearts. The Holy Spirit is like a searchlight inside of us, he can help us to be more aware of what is going on inside of us. We have blind spots in our attitudes, our emotions, our beliefs, and our motives that we are just not fully aware of. Just as our relationship with the Lord and obedience to his Word has impacted our behavior and our conscious decisions, there is an impact that the Holy Spirit makes in our subconscious. The Lord can reveal to us attitudes and beliefs that we did not understand we had before. He can help us become more aware of sinful attitudes such as selfishness or pride. He will help us process the impact of feelings such as hurt or anger. He will help us work through troubling experiences and responses such as anxiety or insecurity. As we grow in our relationship with the Lord, the Holy Spirit ministers to the deep parts within us. The Holy Spirit brings healing to emotions that we may have never fully processed. The Holy Spirit helps us cleanse our hearts and minds of impurity based on selfishness, hurt, or fear. The Holy Spirit can help us distinguish the subtle influences of the flesh from the guidance of the Holy Spirit. When we pray, we have an openness and a willingness in our hearts for the Lord to search us and renew our thoughts, attitudes, and emotions with the truth and love of God by the power of the Holy Spirit.

Search me, God, and know my heart; test me and know my anxious thoughts. See if there is any offensive way in me, and lead me in the way everlasting. In Jesus' name, amen.

August 8

Wisdom in Friendship

"Do not be misled: 'Bad company corrupts good character.'"
1 Corinthians 15:33

Friendships are important. The people with whom we get close in friendship influence our lives. That can be a positive or a negative influence. When we become Christians, the Lord brings changes in every area of our lives, including our friendships. We may have friendships that we need to end or change when we become Christians. We do not continue friendships that interfere with our relationship with the Lord or influence us in an unhealthy manner. We can have a positive influence on our friends rather than allowing friendships to have a negative influence on us. It is awesome for us to have friends who are not Christians. However, we need to be cautious and aware that those friendships do not negatively influence us. It is at that point that we can set boundaries to continue the friendship while guarding our hearts. Friendships are based on shared values and interests. The most important value that we can share with our friends is our love for the Lord. As Christians, we are blessed to have Christ-centered friendships. These friendships become an integral part of our life in the Lord. When we have difficulties in life, our friends can be there to help us. When we are doing well, we can help them. There is this mutual benefit of enjoying each other as friends. We can have friendships that bless our lives and positively influence us. We can enjoy having friends without allowing those friendships to compromise our friendship with Jesus.

Dear Lord, help me to have the wisdom to set boundaries so that my friendships honor you and that they do not corrupt the good character that you are developing in my life.
In Jesus' name, amen.

August 9

God's Word in My Heart

"I have hidden your word in my heart that I might not sin against you." Psalm 119:11

The Word of God provides instruction and principles to live by, and a framework for which we establish a worldview. We can see the world, ourselves, others, and the Lord through the lens of truth that the Word of God provides for us. The Word of God enables us to see the way of life that God has for us. The Word of God and the Spirit of God work together to minister to our hearts and minds. God's Word brings peace and stability to our thoughts when we are troubled. God's Word brings strength to our souls when we feel an emptiness inside. Just as our bodies receive nourishment from healthy food, the Word of God provides nourishment, sustenance, and strength to our souls. Reading the Bible is not just a mental exercise to gain knowledge. Learning and understanding the Word of God is part of it, but God's Word reaches beyond our minds to our hearts and our souls. We take time to prayerfully meditate on the Word of God rather than reading through it quickly. When we pray and meditate over God's Word, the Holy Spirit can use it to speak to our hearts. We also memorize the Word of God, not just to know it mentally, but to allow it to sink into our hearts and become part of our thinking, our beliefs, and who we are. The Word of God can help transform our lives and become a source of God's strength inside of us to keep us from sin and to empower us to live the fulfilled life that God has for us.

Dear Heavenly Father, I pray that when I read and meditate on your Word, that you hide it in my heart so that I might not sin against you. In Jesus' name, amen.

August 10

Jesus Gave It All

"But God demonstrates his own love for us in this: While we were still sinners, Christ died for us." Romans 5:8

Jesus loves us so much that he died for us while we were still sinners. His love motivated him to rescue us from the bondage of our sins. The Lord's love is full of compassion and mercy. Jesus rescued us from the despair and bondage of our sins even though we did it to ourselves. He forgave us and gave us a new life because of his great love. What is even more incredible about his love is that there was no guarantee that we would receive his love. Jesus gave it all for us without the assurance that we would love him back. We were already in rebellion and defiance of him when we started down the path of sin. Our sin did not stop him from loving us. He gave his life to save us from the hopeless despair of our rebellious and sinful state. Jesus held nothing back for us. He did not check to see if we were ready to change our lives. He did not ask us to show him that we wanted to change. We did nothing to deserve his sacrifice. There was nothing we could do to be free. He went the total distance for us. The Lord's gift of salvation is unconditional. There are no strings attached to his gift. How great is the gift of salvation that Jesus gave us by sacrificing his own life while we were still in sin. Because of his love, we can live a life free from the bondage and penalty of sin.

Dear Jesus, thank you for demonstrating your love by dying for me while I was still a sinner. Help me to live in the freedom of your love and to show your love to others.
In Jesus' name, amen.

August 11

The Splendor of His Holiness

"Worship the Lord in the splendor of his holiness..."
Psalm 96:9

When we worship in the Lord's presence, we engage in the spiritual realm. The holiness of the Lord is beyond measure. He is outside the realm of our natural existence. The presence of the Lord is splendorous. He is radiant and glorious. The Lord is majestic and mighty; he is beautiful beyond description. The presence of the Lord is breathtaking and overwhelming. He is pure and holy. He is powerful and loving. He is the source of all life and love. When we come into the presence of the Lord, we worship him in the beauty of his holiness. Worship in the Lord's presence is beautiful because he is beautiful. Our singing, the music, our shouts of praise, our whispers of love, and our reverent quiet stillness all respond to and reflect the beauty of his presence. This connection and engagement of worship in God's presence is foundational in our life as Christians. We become busy and active; we serve, we work, we love others, we pray, we read, and we attend church. Life can become busy, but we must lay everything aside and simply worship him in his magnificent holy presence. When we are going through a trial or struggling with a problem, when we do not know what to do or even how to pray, we can just come and worship him in the splendor of his presence. We have no other agenda but to ascribe to him the glory due to his name. We can put all of our plans, worries, problems, and issues on the back burner and focus fully on basking in the beauty and magnificence of his presence; loving and worshipping his holy name. We live life to its fullest. We need to take time to just abide in the Lord's presence and worship him in the beauty and splendor of his holiness.

Dear Heavenly Father, you are holy, mighty, majestic, and beautiful. I worship you in the beauty and splendor of your holiness. In Jesus' name, amen.

August 12

Soul Sickness

"But the Pharisees and the teachers of the law who belonged to their sect complained to his disciples, 'Why do you eat and drink with tax collectors and sinners?' Jesus answered them, 'It is not the healthy who need a doctor, but the sick. I have not come to call the righteous, but sinners to repentance.'"
Luke 5:30–32

Jesus was criticized by the religious leaders of his day because he was a friend to sinners. Jesus came to save us from our sins. He befriended the people who needed him most. Jesus came out of his love for us. He had compassion on us for our sins; he did not get angry and come to earth to punish sinners. He came to seek and save those who were lost. Jesus uses the illustration of a doctor who helps bring healing to the sick. He not only brought miraculous healing to people's physical bodies, but he also brought healing to our souls. When it comes to his response to sin, Jesus did not come as a judge or a policeman. From this perspective, Jesus' response is not that we are bad people who need to be punished, but instead, we are sick people who need to be healed. Jesus heals the sickness of our souls with his love. He applies his blood for our forgiveness, he cleanses the guilt and shame of our sins, and he heals the depravity of our sinful minds through his Word. He gives us a heart transplant, removing our hardened sinful hearts and giving us a new heart. He gives us the healing virtue of the Holy Spirit inside of us. He prescribes hope, joy, and peace in our lives and a new way of living for us based on his Word. Jesus is our Great Physician. He heals the sickness of our souls.

Dear Jesus, thank you for being a friend to sinners. Thank you that you brought healing from the sin sickness in my soul. You are my healer and my Great Physician. In your name, amen.

August 13

It Bites Like a Snake

"Do not gaze at wine when it is red, when it sparkles in the cup, when it goes down smoothly! In the end it bites like a snake and poisons like a viper." Proverbs 23:31–32

A drink of alcohol may look good on a hot day when we are thirsty. We may even like the taste and find it pleasing. We may like the effect it has on us. Alcohol is a drug. It is a depressant that has an initial effect of calming us, it lowers our inhibitions and has a relaxing effect. Alcohol appears pleasurable at the moment, but in the long term, it does harm, not good. The Bible states that drunkenness is sinful; not alcohol itself. Yet alcohol has an express lane to sinful drunkenness. Alcohol impairs our judgment and affects our ability to make right choices. Alcohol is a highly addictive drug. It consumes a person's life and causes a destructive impact on relationships, health, and career. Alcohol abuse is a factor in terminal illnesses. In its full-blown state of dependence, withdrawal from alcohol may be deadly. Alcohol is also a leading factor in car crash deaths. Alcohol is just one example of how something seems pleasurable at first but causes pain and destruction. What feels good is not always what is best for us. We turn to drunkenness and other sinful pleasures because there is a thirst in our souls. Sinful pleasures do not satisfy that thirst; we will always need more and more, never being satisfied. The love of God and our relationship with Jesus can bring fulfillment and satisfaction to our lives that alcohol, drugs, or any other sinful pleasure cannot bring. Jesus fills the longing in our souls.

*Dear Lord, thank you that you satisfy the thirst in my soul. Help me to remember the pain and consequences of seeking pleasure in sin, and help me to seek more of you instead.
In Jesus' name, amen.*

August 14

Journey with God

"Blessed are those whose strength is in you, whose hearts are set on pilgrimage." Psalm 84:5

A pilgrimage is a spiritual journey. When we become Christians, we begin a spiritual journey with the Lord. The Lord is the source of our strength on our journey. We have a personal relationship with Jesus Christ and he journeys with us. He is always there on every step of our journey. He walks with us and he talks with us. He will never leave us nor forsake us. He journeys with us day and night, when it is hot and when it is cold, when we are on a mountain or we are in a valley. He is there with us. We make mistakes along the way. He loves us and teaches us wisdom when we walk through those mistakes with him. We have setbacks and struggles. We become stronger when we turn to him for help and strength. Heaven is our destination on this journey. We have an upward calling there. He walks with us on our way and brings purpose to our journey with him. He walks beside us, but we let him choose the direction we go in. He encourages us when we become tired, weary, or discouraged. He has a plan for our journey and he wants to lead us on a journey of discovery. We learn more about him, about ourselves, and about life. Our relationship with him strengthens as we journey and walk through life together. The path we take may have twists and turns but we know we are heading in the right direction as long as we stay by his side. We cannot see the path ahead because we walk by faith, not by sight. We just stay focused on Jesus and he will show us where to go and how to get there.

Dear Heavenly Father, you are my strength. Lead me on the path of life and your plans and purpose for me. Help me to grow closer to you on my spiritual journey. In Jesus' name, amen.

227

August 15

Sacrificial Love

"Husbands, love your wives, just as Christ loved the church and gave himself up for her" Ephesians 5:25

The apostle Paul compares the relationship between a husband and wife to that of Jesus and his church. The church is the bride of Christ. Jesus loves us so much that he sacrificed his life by dying on the cross to bring forgiveness for our sins and save us from the penalty of our sins. Paul writes that husbands should love their wives in the same way Christ loved the church and gave himself up for her. This is our call as husbands, to give ourselves up in love for our wives. We love our wives so much we are willing to die for them. Although we may not be put in the dramatic position to physically die for our wives, we die to ourselves through our sacrificial love for them. We are fully devoted to loving her and do anything it takes for her well being. This type of love holds nothing back, just like Jesus held nothing back when he went to the cross for our sins. Sacrificial love also does not expect or require anything back. Giving is an expression of love. We give ourselves to our wives and become one with her. Sacrificial love is giving even when it hurts. It does not seek personal rights but puts the other person before ourselves.

As Christians, we can learn to have sacrificial love in our relationships with the Lord and other people. Jesus sacrificed himself for us, so we love him back the same way. He gave us a new life so the life we live is his; it is not our own. We give ourselves fully to him. With God's help, we can share his sacrificial love with others by giving of ourselves without strings attached and without requiring anything back for ourselves.

Lord Jesus, thank you for sacrificing your life for me. Help me to love you and others with your sacrificial love.
In Jesus' name, amen.

August 16

Washed through the Word

"Husbands, love your wives, just as Christ loved the church and gave himself up for her to make her holy, cleansing her by the washing with water through the word,"
Ephesians 5:25–26

Just as our bodies get washed by water, the Word of God washes and cleanses our minds. The Word of God, working together with the Holy Spirit, purifies our minds and cleanses our thoughts. We all deal with patterns of thinking such as pride, resentment, selfishness, greed, lust, and temptations to sin in many different ways. We have had experiences that have impacted our minds and the way we think. People may have said things to us or about us that have had a deep effect on how we think and how we see ourselves. The Word of God can cleanse our minds from troubling thoughts and disturbing memories. The Word of God is pure. It brings new thoughts and a new way to think for us. God uses his Word to sanctify us. Jesus prayed that the Lord would sanctify us by the truth. God's Word is truth. God's Word brings healing to the corruption and depravity in our minds caused by sin. Because God's Word is living and active through the anointing of the Holy Spirit, the Word of God renews our minds and transforms the way we think. The truth in God's Word cleanses away the lies of the enemy in our thoughts. The Lord desires truth in our inner parts, he gives us wisdom in the inmost place. God's Word washes away impure, unhealthy, and sinful thoughts and establishes God's truth in our thoughts so that we may have a sound mind. The Word of God will change the way we think.

Dear Heavenly Father, thank you for cleansing me by washing with water through the Word. Let your Word continue to cleanse, renew, and transform my mind by the power of your Holy Spirit. In Jesus' name, amen.

August 17

A Gentle Answer

"A gentle answer turns away wrath, but a harsh word stirs up anger." Proverbs 15:1

Gentleness is a fruit of the Holy Spirit that benefits our own lives and ministers to the lives of others. To be gentle is to be considerate, kind, and tender. Gentleness exercises restraint and remains calm even in the face of conflict or adversity. When we are faced with conflict or addressing a person who is offended or angry, a gentle answer will help calm them down. Harsh reactions to an angry person often result in escalation. This makes a challenging situation worse instead of better. When dealing with an angry person, it is as if the person is on fire. We have a bucket in each hand. One bucket is filled with gasoline, the other bucket is filled with water. When we react harshly or angrily, we are throwing gasoline on the fire. When we respond gently, we are throwing water on the fire.

Some practical steps we can take to practice gentleness include: sitting down and calmly reasoning together with another person rather than dealing with conflict while standing or in a busy, loud, or public place; taking time out in the conversation to pray; listening to the other person and not interrupting them; maintaining calmness by not raising our voice; empathizing with the other person and validating their feelings rather than defending ourselves. When somebody cuts us off on the highway, we can wave, let them go, and whisper a prayer for them, rather than honking, yelling, or driving aggressively. With God's help, the Holy Spirit can develop the fruit of gentleness in our lives.

Dear Lord, I pray that you develop the fruit of gentleness in my life. Help me to remember that a gentle answer turns away wrath, but a harsh word stirs up strife.
In Jesus' name, amen.

August 18

Pleasing God

"No one serving as a soldier gets entangled in civilian affairs, but rather tries to please his commanding officer."
2 Timothy 2:4

When we become Christians, we enlist in the Lord's army. Just as soldiers are called away from civilian life to be devoted to serving in the army, we are called out from the world to be devoted to serving the Lord. The Lord is our commanding officer. We are set apart to serve him and to please him. A soldier does not get entangled in civilian affairs. A Christian does not get entangled in worldly affairs but lives a life of holiness, set apart for God. Soldiers are focused on doing what their commanding officer has told them to do. Life as a soldier is disciplined and focused. Our lives as Christians are also disciplined through adherence to the Word of God and focused on pleasing and serving the Lord. We cannot allow ourselves to get caught up in the distractions of the world, but we remain true to our mission and purpose that the Lord has for us. Just as soldiers are called to battle, we also are called into spiritual battle as Christians. When we became Christians, we entered into a war. We walk in the victory of Jesus Christ our Lord, but we fight along the way. We have a focus and a purpose in our lives that surpasses the distractions, pleasures, and comforts of the world. We rise above the affairs of the world because we have a higher calling. At the end of the day, our fulfillment is in knowing that we please the Lord. When we know we please the Lord, then nothing else really matters.

Dear Lord, today I seek to please you and accomplish your will and pleasure in my life, help me to focus on you, and keep me from getting entangled in worldly affairs.
In Jesus' name, amen.

August 19

The Pillar Moves

"In all the travels of the Israelites, whenever the cloud lifted from above the tabernacle, they would set out; but if the cloud did not lift, they did not set out—until the day it lifted."
Exodus 40:36–37

When Moses led the Israelites from Egypt to the Promised Land, the Lord went ahead of them to guide them in their way in a pillar of cloud by day and a pillar of fire by night. We too are on a journey with Christ and the Lord will provide guidance and direction for our lives. We want to do what God wants us to do. We want to go where God wants us to go. We want to stay when God wants us to stay. We do not want to get ahead of God and move when he does not want us to move. We do not want to remain still and do what we have always done when the Lord wants us to move and do something different. We want to be sensitive to the leading of the Lord and obedient to his direction in our lives. The Lord provides guidance and direction to us by his Word in the Bible. The Bible gives us instructions for the choices we need to make. As we seek direction from God's Word, we are also sensitive to the guidance of the Holy Spirit. The Lord also puts spiritual leaders in our lives to provide wise counsel when we are making decisions. We are mindful that the Lord may orchestrate circumstances to guide us regarding his will in our lives. The Lord can open doors that no one can shut, and he can close doors that no one can open. God is faithful to guide us as we put our hope and our faith in him.

Dear Heavenly Father, I pray for your guidance and direction in my life according to your will. In Jesus' name, amen.

August 20

An Eternal Perspective

"For our light and momentary troubles are achieving for us an eternal glory that far outweighs them all. So we fix our eyes not on what is seen, but on what is unseen, since what is seen is temporary, but what is unseen is eternal."
2 Corinthians 4:17–18

Life as a Christian includes difficult and troublesome times. These trials and hardships are uncomfortable to experience. It is during these difficult times that our faith in God grants us hope and strength to endure. The nature of faith is to believe and trust in the Lord, whom we cannot see. Rather than focusing on our trials, we focus on our unseen, loving, and powerful, mighty God who will never leave us nor forsake us. We do not fall apart or give up because we know that the Lord is with us through the trials and difficulties we face. We know that these trials we face are temporary. Our life on earth is temporary, our eternal destiny is in heaven. In heaven, we will be in the presence of our Lord Jesus. There will be no more pain or sorrow, sickness, or sadness, sin or evil. In heaven, we will have our eternal rest and experience joy in the Lord's presence. The joy and freedom we look forward to in heaven far outweigh the discomfort and hardship of the trials we face in this life. When we have an eternal mindset, it helps us to keep our challenges and difficulties in perspective. With the Lord's help, we can endure troublesome times with strength, and gratitude for the hope we have for our eternal destiny with Jesus our Lord.

Dear Heavenly Father, help me to remember that my light and momentary troubles are achieving for me an eternal glory that far outweighs them all. Help me to fix my eyes not on what is seen, but on what is unseen, since what is seen is temporary, but what is unseen is eternal. In Jesus' name, amen.

August 21

An Undivided Heart

*"Teach me your way, LORD, that I may rely on your faithfulness;
give me an undivided heart, that I may fear your name."*
Psalm 86:11

We give our whole heart in our personal relationship with our Lord Jesus Christ. We hold nothing back. To have a divided heart is to love the Lord, but also love something or someone else that interferes with our love for the Lord. When our heart is divided, we give the Lord a part of our hearts, but we set aside another part of our hearts for something or someone else that we value and cherish more than we love the Lord. This part of our heart that we hold back from the Lord will ultimately interfere with our ability and capacity to experience fully our spiritual relationship with him and all that he has planned and in store for us. When our hearts are undivided toward the Lord, we continue to engage in fulfilling love relationships with other people and interests in life that do not interfere with or detract from our relationship with God. We get out of our spiritual relationship with the Lord what we put in to it. Half-hearted measures result in half-hearted results. When we trust the Lord wholeheartedly, he will meet our needs and satisfy the longings in our hearts for whatever it is we are reluctant to give up for him. When we surrender all to the Lord, we can love him with an undivided heart. The Lord will put his finger on those areas of our hearts and our lives that interfere with our ability to love him with an undivided heart. The Lord loves us with all of his heart. Jesus gave his life for us on the cross. He gave us a new life and he wants us to give our hearts fully to him.

Dear Lord, show me anything in my life or in my heart that is interfering with my relationship with you and your purpose for my life. Give me an undivided heart that I may love you without holding anything back. In Jesus' name, amen.

August 22

Treasures in Heaven

*"Do not store up for yourselves treasures on earth, where moths
and vermin destroy, and where thieves break in and steal.
But store up for yourselves treasures in heaven, where moths
and vermin do not destroy, and where thieves do not break in
and steal." Matthew 6:19–20*

Jesus encourages us to store up treasures in heaven rather
than treasures on earth. Jesus points to the temporal value
of material things. Material things break down and lose their
value over time. Material things may be stolen from us. That
which we value can be taken away. These descriptions are
in contrast to treasures in heaven. Spiritual treasures do not
break down and lose their value as material treasures do. No
one can ever take away or steal our spiritual treasures such
as God's love and the spiritual impact the Lord can make on
others through us as we serve him. We cannot take our material treasures with us when we die and go to heaven. When we
serve the Lord and share his love with others, we lay up treasures in heaven. When we share the gospel and lead others to
Christ, we take part in building the kingdom of God and storing up treasures in heaven. Our eternal life will be in heaven
in the spiritual realm so that is where we can focus on storing
up treasures while we are here on earth. We can be spiritually
and eternally minded rather than earthly minded. The Lord
can help us to focus on spiritual things and the kingdom of
God rather than on earthly material things that do not last.
When we value spiritual things more than material things, we
can store up treasures in heaven.

*Dear Lord, help me today to store up for myself treasures in
heaven, where moths and vermin do not destroy, and where
thieves do not break in and steal. In Jesus' name, amen.*

August 23

God Keeps Us in His Peace

"You will keep in perfect peace those whose minds are steadfast, because they trust in you." Isaiah 26:3

We have peace in our hearts when our trust is in the Lord. He can solve any problem we are facing; win any battle we are fighting, or provide for any need we are lacking. We can be going through a tumultuous experience but still have God's peace in our hearts and our minds because we trust in him. God loves us. He knows our needs and will take care of us according to his great love and power. When we trust in the Lord, we can breathe a sigh of relief and be at ease because we know that the Lord is trustworthy and that he will not let us down. We trust that no matter what happens, God has us in the palm of his hand. He gives us peace in our hearts because of the security we have in his care. Peace is a fruit of the Spirit whom the Lord has given us in our hearts. God's peace can calm our worries, doubts, fears, and insecurities. The Lord's peace strengthens us to walk in faith, believing in his ability to meet our needs. We trust in God's power to overcome obstacles that are in our path and see us through rough times on our journey. We trust in the Lord's power over the forces of evil around us and we trust in him for victory. We know that we are not on our own, but we are under his watchful eye and mighty hand. When we consider our future, we have peace because we know that our future is in his hands and that he who has been faithful in our lives thus far will continue to be faithful in the days to come. Rather than focus on our problems or worry about what might happen, we focus on the Lord and his faithful love and power, and he keeps us in his peace.

Dear Heavenly Father, I pray that you keep me in your perfect peace as my mind is steadfast because I trust in you.
In Jesus' name, amen.

August 24

Fearfully and Wonderfully Made

"I praise you because I am fearfully and wonderfully made; your works are wonderful, I know that full well."
Psalm 139:14

We can get distracted and caught up in things we don't like about ourselves in such a way that we become insecure about ourselves. We compare ourselves to others and wish that we were more like them. We magnify the things we do not like about ourselves and allow that focus to cause us to feel negative about ourselves. This affects our confidence to engage in relationships with others and to engage in life to its fullest. We have this underlying belief that we are not good enough or are unworthy. We become stagnated by our feelings of inadequacy. This mindset of being self-critical and putting ourselves down is not healthy and it is not the way the Lord sees us. He created us and he loves us so much the way we are. The Lord can help us to see ourselves the way he sees us and love ourselves the way he loves us. God does not see us according to our flaws but according to his love for the beautiful expression of his creativity that we are. We all have strengths and weaknesses, assets and shortcomings. The Lord accepts us and loves us for all of who we are. The Lord can help us to stop being so hard on ourselves and critical of ourselves. We do not deserve that. The Lord wants us to see ourselves and treat ourselves like the precious apple of his eye that we are. We can receive God's love and turn it on ourselves today.

Dear Lord, help me to see myself the way you see me and love myself the way you love me. I praise you because I am fearfully and wonderfully made; your works are wonderful; I know that full well. In Jesus' name, amen.

August 25

Angels from the Lord

"Are not all angels ministering spirits sent to serve those who will inherit salvation?" Hebrews 1:14

Angels are mentioned throughout the Bible in various roles and circumstances. Angels were created by God and are subject to God. Angels exist in spiritual form in the spiritual realm. The Lord has power and authority over all angelic beings including Satan and his demons. Angels are supernatural beings yet they are not to be worshipped and they also worship the Lord. Angels are described as having structure and order similar to that of a military regime. God is the Commander and Lord of Hosts over all angelic beings. Angels do the bidding of the Lord in obedience to him. A common role that angels have played regarding interaction with humans is that of being a messenger for the Lord. Angels are also guards and warriors in spiritual warfare, they worship the Lord in his presence, and they watch over and protect us as the Lord sends them to do so. The writer of the book of Hebrews states that angels are sent by God to serve those of us who have inherited salvation through Jesus Christ our Lord. The presence and the ministry of angels in our lives is another way that the Lord shows his love and his power in our lives. Angels are another resource of the Lord to watch over us and accomplish his will and purpose in our lives. The existence of angels is another reason for us to give God glory and to be assured of his love and his power to watch over us and accomplish his will.

Dear Heavenly Father, you are the Lord of hosts of all angels. I thank you for sending angels in my life. I pray that you send angels to watch over my loved ones today. In Jesus' name, amen.

August 26

Times and Seasons

"There is a time for everything, and a season for every activity under the heavens:" Ecclesiastes 3:1

While we are on this journey with Jesus, we experience changes in seasons in our lives. Varying seasons may be distinguished by where we live, what we do for work, our goals, our financial status, relationships with others, membership at a particular church, participation in a particular ministry, hobbies, interests, and even stages in development as we grow older. Events and circumstances may mark seasons in our lives. Some of these are pleasant and positive, other seasons are challenging and difficult. Some events we experience mark heartbreaking or traumatic seasons. Seasons remain for different lengths of time; some transition sooner than others, and some seasons remain long-term. Whether long-term or short-term, whether pleasant or difficult, our times and seasons are in the hands of the Lord. We trust him with the seasons and chapters of our lives. We look to the Lord in times of transition because he is the Lord over all the times and seasons of our lives. We may experience a sense of loss as we recognize that the Lord is bringing a season of our life to a close, but we let go and thank the Lord for the seasons he has given us, moving forward to embrace the next season he has in store for us with enthusiasm and eager anticipation for the new experiences we will have in him!

Dear Heavenly Father, thank you that there is a time for everything and a season for every activity under the heavens. My times and seasons are in your hands. Give me your strength to endure the difficult seasons, grant me the grace to let go of the past and embrace the changing seasons of life.
In Jesus' name, amen.

August 27

Trust and Obey

"By faith Abraham, when called to go to a place he would later receive as his inheritance, obeyed and went, even though he did not know where he was going." Hebrews 11:8

To walk in faith is to do what the Lord wants us to do even though we do not know where we are going, what we are doing, or why we are doing it. We may like to have our plans lined out for us in advance and know the details of what we are going to do and how we are going to do it. The Lord does not always allow us the luxury of knowing the details of his plans. He asks us to step forward in faith trusting him for results as we obey him. We have confidence as we step out in faith, because our faith is not in our destination, or the accomplishment of an endeavor, or in our abilities or resources. Our faith is in our Lord God Almighty. He is faithful. If we knew all the answers to our questions, had all of our plans and the details of our plans laid out for us, and had the Lord's assurance of results, then we would not even need to have faith. On the contrary, without faith, it is impossible to please God. When we are faced with the uncertainty of results, the hesitancy of the unknown, and the burden of unanswered questions, then we are right where the Lord wants us to be so we can step out in faith in him. By faith in God, we overcome all of our hesitancies and resistance to be obedient to the Lord and we move forward in obedience. When we obey the Lord and follow him in faith, he can bless us and surprise us with his results, which are better than we can imagine.

Dear Heavenly Father, help me to have the faith to obey you when I don't know where I am going. Help me to walk in faith and obedience as I put my trust in you. In Jesus' name, amen.

August 28

The Lord Looks at the Heart

"But the LORD said to Samuel, 'Do not consider his appearance or his height, for I have rejected him. The LORD does not look at the things people look at. People look at the outward appearance, but the LORD looks at the heart.'" 1 Samuel 16:7

The Lord told the prophet Samuel to go to the house of Jesse to anoint one of his sons as the king of Israel. When Samuel saw Jesse's oldest son, Eliab, he thought to himself, "Surely the Lord's anointed stands here before the Lord." But the Lord rejected Eliab. Finally, Samuel anointed Jesse's youngest son David as king. The Lord does not get caught up in outward appearances like we tend to do. The Lord looks at a person's heart. A true expression of a person is their inner qualities, not how they look. Appearances can be deceiving. We do not want to make the mistake Samuel made by judging someone by the way they look. We need to give a person a chance and get to know them to know what kind of person they are rather than just going by their appearance. The Lord may choose the person we least expect to do mighty things for him because the Lord looks at the heart. How we look on the outside is not as important to the Lord as who we are on the inside. We are wiser to focus on developing our inner qualities and character than focusing our effort on how we look. The Lord looks at our hearts. The condition of our hearts is much more valuable in God's sight than our outward appearance.

Dear Heavenly Father, help me to get to know people by their hearts rather than their appearance. Help me to place more value on the condition of my own heart than on how I look. In Jesus' name, amen.

August 29

Struggle with Sin

"I do not understand what I do. For what I want to do I do not do, but what I hate I do....For I do not do the good I want to do, but the evil I do not want to do—this I keep on doing."
Romans 7:15, 19

The apostle Paul shares his own experience regarding his struggle with sin. He knows what is right and wants to do what is right. He also knows what is wrong and does not want to do what is wrong. Yet he keeps doing what is wrong even though he does not want to. Paul says he does not understand why he keeps sinning when he does not want to. It is comforting for us to read these words from Paul, the man of God, because we know what it is like to struggle with sin and it is helpful to know that we are not the only ones who experience this struggle. Sin does take on a power of its own in our sinful nature, that part of us that is inclined to give in to sin. The power of sin can take control over our lives to the point that we feel like we cannot stop ourselves. Paul addresses a point of despair in this passage. He asks, "What a wretched man I am! Who will rescue me from this body that is subject to death?" Paul answers his own question: "Thanks be to God, who delivers me through Jesus Christ our Lord!" We know that Jesus is the answer for our struggle with sin. He died on the cross to save us from the penalty of our sins. He shed his blood for the forgiveness of our sins. Jesus rose from the dead to lead us in victory over sin and in eternal life. The power of God is greater than the power of sin in our lives. There is hope and victory in Jesus Christ our Lord.

Dear Heavenly Father, I turn to you for help with the struggle of sin in my life. Grant me your victory over sin through Jesus Christ my Lord. In Jesus' name, amen.

August 30

Open My Eyes

"Open my eyes that I may see wonderful things in your law."
Psalm 119:18

We stop and pray before we read God's Word. We pray that the Lord will open our eyes so that we may see wonderful things in his Word. This is a ministry of the Holy Spirit. The Holy Spirit is the Spirit of Truth. He guides us into all truth. As we read and study the Word of God, the Holy Spirit helps us to understand the Word. The Holy Spirit helps us to receive what the Lord is speaking to our hearts today through his Word. The Lord reveals to us how his Word, written centuries ago, applies to our daily lives. The Lord uses his Word to encourage us, strengthen us, guide us, and build our faith. The Lord helps us draw closer to him through his Word. He also helps us understand ourselves and others better through the insight and understanding we receive through the Word of God. The Holy Spirit helps us by bringing back to remembrance the Word of God so that we may apply it in our daily lives. We may have hindrances from seeing what the Lord wants to reveal to us in his Word, such as denial, troubling thoughts, memories, and preconceived ideas that limit our understanding of the Word of God. The Lord can remove those hindrances and open our eyes to see new things in his Word to expand our thinking, our understanding, and our spiritual growth. God will use his Word to help us see things we did not see, to know things we did not know, and to understand things we did not understand.

Dear Lord, I pray that your Holy Spirit ministers to me as I read your Word. Open my eyes so that I may see wonderful things in your Word. In Jesus' name, amen.

August 31

The Battle Is Won

"They triumphed over him by the blood of the Lamb and by the word of their testimony; they did not love their lives so much as to shrink from death." Revelation 12:11

John the Revelator shares his vision of the battle in the heavens. The devil is defeated and cast down by the army of angels in the authority of Jesus the Messiah and the kingdom of God. Those whom the devil accuses triumph over him by the blood of the Lamb and the word of their testimony. This victory over Satan applies to us because of what Jesus did on the cross. Jesus shed his blood and died on the cross to save us from the penalty of our sins. Our sins are forgiven and washed away by the blood of the Lamb of God, Jesus Christ our Lord. The accusations that Satan tries to make against us are overcome by the blood of Christ. Jesus defeated Satan for us by taking the penalty of our sins for us and then rising from the dead. Jesus overcame death, hell, and Satan when he rose victoriously from the dead. Jesus ascended to heaven and is seated at the right hand of the throne of God. Jesus is coming back, and we will be with him forever. Jesus' victory is our victory. We have triumphed over the devil because of Jesus. We stand in victory in spiritual warfare and triumph over the enemy when we share our testimony. When we share our testimony about what Jesus has done and is doing in our lives, we give him glory as we stand in victory over the devil and sin, having confidence and faith in Jesus our Lord.

Dear Jesus, I thank you that you have triumphed over the devil, sin, and hell by shedding your blood. I stand on my testimony of your forgiveness, salvation, and deliverance in my life.
In Jesus' name, amen.

September 1

Eternal Destiny

"For the wages of sin is death, but the gift of God is eternal life in Christ Jesus our Lord." Romans 6:23

The Bible teaches that there is a heaven and a hell. Those who have been saved through Jesus Christ will have eternal life in heaven. Those who rebel against God and reject Jesus Christ will have eternal death in hell. The Bible describes hell as eternal punishment, a place of torment, outer darkness, and eternal separation from God. This is in contrast to heaven, which is described as paradise, eternal rest, and the dwelling place of the Lord, where we will be in the Lord's presence for eternity. Eternal life is a gift from God offered to all humankind. God created all human beings and loves us so much that he gave his only Son, Jesus, to live as a man and die on the cross to save us from the penalty of our sins. Jesus shed his blood on the cross for the remission of our sins so that we may be forgiven and have eternal life in heaven with Jesus. This is the greatest expression of love because of the sacrifice Jesus made by dying for us so that we may live. This is also the greatest expression of God's grace because this is a gift that we did not deserve and did nothing to earn. All we have to do is turn to Jesus Christ, believing in him with the faith that God also gives us as a gift, and ask him to forgive us of our sins. God is loving, compassionate, and gracious. We are so grateful and blessed to receive the gift of eternal life through Jesus Christ. We can share his love and the hope for eternity with others so that they too, may receive God's gift of eternal life through Jesus Christ.

Dear Heavenly Father, thank you for the gift of eternal life in Christ Jesus my Lord. Have mercy, Lord, and help me to share your gift of salvation with those who are lost without you. In Jesus' name, amen.

245

September 2

A Prayer for Our Eyes

"Turn my eyes away from worthless things; preserve my life according to your word." Psalm 119:37

The things we look at can have an impact on our hearts. As Christians devoted to the Lord, we guard our hearts from becoming contaminated by the world, by sin, and by evil. In order to guard our hearts, we need to guard our eyes. The things we look at transfer to our hearts and our minds. We can look at something that catches our eye and then it can appeal to our flesh and our sinful nature. Our flesh and sinful desires may be awakened by what we look at. Covetousness kicks in and we begin to desire what we are looking at. This covetousness is lust of the eyes. This can lead to temptation to sin, either in our thought life, or in our actions. The Lord can help us by turning our eyes away from worthless things. We become aware of our propensity to covet and lust and stand on the conviction that there are some things we have no business looking at. Lust of the eyes is from the world. Our enemy the devil can wave temptations in front of our eyes in an attempt to trip us up and turn us away from the Lord. To avoid the luring appeal of lust of the eyes, we fix our eyes on Jesus. We turn to the Word of God to give us pure and godly thoughts rather than the impulsive temptation to drink in pleasure with our eyes. We ask the Lord in prayer for his help to do this.

Dear Lord, turn my eyes away from worthless things; preserve my life according to your Word. In Jesus' name, amen.

September 3

Rest from Our Labor

"Those who work their land will have abundant food, but those who chase fantasies have no sense." Proverbs 12:11

Labor Day is a national holiday celebrated in the United States on the first Monday of September. This holiday honors workers and laborers in our country and recognizes their contribution to society. Hard work can bring positive results. A hard-working farmer brings in a bountiful harvest. A hard-working builder constructs a secure building. A diligent teacher helps to educate students. All of the various types of work that people do contribute to society and bring productive results. Work is also a means to generate an income and support our families as well as the Christian ministries through our giving. A person who works hard is in contrast to a person who just daydreams and chases fantasies but never gets anything done. Whatever type of work we do, we can do it in a way that brings glory and honor to the Lord. As Christians, we practice a work ethic that honors the Lord. We display qualities such as responsibility, faithfulness, diligence, trustworthiness, and working well with others. Our work allows us to do something that makes a difference in people's lives. Our work is important, but it does not define our lives. As Christians, our relationship with the Lord, family relationships, and health are areas of life that are more important than work. The Lord can help us have a spirit of excellence with our work while keeping a balance in these other priorities and also taking time to rest. We commit our work to the Lord and trust him for success.

Dear Heavenly Father, I dedicate and commit my work to you. I pray that you bless the work of my hands. I pray for your success at whatever work I do. In Jesus' name, amen.

September 4

Our God of Justice

"The LORD is slow to anger but great in power; the LORD will not leave the guilty unpunished...." Nahum 1:3

The prophet Nahum pronounced judgment on Nineveh, the capital of the Assyrian empire. The Assyrians were wicked, cruel, and oppressive as they took Israel captive in their reign. The Lord's judgment on Nineveh reveals that justice is an attribute of God. The Lord brings punishment on those who are wicked. The justice of God's character is a factor in his motivation to send his Son, Jesus the Messiah, to save us from our sins. We all have sinned and fallen short of the glory of God. Jesus, the eternal God, took on the form of a man and died on the cross in our place to take the punishment for our sins that we deserved. This satisfied the judgment of God so that we may be free from the penalty of our sin.

The attribute of God's justice assures us that the Lord will make things right for those who have been wronged. The Lord does not turn a blind eye to wrongdoing and injustice. The Bible tells us that God will bring justice and punishment to those who do wrong. In those times when we have been treated wrongly, we forgive those who have wronged us as the Lord has forgiven us. We also entrust the punishment of wrongdoers into the hands of the Lord. We do not take justice or revenge into our own hands. The Lord will not leave the guilty unpunished. We entrust justice into his hands. Our Lord is a God of justice.

Dear Lord, you are righteous and just. You are slow to anger but great in power and you will not leave the guilty unpunished. I pray for justice for those who are oppressed. I entrust justice into your mighty hands. In Jesus' name, amen.

September 5

Strength Sapper

"...my strength was sapped as in the heat of summer."
Psalm 32:4

The summer heat will cause us to feel exhausted, drained, and weak—as if all our strength was gone. In the context of this psalm, David is recounting his experience when he had unconfessed sin—something that always separates us from God. We jeopardize the benefit of receiving God's spiritual power when we allow sin to stand between us and the Lord. Unconfessed sin also has the burden of guilt and shame, which wears us down and continues to drain our strength. The profoundly sad irony is that we turn to more sin as a relief from the burden of the sin we are bearing, only to make matters worse and drain our strength all the more. We can get into a repetitive cycle of sin and shame when we feel shame for our sin and then turn to sin to escape our shame, then we experience more shame, so we turn to more sin. This puts us on a downward spiral of sin and shame. The solution to this madness is to turn to Jesus and ask him to forgive us of our sins. We do not have to live in that place of carrying sin and shame that saps our strength. Jesus shed his blood and died on the cross so that we may be forgiven of our sins. The Lord's forgiveness lifts the burden of our sins. We can experience the freedom of guilt, shame, and the burden of sin when we receive forgiveness through Jesus. When we ask the Lord for forgiveness, he gives us strength. The Lord is our strength when we turn to him and rely on him.

Dear Lord, I confess my sin to you and ask for your forgiveness through the blood of Jesus. I thank you that when I am weak, you are my strength. I pray for your strength in my life today.
In Jesus' name, amen.

September 6

Easy Does It

"Fathers, do not exasperate your children; instead, bring them up in the training and instruction of the Lord."
Ephesians 6:4

The apostle Paul provides wise advice to refrain from exasperating our children. To "exasperate" means to irritate or provoke to a high degree, and to annoy extremely. This principle applies to both mothers and fathers who are raising children. We do not want to provoke our children to the point that they are overwhelmed and become upset. This can happen when we push them too hard. We need to provide discipline and instruction for our children lovingly rather than becoming harsh and insensitive to their feelings. This same principle carries over to our workplace for those of us in leadership positions. We need to be aware of how we treat other people and be mindful that we are not overwhelming or exasperating others by how we treat them. This also applies to our relationships with our spouse and with our friends. We can overwhelm or exasperate others by placing unreasonable expectations on them. Each of us has different levels of capabilities and limitations. To overwhelm others to the point of exasperation is not what God wants us to do. Jesus criticized the spiritual leaders of his day because they placed a heavy burden on people and did not lift a finger to help them. In contrast, Jesus said that his yoke is easy and his burden is light. We can be more like Jesus when we practice love, patience, and gentleness with others rather than overwhelming and exasperating others with harshness or unrealistic expectations.

Dear Lord, thank you that your yoke is easy and your burden is light. Help me to reflect your love and gentleness in how I treat others today. In Jesus' name, amen.

September 7

A Shield about Me

"But you, LORD, are a shield around me, my glory, the One who lifts my head high." Psalm 3:3

We praise and worship the Lord because he is a shield around us. God loves us so much that he protects us by his mighty power. We are precious to him. He watches over us and guards our lives with his love and strength. The Lord is a mighty God. No one or nothing can stand against him. He treasures us and provides security for us by his great power. We are safe in the Lord's hands. He protects us from harm and evil. We have refuge and security in the secret place of the Most High God. We have confidence in him because of his love and power. His love casts out our fear because of the security that we have in him. We trust in God's protection as we walk through life. This gives us confidence in him.

The Lord is our glory. He is the greatest source of joy in our lives. The good things in our life flow from our relationship with the Lord. He is a glorious God. Anything good in us or in our lives comes from him. We are blessed to have the Lord's love and goodness in our lives. We give him thanks and all glory and honor go to God. When we are discouraged or disappointed, we keep our chin up and our knees down. The Holy Spirit inside of us gives us hope and encouragement to lift our hearts as we trust in the Lord. We do not stay down in a place of discouragement or sadness, even when faced with difficulty. Our faith in God strengthens us to worship him because of who he is. Our relationship with him gives us strength and encouragement. The Lord is the lifter of our heads!

Dear Heavenly Father, I praise you because you, Lord, are a shield around me, my glory, the One who lifts my head high. In Jesus' name, amen.

September 8

Walk It Out

*"When he saw them, he said, 'Go, show yourselves to the priests.'
And as they went, they were cleansed." Luke 17:14*

Jesus came upon ten men who had leprosy. They were crying out to him for mercy. Jesus responded to their cries by telling them to go and show themselves to the priests. This instruction was following Old Testament law. A person who was healed from leprosy was required to be examined by a priest and then pronounced clean. Jesus told them to show themselves to the priests so that they could be pronounced clean even though they were not healed yet. The men who had leprosy could have looked at themselves and asked, "Why should I show myself to the priest? I am not even healed!" The lepers followed the instructions of Jesus even though they had not experienced healing yet. This was a step of faith on their part. The Lord requires us to step out in faith to believe in him and to trust and obey him even when we do not see results. Jesus did not heal them immediately and instantly, although he could have. They were cleansed as they went. The Lord healed them as they followed his word. The Lord often does his work of deliverance, healing, renewal, and transformation in our lives as we follow him in faith and obedience. He transforms us as we walk with him in faith. He cleanses us as we go, like he did to the ten men who had leprosy. This is a process that the Lord is doing in our lives as we follow him in faith and focus on our personal relationship with him. Every day is a new day of healing and growing in Jesus.

Dear Jesus, thank you for the cleansing, healing, and renewal you are doing in my heart and my life every day as I walk in faith with you. In Jesus' name, amen.

September 9

A Tough Lesson Learned

"Before I was afflicted I went astray, but now I obey your word."
Psalm 119:67

As followers of Christ, to become disobedient is to go astray. The Lord loves us and he has provided guidelines in his Word for us to live a safe and healthy life. When we are disobedient, we break the Lord's commandments and we also remove ourselves from under his covering of protection and blessing on our lives. When we are disobedient, we set ourselves up for negative consequences. Negative consequences that are a result of disobedience are self-inflicted because we did it to ourselves by being disobedient. Although the experience of negative consequences is uncomfortable and unpleasant, that experience can bring about positive results. The discomfort of negative consequences can teach us deep within to prevent future disobedience that will bring further hardship. We need to connect the dots and know that disobedience leads to negative consequences. We need to let our consequences help us to hate sin. The consequences we experience as a result of our sin should cause us to be mad at that sin and disgusted at the temptation to sin rather than being seduced by the deceptive appeal to sin's pleasure. We need to embrace the consequences and take ownership of our choices and actions rather than blaming others and minimizing our sin and disobedience. Those negative consequences as a result of our disobedience may be the best thing that happened to us when they cause us to turn to the Lord and allow him to change our hearts.

Dear Heavenly Father, help me to draw close to you and learn from the consequences that come from my sin and disobedience. Before I was afflicted, I went astray, but now I obey your word. In Jesus' name, amen.

September 10

Live at Peace

"If it is possible, as far as it depends on you, live at peace with everyone." Romans 12:18

The Lord has called us to a life of love. He has given us a message and a ministry of reconciliation. His Word teaches us to live in peaceful unity with others. However, sadly, in this fallen world we will not always have peace, unity, and reconciliation. The gospel itself is a divisive factor for some people in this world. We have no control over those who are hostile toward Christ and the gospel. We also may encounter conflict and division over other issues from personal relationships to politics within and outside of the body of Christ. Jesus calls us to be peacemakers. Harmonious relationships require both parties to seek peace. Unfortunately, this does not always happen. We have no control over the actions of others. We can seek peace, but they may continue to be hostile. We may seek reconciliation, but they may reject our efforts. We may desire to get along, and they may respond with contention. The apostle Paul recognizes this reality and instructs us that if it is possible, as far as it depends on us, to live at peace with everyone. We do our part to live in peace even when others remain hostile. Jesus taught us to forgive others the same way that God has forgiven us. He also taught us to bless those who curse us and pray for those who mistreat us. We refrain from engaging in anger and hostility even when others are offensive or hurtful toward us. We turn to the Lord in times of offense or hurt for his love and strength to respond with love and live at peace.

Dear Heavenly Father, I pray for peace and reconciliation in all of my relationships. I pray for those with whom I am in conflict. I pray that as much as it depends on me, I will live at peace with everyone. In Jesus' name, amen.

September 11

Day of Rest

"Then God blessed the seventh day and made it holy, because on it he rested from all the work of creating that he had done."
Genesis 2:3

The Lord set forth an example by taking a day of rest in the creation story told in the book of Genesis. In the Mosaic Law, the Lord instituted the Sabbath as a day of rest for the Israelites. Although all of the Old Testament laws do not carry over into the New Testament church, there is a moral principle found in the law of the Sabbath that is important for us today. The primary focus of the Sabbath is to rest. This is a clear purpose of the Sabbath. The Lord took a day of rest after creating the universe in six days. How much more do we need to take a day of rest and refresh our bodies, minds, and spirits? To push ourselves at work every day is not healthy for us. That is not the way the Lord wants us to live. To have a day of rest lays a foundation for balance between work and rest in our lives. The other element of a day of rest without work is to have a day devoted to worshiping the Lord in church with other believers. The Sabbath in the Old Testament was kept on the last day of the week. The New Testament reveals that Jesus rose from the dead on the first day of the week. There is New Testament scriptural support for the first day of the week being called "The Lord's Day." It is widely practiced among contemporary Christian churches to gather for worship on Sunday, the first day of the week. The New Testament does not specify requirements regarding the day as in the Old Testament. However, the principle remains true. It is important for us to have dedicated times of rest and worship. The Lord will help us to live in balance in our relationship with him.

Dear Lord, thank you for the rest that I have in you. Help me to live a life in balance with work, rest, and worship.
In Jesus' name, amen.

255

September 12

Go and Be Reconciled

"Therefore, if you are offering your gift at the altar and there remember that your brother or sister has something against you, leave your gift there in front of the altar. First go and be reconciled to them; then come and offer your gift."
Matthew 5:23–24

Jesus teaches us that our relationships with each other are important to him. Reconciliation is the mending of broken relationships. Jesus' teaching implies the priority that God places on our relationships with others. Jesus puts the responsibility on us. He said that we need to go and be reconciled when we know someone is hurt or offended by us. We take responsibility for our part in any conflict. To go and be reconciled is to admit our wrongdoing and abstain from pointing the finger at the other person. We need to take ownership of our wrongs. To go and be reconciled takes humility because we admit that we were wrong. To go and be reconciled requires us to ask for forgiveness. Forgiveness is the threshold to reconciliation. Once we have been forgiven, then the process of mending the relationship can take place. The Lord wants us to be in a right relationship with others. To hold grudges and resentment, to have friends or family members that refuse to talk with each other is not what God wants. The Lord is a God of reconciliation. He wants us to be ministers of reconciliation as well. Whether we are offended by someone, or we know they are offended by us, we need to go and be reconciled. Jesus puts the responsibility on us to be the one to reach out and make things right. That is what God wants.

Dear Heavenly Father, help me to be in a right relationship with other people. Help me to reach out to others with whom I have conflict. Help me to go and be reconciled. In Jesus' name, amen.

September 13

Dependence on God

"The Lᴏʀᴅ said to Gideon, 'You have too many men. I cannot deliver Midian into their hands, or Israel would boast against me, "My own strength has saved me."'"
Judges 7:2

The Lord called Gideon to lead the army of Israel in battle against the Midianites. Israel's army had over 30,000 soldiers. The Lord stopped Gideon and told Gideon that the army was too big because when they won the battle, they would think that they did it by the size of their army. The Lord told Gideon to reduce the size of the army. When the army got down to just 300 men, the Lord was pleased to use that army to defeat the Midianites. The Lord wants us to depend on him, rather than relying on our own strength. We need to depend on God and give God glory for our victories rather than taking it upon ourselves and giving ourselves credit for the victory in our lives. It is not because the Lord needs credit for his ego, but that he wants to save us from our ego. When we are full of self-reliance, it often leads to pride. When we become prideful, we think we can do things on our own and we do not need God anymore. We need to remain dependent on God for our victory. The Lord helps us by putting us in a position of relying on him. God calls us to do things that we cannot possibly do on our own so that we will depend on him and give him the glory for the results. When we feel that we are in an impossible situation, that the odds are against us, and that there is no way for us to accomplish the task set before us, we are in a perfect place to depend on God. The Lord makes all things possible when we depend on him.

Dear Heavenly Father, today I declare my dependence on you. I can do nothing without you. I thank you for your help, and I give you glory for victory in my life today. In Jesus' name, amen.

September 14

A Depraved Mind

"Furthermore, just as they did not think it worthwhile to retain the knowledge of God, so God gave them over to a depraved mind, so that they do what ought not to be done."
Romans 1:28

We hear about some of the violent, perverse, and evil atrocities in the world today and we wonder how people can ever come to a place where they commit such acts. The apostle Paul describes a progressive degradation that takes place when people reject God and turn to sin. Paul wrote that God gave them over to the sinful desires of their hearts, then God gave them over to shameful lusts, and then God gave them over to depraved minds. God does not impose this on people but he allows people to decide to go down this path of depravity. Sin is like a poison that increasingly causes corruption in a person's mind. Paul describes that when people go down this path, they exchange the truth of God for a lie. Their thinking is based on lies and falsehoods and they believe their own lies. This progressive pattern leads to irrational and delusional thinking. This process becomes increasingly worse to the point that a person's thinking becomes deranged. There is a sin-induced madness that can take place in a person's mind that leads a person down a spiral of degradation and depravity. The good news is that when we turn to Jesus, he can renew and heal our minds. The Word of God can bring truth and healing to the impact of sin's corruption and lies. The Holy Spirit can cleanse our minds of the impurity of sin. Rather than rejecting God and turning to sin on a path of depravity, we reject sin and turn to God on a path of renewal, hope, and purity.

Dear Lord, I pray that you help me to overcome the negative impact that sin has had on my mind. Renew and heal my mind through your Word and the power of your Holy Spirit. In Jesus' name, amen.

September 15

Rise Again

"for though the righteous fall seven times, they rise again, but the wicked stumble when calamity strikes."
Proverbs 24:16

Being a Christian does not mean that we do not make mistakes. When we experience setbacks and failures, we do not give up. A Christian is either up or getting up. We don't stay down. Our Lord is a God of second chances. Failure can be so discouraging. The enemy of our soul wants to see us stay down and get discouraged so we give up on ourselves and give up on God. God will never give up on us. We turn from our sin and failure and turn to the Lord in repentance. God's forgiveness through Jesus Christ frees us from the burden of our guilt and shame from our sins and failures. The Lord gives us hope that we can move forward and rise again rather than being stuck in the despair of sin and failure. The Holy Spirit inside of us gives us strength to rise again. The same Spirit that raised Jesus from the dead is inside of us. He gives us that resurrection power to rise again from our failures and setbacks. We learn from our mistakes and grow in the areas where we are weak with the Lord's help. We grow closer to the Lord in our relationship with him. We turn to the Word of God to give us truth and to overcome the confusion, fear, doubts, and lies of the enemy that fill our heads when we have failed. We stand on the promises of God for strength. We also strengthen our relationships with other believers to receive support, prayer, and encouragement. We overcome the attempts of the enemy to isolate, give up, feel sorry for ourselves, or go backward in our spiritual journey. The Lord helps us to rise again and continue to serve and follow him.

Dear Heavenly Father, thank you for your strength to rise again from failure. I pray for your wisdom to learn from failure, to draw closer to you, and to walk in your victory.
In Jesus' name, amen.

September 16

Begin by Giving Thanks

"Enter his gates with thanksgiving and his courts with praise; give thanks to him and praise his name." Psalm 100:4

This psalm presents a picture of Old Testament tabernacle and temple worship. To go into the Tabernacle or the Temple, people would have to first go through a gate and then through the court to approach the Holy Place to worship. This psalm instructs us that even as we enter the gate to worship, we should have thanksgiving in our hearts to the Lord. This is an illustration of entering into the presence of the Lord. When we enter into the Lord's presence in our personal time of prayer or when we gather with other believers, we begin by giving thanks. We don't bombard the presence of the Lord with our requests of what we want or need or our struggles with our problems. We begin our time of entering the Lord's presence with thanksgiving and praise. This psalm tells us that we can thank the Lord because he made us. He gave us life and a purpose for living. We thank the Lord because he is our shepherd and we are the sheep of his pasture. He takes care of us and watches over us. We thank the Lord for his goodness, his love, and his faithfulness. There are so many things we can be thankful for. As we enter the Lord's presence, and as we enter a new day that God has given us, we begin by thanking God and praising him. We can begin our day and our prayers by telling the Lord the many reasons we are thankful.

Dear Heavenly Father, I enter your presence with thanksgiving in my heart. Help me to always begin my day and my prayers by giving thanks for your love, your goodness, and your faithfulness. In Jesus' name, amen.

September 17

Restore Gently

"Brothers and sisters, if someone is caught in a sin, you who live by the Spirit should restore that person gently. But watch yourselves, or you also may be tempted."
Galatians 6:1

Four guidelines help us to respond to others who are caught in sin: that we live by the Spirit, that we restore them, that we are gentle, and that we watch ourselves or we may also be tempted. When we live by the Spirit, we are people of prayer. We need to pray for those we know who struggle with sin, and we need to pray about our response to them. We need to respond with the love and compassion of our Lord. Our focus is on helping them be restored to a right relationship with the Lord and others. Jesus came to bring restoration with God for sinful people. When we respond to those who are struggling with sin, their restoration always needs to be our focus. Those who are caught in sin are people who are hurting. We do not need to react to them with anger or condemnation. We do not react in such a way to cause them to feel guilt and shame. These are tactics of the enemy to push them away from the Lord. When we are gentle with people who are hurting from sin, we can help them receive God's healing in their lives. We also need to watch ourselves or we may be tempted. We set wise and healthy boundaries so that we do not also get entangled in that sin and we will not encourage them to rely on us but for them to rely on our Lord Jesus for their restoration.

Dear Heavenly Father, help me to respond to those who are caught in sin the same way that I would need others to respond to me. Help me to live in the Spirit, to focus on restoration, to be gentle, and to watch myself so that I also will not be tempted to sin. In Jesus' name, amen.

September 18

Trinity Ministry

"And I will ask the Father, and he will give you another advocate to help you and be with you forever—the Spirit of truth...."
John 14:16–17

God eternally exists through three separate but equal members of the Trinity: God the Father, God the Son, and God the Holy Spirit. This verse not only mentions the three members of the Trinity, it provides insight into each of their distinct ministries and roles in our lives. Jesus states that he will ask the Father. This describes a ministry role of Jesus. He intercedes for us. He speaks to the Father on our behalf. Jesus represented us when he died on the cross to save us from the penalty of our sins. Jesus rose from the dead. He ascended to heaven, and now he is seated at the right hand of the throne of God, interceding for us. He continues to speak to the Father on our behalf. Jesus said that the Father will give us the Holy Spirit. This describes a ministry role of our Heavenly Father. He is our heavenly provider. Our Father loved the world so much that he gave his one and only Son, Jesus. Our Father gives us his Holy Spirit. The Holy Spirit is our advocate. He is called alongside us to help us. The Holy Spirit gives us God's comfort and strength. He is the Spirit of truth. He guides us into all truth. The Holy Spirit helps us to understand God's Word, to apply God's Word, and to hide it in our hearts. Jesus said that the Holy Spirit will be with us forever. The Holy Spirit is a deposit of the eternal life that we have in Jesus Christ. We have eternity in our hearts because of the presence of the Holy Spirit inside of us. The members of the Trinity, God our Father, his Son Jesus, and the Holy Spirit, continue to minister to us in their distinct roles and ministries today.

Dear Lord, I thank you for your ministry and presence in my life through the Father, the Son Jesus, and the Holy Spirit.
In Jesus' name, amen.

September 19

God Answers

"Call to me and I will answer you and tell you great and unsearchable things you do not know." Jeremiah 33:3

We have a personal spiritual relationship with the Lord based on his love for us and developed through our capacity to communicate with him. We talk with God through our prayers and he answers us. God hears us when we call out to him. We are important to him. He does not ignore our cries. He is not too busy for us. He does not feel bothered by us. He listens intently to our prayers. The Lord answers us when we call to him. The Lord answers us through his Word. When we are in prayer and reading the Bible, we will find answers from the Lord regarding our prayers. The Lord also answers our prayers through the Holy Spirit inside of us. The Holy Spirit reveals the truth in God's Word to help us understand his will and his answers to the requests of our hearts. He speaks to our hearts with the gentle leading of his Holy Spirit. The Lord will also use other people to answer our prayers. He will use his Word as shared by our pastor or our Bible study leader to give us answers to our prayers. As we seek wise counsel and pray with others, the Lord will guide us regarding his will. The Lord can also answer us by supernatural means including open and closed doors, and miraculous signs and solutions that cannot be explained. It is important when we pray to the Lord that we are then paying attention and listening with our spirits and our hearts for his answers. He told us he will answer. As we continue to pray, we wait, watch, and listen.

Dear Heavenly Father, thank you for hearing my prayers and answering them. Help me to listen and hear your answers. Tell me great and unsearchable things I did not know.
In Jesus' name, amen.

September 20

God Brings Order to Chaos

"For God is not a God of disorder but of peace—as in all the congregations of the Lord's people." 1 Corinthians 14:33

The apostle Paul addresses the church in Corinth because there was so much disorder in their gatherings to worship that it was confusing to people who attended. Paul clarifies that God is not the author of confusion and disorder. The Lord works in order and peace. Paul offers correction and practical guidelines to the church so that everything can be done in a good and orderly fashion. That way, people who attend can worship the Lord in peace rather than be turned away from the Lord in confusion. These principles carry over to our lives beyond the worship service. Our lives do not have to be filled with confusion and chaos. That is not the way the Lord wants us to live. Being a Christian does not mean we will not have times of confusion or storms in life, but we do not have to live life from chaos to chaos. God offers order to our chaos and peace to our confusion. When we do face confusion or chaos, the Lord guides us through the storm to a peaceful haven. The Word of God is a source of stability and peace in our lives. We have soundness and a firm foundation in our relationship with the Lord when we live by the Word of God. We can enter into confusion when we depart from the Word and lean on our own understanding. We can cause our own confusion when we neglect to seek God's Word for answers. We can resolve our confusion by asking what the Bible has to say and relying on that direction in faith and trust in the Lord.

Dear Heavenly Father, thank you that you are not a God of disorder but of peace. I pray for your peace and your order in the confusion and disorder in my life. In Jesus' name, amen.

September 21

Abounding in Love

"The LORD is compassionate and gracious, slow to anger, abounding in love." Psalm 103:8

We may know good people who are loving, kind, and gracious. They are but mere splinter reflections of the goodness and love of God. He has infinite and unfathomable love for us. We also may have had experiences with people who were not compassionate, not gracious, not loving, and quick to anger. Perhaps that is why we think that God will be intolerant or angry with us when we fall short. We feel guilt and shame over our failures and shortcomings. We become afraid that God will be angry with us and judge us or reject us for our failures or our problems. God is not like that. He is the complete opposite. He is slow to anger. He has great patience with us. He has compassion for us when we are hurting. The Lord is like a loving parent who watches over a toddler taking their first steps. He is proudly and lovingly watching over us. The parent does not get mad when the toddler falls. That parent is quick to pick that toddler up with love and compassion and embrace that child. That's the way the Lord feels about us when we fall. He is abounding in love. We can turn to the Lord with our hurts and our problems rather than trying to cover them up because of our guilt, shame, or fear. He will not be angry with us. He wants to love us so that we can overcome, heal, and grow. God does not hold our sins and problems against us. When we come to him with our hurts and our weaknesses, he is gracious and compassionate toward us. He lovingly draws close to us as we turn to him in faith. We need to allow ourselves to receive his love.

Dear Lord, you are compassionate and gracious, slow to anger and abounding in love. I give myself to you today. I receive your love. In Jesus' name, amen.

265

September 22

But I Am a Person of Prayer

"In return for my friendship they accuse me, but I am a man of prayer." Psalm 109:4

David shares about the unfortunate position of being betrayed by others. It is an awful place to be when we reach out to others and do our best to be a friend, yet they betray our friendship by accusing us or slandering us and talking about us behind our backs. That hurts. David had a great response to this situation. He said, "...but I am a man of prayer." When we respond in prayer, we overcome the temptation to react in our flesh. Our initial reaction might be to want to become angry and lash out to hurt others the way that we have been hurt. When we pray, we turn our emotional release to the Lord. It is okay to tell God how we feel. Throughout the Psalms, David exhibits his ability to articulate his emotions before the Lord rather than react to them. When we pray, we not only have the opportunity to express our feelings; we also have the opportunity to have our hearts met by the Spirit of God to bring healing to our hurts and to empower us to handle our situation in a healthy and godly manner. With God's help, we forgive those who have betrayed us as the Bible instructs us to. When we turn to God in prayer, we receive his love in such a way that we do not fall apart when other people hurt us. The love of God holds us together. Our relationship with the Lord is our primary relationship and although betrayal from others hurts, no one can take away the strength we have in God's love. Other people may hurt us, reject us, or betray us, but we are people of prayer.

*Dear Heavenly Father, other people have returned my friendship by hurting me, but I am a person of prayer. I entrust my feelings and relationships into your hands. I forgive those who have betrayed me. Heal my hurts with your love.
In Jesus' name, amen.*

September 23

Ask, Seek, Knock

"Ask and it will be given to you; seek and you will find; knock and the door will be opened to you. For everyone who asks receives; the one who seeks finds; and to the one who knocks, the door will be opened." Matthew 7:7–8

Jesus teaches us how to pray. He tells us that when we ask in prayer, we will receive what we asked for. When we seek in prayer, we will find what we are looking for. When we knock on the door in prayer, the door will be opened for us. This encourages us to turn to the Lord in prayer rather than trying to do things on our own without the Lord's help. The Lord did not leave us to our own devices to manage life on our own. He is there for us when we pray. The Lord is mighty in power to answer our prayers and make things happen. This not only indicates the power of God, but it also shows his great love for us. God hears and answers our prayers as an expression of his love. Jesus' three-fold description of prayer as asking, seeking, and knocking lets us know that prayer is a process in which we need to be actively involved. Prayer for a Christian is not depicted as the Lord always automatically, instantaneously, miraculously giving us everything we ask for. Prayer is a journey of drawing close to God and making requests according to his will. Prayer requires persistence on our part. When we pray, we ask and keep asking, we seek and keep seeking, we knock and keep knocking; then we will receive, we will find, and the door will be opened. Prayer is a journey of drawing close to God, sharing our hearts with him, and trusting him for the results and for his will to be done.

Dear Lord, help me to have a stronger prayer life as I turn to you in faith and trust. Thank you that when I ask, I will receive, when I seek, I will find, and when I knock, the door shall be opened. In Jesus' name, amen.

September 24

Like a City with Strong Walls

"Like a city whose walls are broken through is a person who lacks self-control." Proverbs 25:28

In Bible times, it was common for cities to have walls around them. The walls protected the inhabitants of the city from attacks by the enemy. A city without walls would be vulnerable to the attacks of the enemy. Solomon wrote this proverb stating that a person who lacks self-control is like a city with its walls broken down. A lack of self-control on our part opens us up to be vulnerable to the attacks of the enemy of our souls. When we become hasty, reckless, or impulsive, we put ourselves out there for the enemy to walk all over us and have his way with us. Just as the walls of a city provide security and sanctity for those in the city, a life of self-control has security and safety for us. Self-control is a fruit of the Holy Spirit. The Lord gives us his strength and wisdom to restrain our appetites, impulses, and emotional reactions. Just as the city walls provide a boundary for the people who live in the city, we learn to develop healthy boundaries in our lives as the Lord develops self-control in us. The Word of God provides healthy boundaries for us as we live by and adhere to the teachings and standards of the Bible. With God's help, we practice self-control through our commitment to our spiritual disciplines such as prayer, Bible reading, and church attendance. We learn to practice prudence and wisdom in our decisions rather than impulsively doing what we want to do or what we feel like doing. With God's help, we can live our lives with self-control and be like that city with strong and secure walls.

Dear Lord, I pray for the fruit of your Spirit of self-control. Help me to have self-discipline, wisdom, and healthy boundaries in my life. In Jesus' name, amen.

September 25

We Are God's Handiwork

"For we are God's handiwork, created in Christ Jesus to do good works, which God prepared in advance for us to do."
Ephesians 2:10

We are God's handiwork. In other words, God is the artist, and we are his masterpiece. That's the way he sees us. We are all the results of the Lord's creative power and genius. He made us the way we are and he loves and cherishes us. He sees each of us as his masterpiece. Anyone who told us anything otherwise was wrong. Life throws its hurtful experiences at us and sometimes we end up seeing ourselves as less than who God created us to be. When we get into the Word of God and the presence of God, we are refreshed and healed by the love of God and the truth of God that we are truly God's masterpiece and that he loves us the way we are. God also made each of us with a plan and a purpose for our lives. The Lord reveals that purpose to us as we seek him and serve him. Some of us understand that purpose sooner than others. For some of us, there is a journey to discover the purpose for which God has created us and the good works that he wants us to accomplish. As we are on our search for more of God, he reveals these things to us in his time. There is fulfillment in receiving God's love for us and finding our identity as his masterpiece. There is more fulfillment and satisfaction in fulfilling God's purpose and plans for which he created us. There is a blessing in serving the Lord and others and doing good works in Jesus' name. God is glorified when we fulfill his purpose for our lives.

Dear Heavenly Father, I am your handiwork, created in Christ Jesus to do good works, which you prepared in advance for me to do. Help me to know and to do those good works for which I am created. In Jesus' name, amen.

269

September 26

Choose Life

"This day I call the heavens and the earth as witnesses against you that I have set before you life and death, blessings and curses. Now choose life, so that you and your children may live"
Deuteronomy 30:19

The Lord has set before us life and death, blessings and curses. He gives us a choice. We decide whether we choose life or death, blessings or curses. God wants us to choose life. God wants that so much that he sacrificed his Son, Jesus, to die for us on the cross so that we can be free from the power and penalty of our sins. Jesus died on the cross to save us from the penalty of our sins. He rose from the dead to lead us in victory over sin and death and to lead the way for us to have eternal life in him. When we choose Jesus, we choose life. God loves us so much that he gave us a choice. When we accept Jesus as our Lord and Savior and ask him to forgive us of our sins through his shed blood, we choose life. We receive God's blessings when we choose to obey him. We choose blessings when we read the Word of God and seek to apply his Word to the standards and direction of our lives. God blesses us when we choose to obey him wholeheartedly. We are in a "bless-able" position when we continue to choose to obey the Lord and his Word. Craziness and chaos are abundant out there in the world today. The Lord wants us to reject worldliness and evil and to choose a life of obedience in a personal relation-ship with Jesus Christ. When we choose Jesus, God blesses us and gives us abundant and eternal life.

Dear Heavenly Father, today I choose life by choosing Jesus and I choose blessings by choosing to obey you and your Word. Dear Jesus, you are my life and you are my blessing.
In your name I pray, amen.

September 27

The Fleeting Pleasures of Sin

"By faith Moses, when he had grown up, refused to be known as the son of Pharaoh's daughter. He chose to be mistreated along with the people of God rather than to enjoy the fleeting pleasures of sin." Hebrews 11:24–25

Moses was raised by Pharaoh's daughter in Pharaoh's palace as a prince of Egypt. When he had grown up, he made the choice to leave Pharaoh's palace and instead he ended up leading the Israelites out of their slavery in Egypt. Moses sets an example to us by practicing the faith to say no to the fleeting pleasure of sin and choosing instead to suffer with the people of God. This description of sin as fleeting pleasure acknowledges that it may be pleasurable for a moment, but the pleasure of sin is not long lasting. In fact, the long-term results of sin are pain, suffering, heartache, and misery. Sin appeals to us as pleasurable or fun at the moment, but there is a price to pay. It is not worth it to throw away God's blessings in life for a fleeting moment of pleasure. Moses' choice to instead suffer with the people of God implies that choosing God's path is not always easy. It does not offer the appealing pleasure that sin does. Following God may involve sacrifice, difficulty, and hardship. However, following God in a personal relationship with Jesus Christ brings long-term fulfillment to our souls. There are blessings from God that endure long after the fleeting pleasures of sin are gone. Our faith in Jesus Christ leads to eternal life in heaven. With God's help we too can practice our faith like Moses did by rejecting the fleeting pleasures of sin and choosing to follow the Lord in faith instead.

Dear Heavenly Father, I choose to follow you by faith rather than to enjoy the fleeting pleasures of sin. Thank you for your victory over sin. In Jesus' name, amen.

September 28

Standing Orders

"Therefore go and make disciples of all nations, baptizing them in the name of the Father and of the Son and of the Holy Spirit,"
Matthew 28:19

After Jesus rose from the dead, he appeared to his disciples and spent more time teaching them. Before he ascended to heaven, he told them to go and make disciples of all nations, baptizing them in the name of the Father and of the Son and of the Holy Spirit. This final instruction of Jesus to his disciples is known as the Great Commission. The Christian Church accepts this as standing orders for the Church today. It is for this reason that there are missionaries in countries all over the world sharing the gospel with those who do not know Christ. If we are not able to serve as missionaries, we can support missionaries through our prayers and our giving. Many of our local churches have opportunities to support missionaries through giving partnerships. If we are not able to serve as full time, long-term missionaries, we can participate in short-term mission trips. It is so important that there are missionaries fulfilling the Great Commission all over the world, but we do not have to leave our country to make disciples either. There is a mission field of people who need Jesus and need to be discipled in our own communities, in our workplace, and perhaps in our own families. Out of obedience to our Lord Jesus, we can do something to fulfill the Great Commission and follow through on his standing orders.

Dear Jesus, I pray that people of all nations will receive the good news about you and become discipled and baptized. I pray for missionaries that are serving in other nations today. Show me how I can take part in fulfilling your Great Commission. In Jesus' name, amen.

September 29

Resist the Devil

"Submit yourselves therefore to God. Resist the devil, and he will flee from you." James 4:7

The influence and the power of the devil is real. When we accepted Jesus, we crossed over from the kingdom of darkness into the kingdom of God. While this world is embroiled in constant spiritual warfare, we have victory over the devil through our conquering King Jesus. The Lord has given us his Holy Spirit, which dwells inside us and gives us power over the devil. The devil will still make attempts to defeat us. One of the tactics the devil will continue to use is to tempt us to go back to our sinful lifestyle. Our greatest defense against the attacks and temptations of the devil is to submit ourselves to God. When we submit to God in surrender, dependence, and obedience, the Lord is our covering and our strength over the devil, giving us victory over temptation, sin, and evil. The Lord is our strength. He is our refuge, our fortress, and our deliverer. The Lord conquers the attempts of the devil to discourage us, to tempt us, and to set us back. When we give in to temptation, we are giving the devil a foothold and allowing him to take back ground in our lives. We want nothing to do with sin and evil. When we resist sin and temptation with God's help, it disarms the strength and power of the devil, and his attempts to draw us back into sin. When we first become Christians and say "No" to sinful habits, the temptations may come on strong. As we draw closer to God and resist those temptations, the power of sin diminishes. The power of temptations to sin will fade when we turn to God for help and resist the devil and say "No" to sin.

Dear Heavenly Father, I submit myself to you. Help me to resist the devil by your strength today. I pray that you overcome the attacks and the influences of sin and the devil in my life today. In Jesus' name, amen.

September 30

The Image of God

"Then God said, 'Let us make mankind in our image, in our likeness, so that they may rule over the fish in the sea and the birds in the sky, over the livestock and all the wild animals, and over all the creatures that move along the ground.'"
Genesis 1:26

The creation story reveals that God created us in his image, reflecting his qualities. The Lord also said we are made in his likeness. This means that we are created to be like him. God is Spirit and we are created beings. We have a spiritual nature that reflects God's image. We do not possess the supernatural spiritual qualities of God such as omniscience, omnipotence, and omnipresence. However, he did create us with the capacity to reflect his attributes such as love, compassion, justice, goodness, and holiness. God created humans to rule over the animals on earth. Our triune God is relational in his essence and he created us to be relational as well. God created us to be in relationship with himself and with each other. Because of the fall of humankind to sin, the image of God in us was corrupted by sin. The Lord sent his Son, Jesus, to die on the cross so that we may be forgiven for our sins. The blood of Jesus cleanses us of the impurity of our sins. The Lord sent his Holy Spirit to be in us. Although we are created beings, the Lord created our souls in his image to exist in eternity. Because of the death and resurrection of our Lord Jesus, we now have eternal life with God in heaven. Until the time that Jesus comes back, or we pass on to be with him in heaven, the Lord will continue to conform us to his image and help us to be more like Jesus Christ.

Dear Heavenly Father, thank you for creating me in your image. I pray that you continue to conform me to your image today. In Jesus' name, amen.

October 1

Jesus Is Our Righteousness

"God made him who had no sin to be sin for us, so that in him we might become the righteousness of God."
2 Corinthians 5:21

We need Jesus. There is no way for us to get right with God without Jesus. There is none righteous, no, not one, except for Jesus. That is why Jesus, the eternal God, became a man so that he could atone for our sins as a human. Jesus took the penalty of our sins on himself for us so that we might be forgiven of our sins. We are forgiven for our sins through the blood of Jesus Christ. We are reconciled to God through Christ. Jesus mended our broken relationship with God. Our sin and unrighteousness separated us from God. Jesus not only took away our sins; he gave us his righteousness. The righteousness that we have is imputed to us by Jesus Christ. God the Father now sees us as cleansed by Jesus' blood and as righteous because of Jesus' righteousness, which has been credited to us. We are not righteous without Jesus. There is no way for us to earn righteousness on our own. We are fallen and imperfect. We cannot earn righteousness by doing good works. This is not attainable for us. It is only through Jesus that we have righteousness. Because Jesus imputed his righteousness to us, God now sees Jesus' righteousness when he looks at us. Jesus became sin for us to die for us. He credited us with his righteousness so that we may be justified in a right relationship with the Father. Jesus is our righteousness.

Dear Jesus, you who had no sin became sin for me, so that I may become the righteousness of God. Thank you, Jesus. You are my righteousness. In Jesus' name, amen.

October 2

You Can't Run from God

"But Jonah ran away from the LORD and headed for Tarshish...."
Jonah 1:3

The Lord told Jonah to preach against the city of Nineveh. Jonah refused to do what God told him to do, and decided to try to run away from God instead. Jonah got on a ship and set out for the high seas, going in the opposite direction of where the Lord told him to go. The Lord caused a severe storm in the waters. The sailors threw Jonah overboard for fear of their own lives. Jonah ended up being swallowed by a great fish. He was inside the fish for three days before the fish vomited Jonah onto dry land. Jonah's story proves the reality that you cannot run away from God!

God is omnipresent. He is everywhere all the time. How can we escape his presence? There is no way. Jonah's example shows us that when we try to run away from the Lord and what he wants us to do, it makes life harder for us. We set ourselves up for hardship and difficulties when we turn from the Lord's will and plan for us. The best response for us to have with the Lord is to surrender to him and his will for our lives and to obey him and do what he wants us to do. We will be miserable until we surrender our will and our ways and follow God's will and his ways. It may not seem pleasant at the time. We may have fears or misgivings about what the Lord is directing us to do. When we turn to him in prayer, he will help us to have the faith to trust and obey him. We will be blessed and most fulfilled when we follow the Lord's plans and do what he tells us to do.

Dear Heavenly Father, I surrender my will and my life to you. Grant me the faith and the grace to follow you and to do whatever you want me to do. I give myself to you. In Jesus' name, amen.

October 3

God Works for the Good

"And we know that in all things God works for the good of those who love him, who have been called according to his purpose."
Romans 8:28

We are in a love relationship with God. This gives us confidence and security that he is watching over us and that he is working for our good. We have peace knowing that we are never alone, and that the Lord is watching over us and working for our good because of our relationship with him. We know his mighty power to provide anything we need and to overcome any difficulty or force that comes against us. We know that he is a mighty God and that nothing is impossible for him. We know that he loves us so much that he is attentive to our situation and our needs. We have faith knowing that we are serving his purpose and that the Lord is able to have his purpose fulfilled. Even when we are facing difficult times, we have faith and trust in God that he is working for our good. This does not mean that we get everything we want. This does not mean that we will not have any problems or difficulties. We trust the Lord during our difficult seasons. There is a difference between faith and optimism. Optimism believes that everything will work out the way we want it to. Faith understands that everything may not be the way we want, but that the Lord is with us through this situation no matter what happens. Our faith is in the Lord, not in favorable results. The big picture for us as Christians is to include eternity. We do not look only at the immediate circumstance. In the long run, we are with Jesus forever in heaven and everything that happens here on earth is a step in that direction.

Dear Heavenly Father, I know that in all things you work for the good for those who love you and are called according to your purpose. My faith and trust are in you. In Jesus' name, amen.

October 4

The One Who Is Wise Saves Lives

"The fruit of the righteous is a tree of life, and the one who is wise saves lives." Proverbs 11:30

The love of God is a gift that the Lord does not want us to keep to ourselves. By the miraculous grace of the Lord, we have been saved from our sins, and we now have a personal relationship with Jesus. We have eternal life in Jesus and we look forward to being in his presence for eternity. God used somebody to share his love with us and pray with us to accept Jesus as Lord. Now God wants to use us to share his love with others. We do not have to be a pastor or an evangelist to share the gospel of Jesus Christ with other people. We can witness to the people in our circle of friendships and relationships as well as to those people whom the Lord puts in our path. There are people around us who are lost without Christ. We can share about Jesus with them so that they can have the same salvation experience that we have had. We can let other people know about how the Lord changed our lives when we accepted Jesus. We can share Scripture verses that unfold the gospel message for them. We can ask others if they would like to accept Jesus Christ as their personal Lord and Savior. We can pray with them to accept Christ. When we do that, the Lord is using us to win souls and save lives. There is rejoicing in heaven when a sinner comes to repentance. God wants to use us to bring more souls to his kingdom. He who wins souls is wise. He who does not is otherwise.

Dear Heavenly Father, thank you for the salvation and the new life you have given me through Jesus Christ. I pray that you will use me to share your good news with others so that they too may have eternal life. In Jesus' name, amen.

October 5

Turn It Over

"Father, if you are willing, take this cup from me; yet not my will, but yours be done." Luke 22:42

Jesus prayed on the night he would be arrested before being tortured and crucified on the cross. Jesus was about to take the sins of the world on his shoulders and he prayed in anguish that the Father would take that cup from him, that God would somehow rescue him from the horror that he was facing. Even in the face of betrayal and death, Jesus prayed, "Yet not my will, but yours be done." This is a prayer that we need to pray every day. Doing things our own way caused us grief and hurt in the past. Now we want to do things God's way, not our own way. We practice our faith and trust in the Lord when we turn our will over to him. We know that God's ways are the best ways. We struggle with the security of knowing and understanding what our will is, and not always fully comprehending the will of God. The Word of God helps us to know the will of God. As we study the Word of God and pray, the Lord reveals his will through his Word. We have confidence when we know what God's Word says and we make the decision to stand on the Word of God and live the way the Bible instructs us to live. There is freedom for us when we surrender our will to the Lord. We can live according to his will and his plans. We do not want to resist the Lord and try to fight against his will. There is freedom from that struggle when we have an attitude of surrender toward the Lord and turn our will over to his mighty loving hands.

Dear Heavenly Father, today I surrender my life and my will to you. I pray in everything I do today, that not my will, but yours be done. In Jesus' name, amen.

October 6

White as Snow

"'Come now, let us settle the matter,' says the LORD. 'Though your sins are like scarlet, they shall be as white as snow; though they are red as crimson, they shall be like wool.'"
Isaiah 1:18

The Lord speaks through the prophet Isaiah to call people out of their sins and to live a life of obedience to the Lord. The Lord provides a descriptive illustration of what it is like to experience his forgiveness. He said, "Though your sins are like scarlet, they shall be as white as snow..." The red color of scarlet is a reference to the Lord's indictment that the people's "hands are full of blood." The deep red color of scarlet is in contrast to the purity of white snow. This illustration depicts the huge difference in our lives that God's forgiveness brings. We do not have to carry around the impurity and guilt of our sins. God's forgiveness purifies our hearts and our lives. This promise of forgiveness was fulfilled by the Messiah Jesus Christ. Jesus shed his blood for the forgiveness of our sins. We experience the cleansing and purifying forgiveness of God through the blood of Jesus. He takes our sins away. Our lives mark the difference between that deep red scarlet and the purity of the white snow when we have been forgiven by Jesus. Just as the Lord was calling his people through Isaiah, he calls our world today to repent of sin, to ask for his forgiveness, and to live in obedience and a right relationship with him. When Jesus forgives us, we are free from the penalty and power of our sins. Our hearts and lives are as pure as white snow through the forgiveness of our Lord Jesus Christ.

Dear Jesus, though my sins were like scarlet, you have made them white as snow, though they were red as crimson, you have made them white as wool. Thank you for your forgiveness. In your holy name, amen.

October 7

Faithful Friends

"Since they could not get him to Jesus because of the crowd, they made an opening in the roof above Jesus by digging through it and then lowered the mat the man was lying on. When Jesus saw their faith, he said to the paralyzed man, 'Son, your sins are forgiven.'" Mark 2:4-5

This encounter shows the compassion of Jesus, his love to forgive, and his power to heal. This encounter also features the remarkable faith of the men who brought the paralytic man to Jesus. Jesus responded to their faith when he forgave and healed the man they brought to him. This shows how the Lord can respond to our faith to move in the lives of other people. The men displayed spiritual qualities as they put their faith in action. They worked together in unity to bring that man to Jesus. We can also benefit by working alongside other believers in unity to accomplish things for God. These men were resourceful. When they could not get to Jesus because of the crowd, they made a way to get to Jesus through the roof. They were creative in finding a way to bring the man to Jesus. We also can apply resourcefulness and creativity in finding ways to bring people to Jesus. These men were also determined to get that man to Jesus. Nothing was going to stop them from getting that man in front of Jesus. We should have the same determination when it comes to bringing people to Jesus. These men serve as an example to us. God can help us to have the same resourcefulness, creativity, determination, and faith to bring other people to Jesus.

Dear Jesus, I pray for those on my heart that need you in their lives. I pray you draw them to you by the power of your Holy Spirit. I pray that you help me to find ways bring others to you to experience your salvation and your love.
In Jesus' name, amen.

October 8

Discouraged by Memory

"We remember the fish we ate in Egypt at no cost—also the cucumbers, melons, leeks, onions and garlic." Numbers 11:5

The Israelites were traveling with Moses on their way to the Promised Land after they were freed from the bondage of slavery in Egypt. The journey was long and difficult. The Lord provided manna for them to eat. This was not a fancy culinary delight; the manna was the same every day, but it did meet the need to provide them sustenance and nourishment on their journey. The people became tired of the manna. They remembered the food they ate in Egypt. They longed to have their taste buds satisfied with good food again. The problem is that their memory of the good food from the past caused them to be dissatisfied with God's provision for their present. Their longing for good food caused them to complain about how they were not happy. They had the attitude that they were happier back in Egypt and they wish they had never left. They lost sight of the hope they had for their future in the Promised Land. They lost sight of gratitude and contentment for the Lord's provision in their lives. They also overlooked the fact that although they had this good food in Egypt, they were in slavery! They longed for a pleasant memory from the past while forgetting the pain and misery of the bondage of slavery in Egypt. We can make the mistake of looking back with sentiment on the "good times" from the past without fully remembering the pain and the hardship that went along with those memories. Our past is behind us. We cannot go back. We can put our past behind us and thank God for his blessings today.

Dear Heavenly Father, help me to put my past behind me and have gratitude for your blessing and provision in my life today. In Jesus' name, amen.

October 9

You Are Not Alone

"He was despised and rejected by mankind, a man of suffering, and familiar with pain...." Isaiah 53:3

Jesus came to love and to save people from their sins, and yet he was met with rejection and hostility. We may experience rejection and hurt in our relationships. The experience of rejection can be devastating and cause us to feel alone. We are not alone. We are in good company with Christ. Jesus was a man of sorrows. He knew what it was like to be rejected, betrayed, and hurt by others. It is during our hurtful times that Jesus wants to draw close to us. It is during our hurt and pain that Jesus is there for us. As followers of Jesus, we may encounter the experience of hurt and pain as he did. He can empathize with our hurt because he went through hurt as well.

Although Jesus was acquainted with sorrow, it was not the totality of his life, nor is the experience of hurt and sorrow the totality of our lives as Christians. Jesus was an overcomer. He rose from the dead to defeat death, hell, and sin. As we follow Christ and we experience suffering, we also follow Christ in his victory. As much as Jesus did experience sorrow and rejection, he also is a God of joy and love. Sorrow and rejection do not define us; love and hope define our lives in Christ. We encounter pain and sorrow, but we do not live there. The Lord walks with us in his love and comfort during our seasons of sorrow. We may experience an incident of rejection, but God does not reject us and he has placed people in our lives who love us with his love as well.

Dear Jesus, I know that you were despised and rejected by mankind, a man of suffering, and familiar with pain. I am comforted by your presence. Draw close to me with your love and strength. My hope and my trust are in you.
In Jesus' name, amen.

283

October 10

When Others Turn Away

"Jesus looked at him and loved him. 'One thing you lack,' he said. 'Go, sell everything you have and give to the poor, and you will have treasure in heaven. Then come, follow me.' At this the man's face fell. He went away sad, because he had great wealth."
Mark 10:21–22

The rich young ruler asked Jesus what he needed to do to inherit eternal life. Jesus put his finger on the issue that he knew was holding the young man back. That was his wealth. Jesus told him to go sell everything he had and give to the poor, then follow him. The young man was not willing to accept Jesus' advice. He went away sad. Jesus loved the young man, but he did not force him to change. He did not plead with him or argue with him. He did not chase after him to make him change his mind. Jesus laid out the truth before the young man, but he let him go to make his own choice. Jesus loved him.

We will have people in our circle of family and friends who need the Lord in their lives. We want them to have the same experience we have had with the salvation of Jesus Christ. We can share the gospel and God's love with others, but we cannot make them accept Christ. We cannot change other people. Only God can. The love and the truth that we share with that person may be seeds that are planted in their heart to grow in the future. The rich young ruler turned down salvation to Jesus himself. We will also encounter people who do not receive God's love or accept God's truth. With God's help, we need to keep loving them, keep praying for them, and let them go, trusting the Lord to open their eyes and draw them to himself.

Dear Jesus, I pray for those who do not know you that they will experience your salvation. Help me to share with them about you. I trust them to your love and your power to save them. In your name, amen.

October 11

Passion for God

"You will seek me and find me when you seek me with all your heart." Jeremiah 29:13

We get out of our relationship with God what we put into it. Half-hearted efforts in our relationship with God end up with half-hearted results. We can have a full, powerful relationship with God when we seek him with all of our hearts. This means we need to be passionate about our relationship with God. When we have passion about the Lord, we can experience a powerful spiritual relationship with him. When we yearn for and desire more of God in our lives, we make him a priority. We put God first in our lives. We spend quality time with the Lord in prayer and Bible reading. We are faithful and devout in our participation in our local church. When we give God more of ourselves, he gives us more of him. Our passion for the Lord impacts our obedience to him. Our love for God gives us passionate conviction in regard to sin. When we become casual about the Lord, we develop a casual attitude about sin as well. On the contrary, our passion for the Lord results in a zero-tolerance attitude for sin and evil. We do not allow other interests to take the place of God in our lives. We do not allow ourselves to become lazy about the things of God or else we can diminish our own passion for the Lord. When we struggle with having passion, God can rekindle the flame of our love. We keep the fire of our passion for God burning when we continue to spend time with him and experience his love and presence. The more passionately we can seek the Lord, the greater experience of his love and power we can have in our lives.

Dear Heavenly Father, I hunger for you. I seek you with all of my heart. I want you more than anything or anyone else. I pray for more passion for you in my life. I pray for more of your love and presence in my life. In Jesus' name, amen.

October 12

Please the Holy Spirit

"And do not grieve the Holy Spirit of God, with whom you were sealed for the day of redemption." Ephesians 4:30

The Holy Spirit has feelings, like we do. The Bible provides examples of God the Father and Jesus experiencing and expressing emotions; the Holy Spirit has emotions as well. When we sin and do things that are contrary to God's will, the Holy Spirit inside of us is saddened, just as we become sad when someone that we love does something wrong or hurtful. The Holy Spirit wants us to move and act in accordance with God's will and in a way that honors God. Because the Holy Spirit resides in our spirit, we can feel it when the Holy Spirit is grieved. We may experience a foreboding sense of sadness when the Holy Spirit is grieved. Our bodies are the temple of the Holy Spirit, so it is possible that we may experience physiological responses such as an upset stomach, muscle tension, fatigue, chills, or shakes when the Holy Spirit is grieved inside of us. The recognition that the Holy Spirit is grieved can help us gain awareness of our sins and areas in our lives where we are falling short and not pleasing God. The Holy Spirit does not condemn us or cause us to be ashamed or embarrassed. The grief of the Holy Spirit is a signal for us to repent and get back on track with the Lord. That is what the Holy Spirit desires. Rather than grieve the Holy Spirit through our sins or doing things that do not please the Lord, we can live a life that pleases the Holy Spirit inside of us and brings glory and honor to God.

Dear Heavenly Father, I thank you for your Holy Spirit inside of me. Help me so that I do not grieve the Holy Spirit. Help me instead to please your Holy Spirit and to honor and glorify you in my life and through my behavior. In Jesus' name, amen.

October 13

God Pleasing, Not People Pleasing

"Am I now trying to win the approval of human beings, or of God? Or am I trying to please people? If I were still trying to please people, I would not be a servant of Christ."
Galatians 1:10

We are blessed to do anything in our means to help or serve other people. However, our relationship with the Lord comes first. We cannot make everybody happy. If we try, we are on a futile effort that will never be achieved. It is ridiculous to try to please everyone. At the end of the day, the most important thing we can do is to please the Lord. We may be motivated to please people to win their approval. We may struggle with insecurities and feelings of unworthiness. There is a temptation to seek self-fulfillment by pleasing others and seeking their approval. That is a false sense of worth that is never satisfied; we will constantly want to win people over and make them happy to feel good about ourselves. This is not how God wants us to live. Our self-worth is not based on how many friends, followers, or likes we have on social media! The Lord loves us and wants us to be filled with his love and to love and accept ourselves. We do not have to make others happy to feel good about ourselves. People-pleasing can put us in the dangerous position of compromising our Christian values for the sake of pleasing others. We also can neglect our own physical, spiritual, and relational health because we are wearing ourselves out to please other people. The Lord can help us to set healthy boundaries so that we serve others in such a way that does not neglect our spiritual relationship with the Lord, our health, or our family relationships. The approval and applause of people is fickle; our priority is to please the Lord.

Dear Heavenly Father, I am not trying to win the approval of human beings over you. If I were still trying to please people, I would not be a servant of Christ. In Jesus' name, amen.

287

October 14

The Heart of the Matter

"Circumcise your hearts, therefore, and do not be stiff-necked any longer." Deuteronomy 10:16

Circumcision was a sign of the covenant that God made with Abraham and his descendants. This was a cutting away of the flesh as an outward sign of their agreement to follow God. Scripture in the Old and New Testaments emphasizes that circumcision is a matter of the heart. The cutting away of the flesh is done more importantly in our hearts than in our outward behavior. What we do outwardly is seen by others and we come across a certain way as demonstrated by our behavior, but our true identity is not based on what we do or how we appear. Our true identity is who we are in our hearts. Our outward behavior is just the tip of the iceberg. Spiritual change is an internal transformation in our hearts that flows out to result in changed behavior. Following Christ is not just about focusing on quitting our sinful habits. Those efforts will not work unless we allow the Lord to change our hearts. There is a spiritual renewal and transformation that takes place in our hearts by the power of the Holy Spirit that changes our behavior. We do not want to get caught up in focusing on our external behavior or appearance to the neglect of matters of the heart. It is more important that we open our hearts up to the Lord and allow him to heal us and cleanse us of matters of the flesh in our hearts. If we just focus on our behavior, those issues remain in our hearts. When we open up our hearts to the Lord and fully surrender our hearts to him, he changes us from the inside out.

Dear Heavenly Father, I open my heart up to you in surrender. I pray that you change my heart with the power of your Holy Spirit. In Jesus' name, amen.

October 15

God Makes Things Grow

"I planted the seed, Apollos watered it, but God has been making it grow. So neither the one who plants nor the one who waters is anything, but only God, who makes things grow."
1 Corinthians 3:6–7

The apostle Paul is responding to division in the church over the people following one leader or the other. Paul is taking the focus off the leaders and placing it on the Lord. A good spiritual leader is not trying to get followers for himself or herself but for the Lord. As we serve the Lord together, it is the Lord who gets the glory for any victory or progress that we make. We are dependent on the Lord for growth and victory. Each of us has our part to do, and we should do our parts to the best of our ability, but we are dependent on the Lord for results and success. We labor in vain without the Lord's help and the Lord's blessing on our efforts. God wants to use us to serve him and serve others while working together with others in unity. God is in charge and is overseeing his work for his plans and purposes to be accomplished. As we serve the Lord together, our goal is to accomplish his will, and to build his kingdom. As laborers unto the Lord, we need to keep a servant spirit while working together with others to accomplish the Lord's purposes for his glory. Our efforts may be tedious at times, and we may toil tirelessly without seeing results, but our hope and our faith is not in our own labor nor in ourselves nor our leaders. Our faith is in our Lord. He can multiply our efforts and bring miraculous results in his time. We remain faithful to do our part while placing our hope and our faith in him.

Dear Heavenly Father, one person plants, another person waters, but you make things grow. Help me to do my part to the best of my ability and to serve humbly along with others. I rely on you for results and give you all the glory.
In Jesus' name, amen.

October 16

Half-Baked

"Ephraim mixes with the nations; Ephraim is a flat loaf not turned over." Hosea 7:8

The Lord is speaking through the prophet Hosea to declare judgment on Ephraim. The half-tribe of Ephraim was one of the ten tribes of the northern kingdom of Israel. Hosea names Ephraim to refer to the northern kingdom of Israel. The Lord calls out Ephraim for mixing with the nations. This was an issue because God's chosen people are called to be separate and holy unto the Lord. Mixing with the nations led the people to worship the false gods of the surrounding nations and oppose their worship and obedience to the Lord. Hosea illustrates this by saying that they are a flat loaf not turned over. This is a loaf of bread cooked over a fire but only cooked on one side. This loaf of bread is not suitable to eat because it is done on one side but uncooked on the other. This bread is only half-baked! This biblical illustration predates the use of the phrase "half-baked" to mean something that is foolish, lacking judgment, and not thought out. This is a timeless illustration of God's people who mix and mingle with the world and allow the ungodliness of the world to enter into their lives. As Christians we are called to be separate from the world. We are called to be in the world but not of the world. We need God's help regarding our tendency to embrace the trends, philosophies, and practices of the world. With God's help, we need to be separate and holy unto the Lord, and not allow the ways of the world to pull us away from the Lord. We do not want to be half-baked Christians!

Dear Lord, help me to live a life holy unto you and not allow the ungodliness of the world around me to pull me away from you or the life of holiness that you have called me to.
In Jesus' name, amen.

October 17

The Secret of Being Content

"I know what it is to be in need, and I know what it is to have plenty. I have learned the secret of being content in any and every situation, whether well fed or hungry, whether living in plenty or in want." Philippians 4:12

To be contented is to be satisfied, pleased, and at peace. To be discontented is to be unsatisfied and to want more than we already have. When we are discontented, whatever we have will not be good enough; we will always want more. It is pleasant to have nice things and to improve our situation, however, getting nice things and having a comfortable lifestyle is not the source of our happiness. When we have the peace and joy of the Holy Spirit from the love of God and our personal relationship with Jesus, we too, like Paul, can be content whether we have a lot or a little. We do not look to material things for our happiness or fulfillment. The love and blessings of God are spiritual. The joy of the Lord is universal and not limited to those who are prosperous. The people who live in impoverished third-world countries also have the love, joy, and peace that come from Jesus Christ our Lord. Most of us in the United States are so blessed that we have not experienced true hunger and poverty. If we did at one time, we likely had the means to improve our situation. There are impoverished people around the world who will never have the opportunities we have in this country, yet they do have the love of God and the spiritual blessing of God's presence. The secret of being content is to be grateful for what we have and to focus on fulfillment in our hearts from our spiritual relationship with the Lord rather than the comfort and pleasure of material things.

Dear Heavenly Father, I pray that you help me to learn the secret of being content in any and every situation, whether well fed or hungry, whether living in plenty or in want.
In Jesus' name, amen.

October 18

The Wisdom to Overlook

"A person's wisdom yields patience; it is to one's glory to overlook an offense." Proverbs 19:11

It is not pleasant to be offended by another person. Unfortunately, people will do things that hurt us or disappoint us. We may be offended by a person because of our dislike, disagreement, or distaste for what they say or do. The Scripture provides instructions for us to deal with conflict and offense. God desires reconciliation. He wants us to love and forgive each other the same way that he loved and forgave us. Jesus taught us that we should go and be reconciled. However, we do not need to go and talk with a person over every minor offense. In some situations, we just need to forgive the person in our hearts and let it go. We do not need to try to confront the person who cut us off in traffic. It is silly for us to confront a person who has thirty items in the express lane at the store for twenty items or less. We just need to forgive and let it go. We make the mistake of holding on to resentment over these small offenses. We become angry over it and let it ruin our day. We can practice patience with others and not get so easily bent out of shape when others offend us or do not meet our expectations. We can be more compassionate toward others and understand that they may have acted offensively because of their own hurt and personal problems. Compassion, patience, and wisdom from God can help us to forgive the person and let it go rather than holding onto the offense and becoming resentful and angry.

Dear Heavenly Father, grant me your wisdom to know when to overlook an offense. Help me to be more patient and compassionate with others so that I may forgive others the same way you have forgiven me. In Jesus' name, amen.

October 19

Confidence and Assurance

"Now faith is confidence in what we hope for and assurance about what we do not see." Hebrews 11:1

The eleventh chapter of the book of Hebrews is known as "The Faith Chapter." The writer of Hebrews honors heroes of faith throughout the Old Testament and provides examples of how they practiced great faith in God. This chapter starts with a biblical description of faith. Having faith is believing in God without seeing him. Faith is undoubtedly necessary to have a relationship with the Lord. The writer of Hebrews goes on to say that without faith it is impossible to please God. Faith is believing in God with full assurance and confidence in him even though we have no evidence or proof of God's presence or his power. The evidence is the faith in our hearts that God gives us. We may describe our trust and confidence in other people and things as having faith in them. We have faith in a friend to not tell others about our personal business. We have faith in our car to get us to our destination. However, there is a distinction in our spiritual faith in Jesus Christ as described in the Bible. The Bible describes faith as a gift from God. Faith is our connection to our spiritual relationship with the Lord. Faith is a power from God that leads to action. As we grow in our relationship with the Lord, our faith grows as well. Our faith in God does not grow old. It took faith to accept Jesus as our Lord and Savior. It takes faith in God to do what he wants us to do today.

Dear Lord, I pray for the confidence of what I hope for, and the assurance about what I do not see. Help me to live by faith in you today. In Jesus' name, amen.

October 20

See for Yourself

"Taste and see that the LORD is good; blessed is the one who takes refuge in him." Psalm 34:8

When we have a serving of food that we have never had before, we may want to taste it first. We take just a small amount in our mouths, chew it a little, and stop to savor the flavors of the food. In doing so, we appreciate the flavors of the food. The psalmist invites us to encounter the Lord the same way, to experience him for ourselves. To taste and see is to intentionally reach out to him and allow him to fill our senses. To taste and see is to enter the presence of the Lord in worship and prayer, to still ourselves and to be open to his love and the ministry of the Holy Spirit inside of us. We taste and see when we turn to his Word, meditate on it, and apply it to our lives. Obeying the Word of God is one of the ways that we show our trust in him. We taste and see when we put our faith and our trust in the Lord. We place our trust in the Lord rather than relying on ourselves. When we trust the Lord with our lives, he shows us that he is trustworthy. We are blessed when we take refuge in the Lord. To take refuge in him means that we turn to him and hide ourselves in him. When we turn to the Lord in prayer, and take refuge in him, we experience his love in our times of hurt and loneliness, his strength in our times of weakness, his comfort in our times of trouble, and his victory in times of temptation. When we reach out to the Lord and trust in him, we can taste and see that the Lord is good.

Dear Heavenly Father, today I taste and see that you are good, I am blessed when I take refuge in you. In Jesus' name, amen.

October 21

Self-Will Run Riot

"'I have the right to do anything,' you say—but not everything is beneficial. 'I have the right to do anything'—but not everything is constructive." 1 Corinthians 10:23

Christ has set us free from the bondage and the penalty of sin, but that does not mean that we are free to do anything we want to do. Doing what we want, when we want to do it is a mindset that can lead us away from the Lord's purpose and plans for us. It may be okay or permissible to do something, but that does not mean that it is the best thing to do. Just because we can do it, does not mean we should do it. We set ourselves up to fall short of God's best when we think only of what we have the right or the freedom to do. It is more important for us to think about what the Lord wants us to do than what we have the right or the freedom to do. There are some decisions we make that are matters of conscience for us based on what we think is right. We need to think about the long-term consequences of our actions before we choose to do something that we feel free to do. Our decisions have an impact on other people. We need to prayerfully and carefully consider how our decisions affect the lives of others and the unity of the Body of Christ rather than carelessly pushing forward, thinking only about our own rights and freedoms. We can prevent the pattern of self-will by seeking the Lord's heart in prayer, studying his Word, and seeking the wise counsel of mature believers before we make decisions based on what we believe we have the right or freedom to do.

Dear Lord, I pray that you give me the wisdom and conviction to make choices that honor you and respect others. Guide me according to your will in matters of freedom and conscience. In Jesus' name, amen.

October 22

The Power of God's Word

"As the rain and the snow come down from heaven, and do not return to it without watering the earth and making it bud and flourish, so that it yields seed for the sower and bread for the eater, so is my word that goes out from my mouth: It will not return to me empty, but will accomplish what I desire and achieve the purpose for which I sent it."
Isaiah 55:10–11

Just as the rain and the snow come down from heaven to water the earth, the Word of God has come down from heaven for us. The water from the rain and snow produces life and fruit for the fields, for the plants, and for the trees. The Word of God also produces life and fruit for us as believers. Just as a plant would shrivel up without water, we need the Word of God for truth and sustenance in our spirits. The Word of God is a means by which the Lord brings spiritual and supernatural change and transformation in our lives. The Lord sends the rain and the snow to the earth for a purpose, and that purpose is fulfilled as the earth soaks in the water for the plants and the trees. The Lord has also sent his Word for a purpose, and that purpose will be fulfilled. Just as the rain and snow do not go back to the heavens without serving their purpose, The Word of God does not return to the Lord empty without serving its purpose. We need to be like the earth that soaks up the rain from heaven and soak up the life-giving, fruit-bearing Word of God to accomplish God's purpose in our lives today and every day.

Dear Heavenly Father, may my heart soak up your Word, that your Word will accomplish what you desire in my life, and achieve the purpose for which you sent it. In Jesus' name, amen.

October 23

Spiritual Family Relationships

"God sets the lonely in families, he leads out the prisoners with singing; but the rebellious live in a sun-scorched land."
Psalm 68:6

When we become Christians, we become adopted sons and daughters by God our Heavenly Father. We become co-heirs with Christ of an eternal inheritance in heaven, and we become members of the family of God. Our spiritual family relationships are particularly developed in the local church that we are a part of. We may have a healthy biological family of origin that also follows Jesus. Our spiritual church family now becomes an extension of that family. For others of us, we may not have an intact relationship with our family of origin, so now we do have a new family in Christ. For others, we have a relationship with our family of origin, but our family does not share our spiritual values, and for that reason, or other reasons, our relationship with our family is limited and can only go so far. We have familial needs that may not be met through our family of origin but can be met in our spiritual family of God. The Lord places spiritual fathers in our lives to show us wisdom, guidance, and fatherly love. The Lord places spiritual mothers in our lives to show us comfort and nurturing love. The Lord also places brothers and sisters in Christ in our lives with whom we share Christ-centered friendships. As we grow in the Lord, he will also give us spiritual sons and daughters to whom we become spiritual parents. The Lord uses these spiritual family relationships in our lives for us to give and receive his love. No matter what our background or differences, we are members of our spiritual family in Christ Jesus our Lord.

Dear Heavenly Father, thank you for setting me in the family of God. Help me to have strong relationships with the spiritual family that you place in my life. In Jesus' name, amen.

October 24

Jesus Our Mediator

"For there is one God and one mediator between God and mankind, the man Christ Jesus," 1 Timothy 2:5

A mediator is a neutral third party who acts as a go-between to resolve a conflict between two other parties. Jesus is our mediator between us and God. We entered into a conflicted and broken relationship with God because of our sins. All of us have sinned and fallen short of the glory of God. Our sin separates us from him. Sin puts a wall between us and God. Jesus came to knock that wall down. Jesus resolves the conflict between us and God. Jesus mediated for us by dying on the cross to save us from the penalty of our sins. Jesus shed his blood on the cross for the forgiveness of our sins so that we would be reconciled to God. Jesus healed our broken relationship with God and now we have forgiveness of our sins from God our Father through his Son, Jesus. Jesus is the only way to the Father for us. We have access to a right relationship with the Father through our one mediator, Jesus Christ. We do not have to go to the Lord through another person. Although angels and spiritual beings are real, they do not provide access to the Lord for us. Only Jesus does. The Bible has no place for us to "pray" to angels or any other spiritual beings except directly to God through Jesus Christ. Jesus continues to act as our one mediator by interceding for us to the Father. He speaks to the Father on our behalf. When we pray to the Father, we pray in the name of Jesus, because it is only through him that we have access to the Father. Jesus is our mediator and our Lord and Savior.

Dear Heavenly Father, I thank you that there is one mediator between God and mankind, Jesus Christ, my Lord.
In Jesus' name, amen.

October 25

In His Presence

"The LORD replied, 'My Presence will go with you, and I will give you rest.'" Exodus 33:14

One of the spiritual attributes of God is his omnipresence. This means that God is everywhere all the time. Wherever we go, God is there with us. When we became Christians, the Lord gave us his Holy Spirit to be with us and in us. We may have that sense of God's presence when we are in our time of prayer and Bible reading or when we are in worship or hearing the Bible preached at church. God is just as present throughout our day when we are at work, driving, or just relaxing. The presence of the Lord is with us at all times and wherever we go, not only physically, but mentally, emotionally, and spiritually. Our thoughts, emotions, and spiritual battles cause us to feel that we are away from the Lord's presence at times. But he is never away from us. The presence of the Lord dispels our fears, fills our hearts with love, and grants us strength and hope to persevere. God's presence enables us to do things we cannot do on our own. The presence of the Lord helps us to make the right choices because we know he sees all things and we do not allow sin to interfere with our relationship with God. We know that he is always watching and that he will help us overcome temptation when we acknowledge his presence. God is always only a prayer away. We are never alone. We acknowledge the presence of the Lord by praying to him in our hearts throughout the day. God has promised to be present with us at all times. He will never leave us nor forsake us. His presence will go with us wherever we go.

Dear Heavenly Father, help me to acknowledge your presence wherever I go and whatever I do today. In Jesus' name, amen.

October 26

The Least of These

"The King will reply, 'Truly I tell you, whatever you did for one of the least of these brothers and sisters of mine, you did for me.'"
Matthew 25:40

The people who are not important to society or culture are important to Jesus. This is the least of those among us: the rejects, the forgotten, the outcasts of society. Jesus died on the cross for all of us. Each person is important and valuable to Jesus. He wants them to be important to us as well. Jesus taught us that God's priorities for us are to love God and love others. Jesus tells us specific ways to show his love to those who are forgotten by us but so important to him: to give food to the person who is hungry, to give drink to the person who is thirsty, to show kindness to a stranger, to provide clothing for the person who needs clothes, to look after the person who is sick, and to visit the person who is in prison. The people who have these needs are the poor, wounded, broken, and disenfranchised among us. Jesus made such a strong point when he said that what we do for these, the least among us, we do for him. We do not have to go to another country to help these people. They are right here in our community. We pass them by on our busy days. It is important to the Lord that we show them love and kindness, and help them in the name of Jesus. It is not hard for us to do; we just need to remember them and care enough to reach out to them in a loving way.

Dear Lord, I pray for the poor, the hungry, the thirsty, the homeless, the sick, and the prisoner. Use me to help them in some way, to meet their needs and show them your love. They are important to you Lord, so they are important to me.
In Jesus' name, amen.

October 27

Say "No" to Gossip

"A gossip betrays a confidence, but a trustworthy person keeps a secret." Proverbs 11:13

To gossip is to talk about other people behind their backs. Talking negatively about others opposes the love and grace of God. Jesus died on the cross to bring forgiveness of sins, so why do we want to bring other people's sins and failures up in our conversation? If we have bad feelings for another person, we need to forgive them rather than talk about them. It is one thing to share our thoughts and feelings with a trusted mentor, who will help us and pray with us; it is another thing to spread gossip. When we gossip, it is spreading negativity about another person. It is dishonoring that person to another. Gossip is not edifying and does not bring grace to the hearer; it is the opposite. It is hurtful for us to learn that another person said negative things about us, or talked about our problems, failures, or things we are not proud of to another person. Knowing those feelings of hurt and betrayal should keep us from gossiping about other people. When we talk about another person or repeat something they shared with us, it betrays their confidence and breaks their trust. We practice trustworthiness when we are able to keep the confidence of another person and not repeat things that are shared with us. This is a discipline and sign of spiritual maturity that is lacking even in our church culture. Trustworthiness is an important and valuable quality and testimony of our Christian integrity and maturity. We can be trustworthy by keeping things to ourselves and saying "No" to gossip.

Dear Heavenly Father, help me to say "No" to gossip and to develop the quality of trustworthiness by keeping other people's personal business to myself. In Jesus' name, amen.

October 28

Touched by God

"But you have an anointing from the Holy One, and all of you know the truth." 1 John 2:20

"Anointing" is a term used throughout the Old and New Testaments. In the Old Testament, kings, priests, and prophets were anointed for their specific roles. Oil was used as a symbol of God's empowerment in their lives. Items used for worship were also anointed with oil to dedicate them for sacred use. Anointing indicates God's consecration for his purposes. Anointing oil is used as symbolic of the Lord's consecration to set a person or thing apart for his use. Anointing oil used for prayer is symbolic of the spiritual empowerment that comes from the Lord.

The most powerful example of anointing is Jesus Christ. The Hebrew word translated "Messiah" and the Greek word translated "Christ" both mean "Anointed One." Jesus is the promised savior of the world. Jesus, the eternal God, took on the form of a man; he died for our sins, and he rose from the dead. Jesus is called the anointed one because he is the only one by whom we can be saved from the penalty of our sins.

All of us who receive Jesus Christ as Lord are anointed by the Holy Spirit. We have the presence of the Lord in us. We are empowered, authorized, and set apart for God's plans and purposes not only for our life on earth but also for eternal life with our Messiah, Jesus Christ our Lord.

Dear Lord, thank you for the anointing of the Holy Spirit on my life. I pray that your anointing teaches me all things as I remain in you. In Jesus' name, amen.

October 29

Walking with Wounds

"The sun rose above him as he passed Peniel, and he was limping because of his hip." Genesis 32:31

Jacob wrestled with God all night long. He walked away with God's blessing and with a limp. We also may have had experiences that we have walked away from with a limp. We may not have had physical wounds but perhaps we had emotional, mental, spiritual, or relational wounds that have impacted us so strongly that we were not the same. We may have gone through experiences that have impacted us with long-term effects. We walk with God, and we are blessed by God, but sometimes we feel like Jacob like we are walking with a limp. We may have days when we feel like the walking wounded. We are moving forward in Christ despite our wounds, weaknesses, and shortcomings. Jesus walks with us. He gives us strength and grace in the areas of our weakness. He can heal our wounds as we walk with him. Even when we continue to limp through the impact of our wounds and weaknesses, Jesus helps us and blesses us. That weak or wounded issue in our lives is the point where we depend on the Lord and give him glory for redeeming our lives. We remain dependent on the Lord in our weaknesses. We also can help others with our experience and our compassion because of our wounds and weaknesses. There are so many others around us walking with wounds. God helps us, and we help each other in the name of Jesus.

Dear Heavenly Father, I pray for your healing for my hurts, your redemption for my failures, and your strength in my weakness. I am dependent on you as I move forward in your grace. In Jesus' name, amen.

October 30

Killer Pride

"Pride goes before destruction, a haughty spirit before a fall."
Proverbs 16:18

Proud people think highly of themselves. Proud people are arrogant, haughty, and conceited. In its full-blown expression, pride ultimately wants to put oneself on the throne instead of God. We need to be aware of the subtle ways that we can allow pride into our lives. Pride creeps in when we start to feel that we do not need the Lord as much as we did when we called out to him in our time of need. We need to maintain our dependence on the Lord instead of thinking that we can do anything without him. Pride creeps when we depart from having a servant spirit and we think that we are above serving others and the Lord. Pride creeps in when we do not want to admit our failures and mistakes and we have a hard time admitting we were wrong. Pride also prevents us from seeking counsel or receiving correction. Pride wants us to put ourselves first before other people and eventually before the Lord. We have become proud when we feel that we are better than anyone else and look down on others. Spiritual pride breeds a "holier than thou" attitude. The truth is that none of us are better than anyone else. We are all in need of our Savior, Jesus Christ, and we stand only by his grace. The opposite of pride is humility. We practice humility when we remain dependent on the Lord, keep a servant spirit toward the Lord and others, see ourselves and others only through the grace of God, and remain willing to receive correction, to ask for help, and to put others before ourselves.

Dear Heavenly Father, I need your help to stop pride from creeping into my life. Help me to keep a humble heart.
In Jesus' name, amen.

October 31

Living by Faith

"For in the gospel the righteousness of God is revealed—a righteousness that is by faith from first to last, just as it is written: 'The righteous will live by faith.'"
Romans 1:17

The gospel declares the good news that Jesus Christ, the eternal God, took on a human form, he lived a sinless life, and he died on the cross to save us from the penalty of our sins. Jesus rose from the dead, he ascended to heaven, and he will return to bring eternal life to all who believe in him by faith. Jesus not only took the penalty that we deserved to justify us from the penalty of sin, but he gave us his righteousness so that we have righteousness before the Lord only through faith in Jesus. Even our faith is a gift from God. The good news is that God loved us so much that he gave his Son, Jesus, to die for our sins. Jesus gave us forgiveness through his shed blood on the cross. He gave us hope for our resurrection by rising from the dead, he gave us the faith we need to believe in him to be saved, and he gave us his righteousness. The good news is that there is nothing that we need to do; there is nothing that we can do to become righteous on our own. We cannot earn salvation or righteousness. Our trust is in Christ alone. We cannot do enough good works to be saved, and we cannot sin enough to not be saved through faith in Jesus Christ. Once we are Christians, we live by faith, not by works. We are never righteous before the Lord for anything good that we do. Even our religious practices do not earn us any favor or righteousness before the Lord. From first to last, we are only righteous through the gift of faith in Jesus Christ our Lord.

Dear Heavenly Father, thank you for revealing your righteousness in Jesus. Help me to live by faith in Jesus, not by anything that I do. In Jesus' name, amen.

November 1

A Pure Heart

"Create in me a pure heart, O God, and renew a steadfast spirit within me." Psalm 51:10

David prayed for a pure heart and a steadfast spirit in his prayer of repentance. Repentance is more than being remorseful for doing something wrong; repentance involves change. Change is not accomplished through behavioral modification. True change occurs inside of us, in our hearts and our spirits. To change our behavior, we need to have a change of heart. David prays that God would create a pure heart in him. The Lord who created the universe can also create in us a pure heart. We need a heart transformation. It is from our hearts that sinful behavior is manifest. There are emotions, inclinations, attitudes, wounds, and desires deep in our hearts that we cannot understand. God can cleanse our hearts of impurities. The blood of Jesus washes away our sins. There is a washing, cleansing, and renewal that takes place in our hearts. God's Holy Spirit brings purity to our hearts. The Holy Spirit can reveal to us the issues in our hearts that are sources of impurity and sin. He can heal and cleanse these impurities within us. The Word of God is a source of cleansing and purity in our hearts. God creates a new heart in us, and with his help, we prayerfully seek to have a pure heart. We guard our hearts from impurities such as selfishness, pride, lust, and bitterness, and we continue to open our hearts before the Lord so that he can keep our hearts pure. We acknowledge any impurities that we become aware of in confession to the Lord. God can change our hearts as we surrender our hearts to him.

Dear Heavenly Father, create in me a pure heart, O God, and renew a right spirit within me. In Jesus' name, amen.

November 2

The Paradox of the Gospel

"Blessed are the poor in spirit, for theirs is the kingdom of heaven." Matthew 5:3

Jesus states that the poor in spirit are blessed for theirs is the kingdom of heaven. This is an example of Jesus' teaching that presents a paradox. A paradox is a statement that seems to contradict itself. Other examples of paradoxes that Jesus taught include: "Anyone who wants to be first must be the very last;" "Whoever finds their life will lose it, and whoever loses their life for my sake will find it;" and "The greatest among you should be like the youngest, and the one who rules like the one who serves." Jesus' teaching does not contradict itself, but it does contradict the philosophy of the world. Being "poor in spirit" does not come across as an appealing quality to have to be blessed and happy. Our worldly culture associates happiness with being strong, confident, and assertive. It seems like being poor in spirit is the opposite of that. It seems like being poor in spirit is a bad thing, a weakness that holds us back from being happy and blessed. Jesus' teaching does contradict the culture of the world today, as it did when he taught over 2,000 years ago. When we are poor in spirit, we are broken and emptied of ourselves in such a way that we can be filled with God. A person who is full of themselves has no room for God. It is not the self-righteous people who inherit the kingdom of God, it is the humble, broken people who know how much we need God in our lives. When we are poor in spirit, we are rich in eternal life through Jesus.

Dear Jesus, I know how much I need you. I am lost without you. You are my strength in my weakness, you are my savior, and I can do nothing without you. In Jesus' name, amen.

November 3

Filled and Being Filled

"Do not get drunk on wine, which leads to debauchery. Instead, be filled with the Spirit," Ephesians 5:18

Being drunk with wine is in contrast to being filled with the Holy Spirit. Rather than drinking from a wine bottle, we drink from the Word of God and the presence of God through his Holy Spirit. Just as alcohol has an intoxicating effect on our bodies, being filled with the Holy Spirit has an empowering effect on our lives. The spiritual virtues of God permeate our lives when we are filled with his Holy Spirit. The fruit of the Spirit—which is love, joy, peace, patience, kindness, goodness, faithfulness, gentleness, and self-control—is developed in and through our lives. The Holy Spirit guides us, encourages us, and strengthens us to grow and mature in our relationship with Jesus Christ. Being filled with the Holy Spirit gives us understanding and remembrance of the Word of God and empowers us to obey God's Word in our lives. We need all the power and help we can get from the Lord. Being filled with the Spirit of God gives us strength to overcome the temptation to sin and victory in spiritual warfare. Being filled with the Holy Spirit also empowers us to serve the Lord, keeping in step with his Spirit and serving others with his love. The Holy Spirit enables us to share the Word of God with others in their time of need. We turn to the Lord in prayer and allow him to fill us with his Spirit. We are not filled with wine. We are not filled with pride, anger, greed, worry, fear, or worldliness. We are filled and being filled with the Holy Spirit.

Dear Heavenly Father, today I turn to you with thirst in my spirit to drink from your Word and your presence. Fill me with your Spirit and empower me to accomplish your will in my life. In Jesus' name, amen.

November 4

God's Joy Is Our Strength

"Nehemiah said, 'Go and enjoy choice food and sweet drinks, and send some to those who have nothing prepared. This day is holy to our Lord. Do not grieve, for the joy of the LORD is your strength.'" Nehemiah 8:10

To commemorate the completion of rebuilding the wall around Jerusalem, Nehemiah called an assembly of the people to honor the Lord by having the Law of Moses read aloud. When the people heard the Word of the Lord, they began to worship the Lord and also to weep in his presence. Although the people were experiencing sorrow at the reading of the Word of the Lord, this was supposed to be a celebratory occasion to honor the Lord at the completion of the wall around Jerusalem. Nehemiah encouraged them that the joy of the Lord was their strength. The spiritual joy of the Lord is different from happiness. Happiness may be based on circumstances that cause us to feel glad such as a sunny day, a promotion at work, or our favorite team winning the big game. Happiness over these circumstances comes and goes. Joy, however, is a deeper experience that does not depend on fortuitous circumstances. Joy is an inner peace that comes from our faith in God. Joy is a fruit of the Holy Spirit. Despite our passing circumstances, the joy of the Lord gives us strength. The Lord takes joy in us. He loves us so much that he feels joy in his heart over us. When we can understand the joy that God has over us, and how pleased he is with us, we know how much he loves us, and that gives us strength and motivates us to persevere. God's joy is our strength.

Dear Heavenly Father, I thank you for your joy in my heart. I thank you for your joy over me. I love you Lord; your joy gives me strength. In Jesus' name, amen.

November 5

The Importance of Love

"If I speak in the tongues of men or of angels, but do not have love, I am only a resounding gong or a clanging cymbal."
1 Corinthians 13:1

If we do not have love in our hearts when we talk with other people, we are just making noise. It does not matter how smart we are, or how eloquent our words are if we do not have love for the people we are speaking with. The way we talk to people is important. How we say something is often more powerful than what we say. People can tell our attitude about them by how we speak to them. If people sense that we do not care about them, or are judging them, or are speaking out of anger or bitterness, they will not receive what we are trying to tell them. The only things they will receive are hurt and offense by us. Love edifies. When we speak out of love, we build other people up with encouragement. Love expresses our care and concern for others. Whatever we do or say needs to be out of a heart of love for God and others. When we put love first, the right words will come. Sometimes the most loving thing to say is nothing at all. Showing love to others is more important than getting our point across. Whatever we do will be different when we do it with love. Having love in our hearts, words, and actions is more important to the Lord than the things we are doing. We can do something seemingly small but it is big in God's eyes when we do it with love. We can also accomplish some great achievement yet if it is not done with love, it is not great in God's eyes. Love is God's priority. Whatever we do, the Lord can help us to do it with his love.

Dear Heavenly Father, whatever I do and whatever I say today, help me to do it and say it with your love.
In Jesus' name, amen.

November 6

Show Me Your Ways

"Show me your ways, LORD, teach me your paths. Guide me in your truth and teach me, for you are God my Savior, and my hope is in you all day long." Psalm 25:4–5

Before we start reading the Word of God, we can pray that the Lord will help us through his Holy Spirit to understand his Word and that the Lord will speak to our hearts and impact our lives through his Word. When we are faced with making a decision in our lives, the Lord can use his Word and his Holy Spirit to show us his will regarding that decision. The Lord can show us his way to handle the tough situations we are dealing with. When God teaches us his paths, he helps us understand how to do what he wants us to do. The Lord wants to help us every step of the way as we open ourselves up to him with trusting hearts, asking for his help and direction. Rather than pushing forward with our minds focused on our own plans, we quiet ourselves in God's presence and look up to him for his help and direction. When we open our hearts before the Lord and ask for his help, he can show us solutions that we did not see before. The Lord can give us insight that we did not understand before. He can give us peace that we did not have before. When we put our hope in the Lord, we are relying on him. Our confidence is in the Lord, as our purpose is to accomplish his will. At times that means remaining still and waiting on him. We trust the Lord to accomplish his will in his way and to guide us and help us to follow him.

Dear Lord, show me your ways, teach me your paths. Guide me in your truth and teach me, for you are God, my Savior, and my hope is in you all day long. In Jesus' name, amen.

November 7

Freely Give

"...Freely you have received; freely give." Matthew 10:8

Jesus wants us to share the good things we have received from him. Rather than receiving blessings from the Lord and keeping them to ourselves, the Lord wants to see his blessings flow through us like water flows through a river. We have been so blessed by the Lord that we should have a generous spirit toward others, not a stingy spirit. We received love by God when we needed love, now we can love others. We received forgiveness from God; we can forgive others. We were shown mercy by the Lord; we can give mercy to others. We received grace from God; we can give grace to others. We were given a second chance; we can give others a second chance. The Lord provides for us and blesses us with finances and material items. We can be generous and give to the needs of others and for the advancement of the kingdom of God rather than clutching on to the material blessings God gives us and hoarding them for ourselves. We already have been blessed; there are others not as fortunate as we are. We can be a blessing to them. The Lord will continue to bless us as we give to others. No matter what point we are at in our journey, there is someone who will benefit from our generous spirit. Whether it is giving our material possessions or simply our time and effort to give the love of God, we can be a channel of the blessings and goodness of God. Freely we have received; freely we can give.

Dear Heavenly Father, thank you for the many blessings in my life that you have given me freely. Let my life be a channel of your blessings to others. Show me how I can give today.
In Jesus' name, amen.

November 8

He Will Lift You Up

"For all those who exalt themselves will be humbled, and those who humble themselves will be exalted."
Luke 14:11

Jesus saw that the religious leaders of his day liked to sit in their places of honor. Jesus responded by telling a parable about a wedding feast. He told his listeners that when they attend a wedding, they should not sit in the front of the room, because the host will tell them that someone else is sitting there, and he will have them move back to another seat. Instead, they should sit all the way in the back of the room, so when the host sees them, he will ask them to move up to a better seat. Jesus brings it home by saying, "For all those who exalt themselves will be humbled, and those who humble themselves will be exalted."

This is a great illustration of the contrast between pride and humility. A proud person pushes himself forward, and a humble person does not seek position or honor for themselves. Humility is not thinking less of ourselves, it is thinking of ourselves less. Humble people seek the glory of God and the best of others over their own self-interest. Humble people are not trying to get credit for themselves, but want to give glory to God and are happy to give other people credit. Humble people do not push their own agenda, because they want God's agenda and they have a spirit of submission and surrender to the Lord and to others. When we trust the Lord with our lives, we can humble ourselves in his sight, because we know that he is able to take care of us in his way in his time. When we humble ourselves in the sight of the Lord, he will lift us up.

Dear Lord, help me to not have any pride in my life to seek honor for myself. Help me to exalt you and not try to exalt myself. Help me to humble myself before you. I trust you to lift me up. In Jesus' name, amen.

313

November 9

Flood Your Mind

"Finally, brothers and sisters, whatever is true, whatever is noble, whatever is right, whatever is pure, whatever is lovely, whatever is admirable—if anything is excellent or praiseworthy—think about such things." Philippians 4:8

We can be troubled by negative and unhealthy thoughts. For example, we may struggle with worry, anger, lust, or regret. These thoughts may become overwhelming. We can become preoccupied with thoughts that affect our emotions and our actions. With the Lord's help, we can overcome negative unhealthy thinking with positive healthy thoughts.

Meditating on the Word of God can help us have better thoughts. The truth of God's Word can intervene in unhealthy thinking. In this verse, Paul provides eight different categories of healthy thinking, specifically, thoughts that are: true, noble, right, pure, lovely, admirable, excellent, or praiseworthy. We can take time to think about specific examples in each of these eight categories. We can flood our minds with good thoughts and overcome unhealthy thoughts. We can take responsibility for our thoughts. The Lord can renew our thinking in the attitude of our minds. The Holy Spirit will help us to be aware of negative thinking and to remember the Word of truth.

Dear Heavenly Father, today I ask for you to help me with my thoughts. May the Truth in your Word be the foundation of my thoughts today. In Jesus' name, amen.

November 10

Hidden Treasure

"Oh, the depth of the riches of the wisdom and knowledge of God! How unsearchable his judgments, and his paths beyond tracing out!" Romans 11:33

The Lord has provided his Word to us in the Bible. We can read the whole Bible, and study it diligently, and yet, when we are done, we cannot conclude that now we know everything. We have so much to learn. The Lord reveals wisdom, knowledge, and understanding to us through his Word and his Holy Spirit, but we have just scratched the surface of the knowledge and mysteries of God. We cannot fully comprehend the mysteries of God. The Lord always has more to teach us. We are blessed to have the Word of God and to have a relationship with God through Jesus Christ. The Lord shares his wisdom, knowledge, and understanding with us. When we draw closer to the Lord, he grants us the riches of understanding him more. As we read the Word of God every day, he blesses us with insight and understanding of our lives and his will and purposes for us. The knowledge of God is a limitless resource of wisdom for us. The Lord can reveal more to us as we seek his face and study his Word. We maintain an open heart and a teachable spirit as the Lord reveals new insights to our limited understanding. Our lives and our relationship with the Lord are enriched as we continue to learn new things from him every day. The Lord shares the unsearchable riches of his wisdom and knowledge with us as we draw closer to him and seek his face. We have so much more to learn!

Dear Heavenly Father, I pray for your wisdom and knowledge in my life every day as I seek your face and study your Word. In Jesus' name, amen.

315

November 11

Giving Honor

"Give to everyone what you owe them: If you owe taxes, pay taxes; if revenue, then revenue; if respect, then respect; if honor, then honor." Romans 13:7

Veterans Day is a holiday celebrated each year in the United States on November 11 to honor the veterans of our armed forces. We honor and celebrate our veterans for serving in the armed forces because of their patriotism and dedication to serve our country and protect our freedoms. Whether veterans served in times of war or times of peace, they made the commitment to serve and protect our country with dedication and the duty to stand up and fight for our country and the freedoms that we enjoy. We owe our military veterans gratitude for their willingness to protect us against our enemies.

To give honor is a concept that is taught throughout the Bible. To honor a person is to give them esteem, value, respect, and gratitude. Honor is an expression of love. Honor requires us to get past our focus on our own selves and our own needs and to practice humility by esteeming another person more than ourselves. The Bible teaches us to honor those in authority over us as well as our parents, the elders in our church, and our spouse. As Christians, our ultimate goal is to give honor to our Lord Jesus Christ. We express our honor to the Lord with a lifestyle of obedience and godliness. We honor God by putting others before ourselves and giving honor to other people as unto the Lord.

Dear Lord, I give you glory and honor because you created all things. Today I thank you for our veterans. I pray that you bless them and their families. In Jesus' name, amen.

November 12

Alive and Active

"For the word of God is alive and active. Sharper than any double-edged sword, it penetrates even to dividing soul and spirit, joints and marrow; it judges the thoughts and attitudes of the heart." Hebrews 4:12

When we read the Bible, we prayerfully ask the Lord to speak to our hearts as we read his Word. The experience of reading God's Word goes beyond a cognitive understanding of the words on the page. There is an opportunity for a spiritual encounter with God through the reading of his Word. The Word of God is alive and active through the power of the Holy Spirit. The Word of God and the Spirit of God work hand in hand. The Word of God is the sword of the Spirit. The Word is the weapon, and the spirit is the arm that yields the weapon, the power behind the instrument of God's Word. Rather than rip into our hearts with bludgeoning blows, the double-edged sword of God's Word reaches to the inner places of our souls with the precision of a surgeon's scalpel. God's Word can minister to the subtle distinctions inside of us between our soul and our spirit. God's Word judges the thoughts and attitudes of our hearts. The Word of God has the power to demolish strongholds in our beliefs and attitudes, along with patterns of thinking that we have had for years. Those beliefs and attitudes may have been based on lies or hurts, and we developed thought patterns that are ultimately in opposition to the Word of God. The living and active power of the Word of God brings renewal and transformation to these issues of our minds, our hearts, and our souls.

Dear Heavenly Father, your Word is alive and active. May your Word renew my heart by the power of your Holy Spirit. In Jesus' name, amen.

November 13

Desire without Knowledge

"Desire without knowledge is not good—how much more will hasty feet miss the way!" Proverbs 19:2

To engage in desire without knowledge is to do what we want to do without thinking it through first. The practice of thinking things through before acting is called prudence. Prudence is a quality of wisdom and the concept of prudence is repeated throughout the book of Proverbs. It is wise to stop and think things through before acting. It is unwise to make emotional, impulsive, or hasty decisions. We need to think about the consequences of our choices before we act. Some of the practical ways for us to practice this type of wisdom is to first stop! Take a "time out" before acting. When we slow down, we can make wiser choices. The next wise thing for us to do is to pray. The Lord wants to be involved in every aspect of our lives. When we pray about our decisions, we open ourselves up to the guidance of the Holy Spirit. The next prudent practice for us is to seek God's Word for answers and direction. It is wise to ask ourselves, "What does the Bible say about this?" There are biblical principles that carry over into every area of our lives. Another prudent practice for us is to seek wise counsel. There is wisdom in a multitude of counsel. Discussing our choices with others who are wiser than we are can help us to think it through and get some feedback to consider things that we did not think of. With God's help, we can make wise choices rather than acting impulsively with haste and doing things we later regret.

Dear Heavenly Father, grant me your wisdom to have prudence in my decisions rather than acting impulsively or in haste. Guide me by your Word and your Spirit. In Jesus' name, amen.

November 14

Jesus Multiplies

*"Here is a boy with five small barley loaves and two small fish,
but how far will they go among so many?"*
John 6:9

Jesus fed over five thousand people from just five barley loaves and two small fish. After the people ate, there was plenty of food left over. That boy had the faith to give what he had for the Lord to use for his purposes. It would have been easy to refrain from giving because he had so little and the need was so great. Jesus will use the little we have and multiply it for his purposes. When we give what we have to the Lord, the Lord can multiply what we give to accomplish his will. We can become overwhelmed by the needs around us or by the task at hand. We consider our own resources and feel inadequate to meet the need. If we are willing to give what we have, then the Lord will make up the difference out of his glorious riches. This principle displayed by the boy who gave his food applies to our spiritual and personal resources as well. We see ourselves as limited when it comes to serving the Lord. We may feel like we do not have the ability that it takes. We do not have the time or the energy. We do not have the love or the patience to help others. When we bring the little we have to the Lord and say "Lord, here I am, use me," he can give us more time, more energy, more gifts, more abilities, more love, and more patience. The Lord can take that little mustard seed of faith we have in him, and make it flourish for his glory.

Dear Heavenly Father, I do not have much, but what I have I give to you, and I pray that you multiply it to accomplish your will for your glory. In Jesus' name, amen.

319

November 15

Stand Firm

"It is for freedom that Christ has set us free. Stand firm, then, and do not let yourselves be burdened again by a yoke of slavery." Galatians 5:1

Jesus set us free from the bondage of sin. When we were enslaved to sin, Jesus redeemed us from our slavery to sin, he bought us back from slavery to freedom by shedding his blood for our sins. Since Jesus set us free from slavery, we do not go back to that slavery again. We stand firm in the freedom that Christ achieved for us through his death on the cross and his resurrection from the dead. We live in freedom through Jesus Christ. The slavery of sin can take away our choice and cause us to do things that displease God and hurt others and ourselves. We get entangled in the yoke and bondage of slavery when we give in to sin and allow that sin to corrupt our hearts and our minds. This leads to disobedient behavior as well. Instead, we can enjoy freedom from all of that misery and slavery to sin. Why would we ever go back? We enjoy life and our freedom to choose and live a joyful life. We are vigilant of the tactics of the enemy and of the desires of our flesh that could cause us to become entangled with sin again. We stay clear of the darkness of sin as we live in the freedom of God's light. We stand firm in our freedom when we cultivate our personal relationship with Jesus. We stay close to him because he is the source of our freedom. We stand firm in freedom when we are reading and meditating on the Word of God every day. God's Word strengthens our hearts and minds with spiritual strength to resist sin and flourish in the freedom of Jesus Christ.

Dear Heavenly Father, it is for freedom that Christ has set me free. Help me to stand firm, then, and not let myself be burdened again by a yoke of slavery. In Jesus' name, amen.

320

November 16

Pleasant Places

"The boundary lines have fallen for me in pleasant places; surely I have a delightful inheritance." Psalm 16:6

The Lord blesses us with a fulfilled and pleasant life in a relationship with Jesus. We have freedom in Christ to live our lives to the fullest. The Lord grants us love and joy in our relationships with others. He blesses us with fun and adventures in life. He provides opportunities for us to experience accomplishments in our goals and dreams. He blesses us with the joy of serving him and other people. He blesses us as we delight in his presence and receive his love in our daily lives. In this full life of freedom and vivacious living, the Lord has boundary lines in place in our lives. The Word of God provides the boundary lines for our lives as Christians. God's Word instructs us on how we live our lives to the fullest according to the will of God. We live that fulfilled life when we live within the boundaries of the commandments and instructions of the Word of God. When we are disobedient, we go out of bounds and subject ourselves to hurt and consequences. Disobedience and sin cause separation between ourselves and the Lord. The boundary lines that the Lord sets in place in our lives also represent his covering, his protection, and his blessing. When we remain within the boundaries of the Word of God, we remain under his covering and his blessing. We enjoy a life of freedom and fulfillment in our lives as Christians. We live our lives within the boundaries of God's Word. The Lord has set his boundary lines in pleasant places!

Dear Heavenly Father, thank you that the boundary lines have fallen for me in pleasant places; surely I have a delightful inheritance through Jesus Christ my Lord.
In Jesus' name, amen.

November 17

Building Others Up

"Do not let any unwholesome talk come out of your mouths, but only what is helpful for building others up according to their needs, that it may benefit those who listen."
Ephesians 4:29

We have a great opportunity every day to bless and encourage other people by what we say. This is a ministry unto the Lord that each of us can participate in. We bless others and honor the Lord by saying things that build other people up. Many people are burdened with issues and problems that cause them weariness and discouragement. Some people are beyond burdened and feel torn down by life's hurts. The things we say can make a difference in someone's day and in that person's life. We can share words of encouragement and hope with others. We can bless others with words of kindness. We can share the love of God with others through our words and the way we speak. This is such a powerful opportunity for us that we can be mindful and intentional about it. With the Lord's help, we can have wisdom and self-control to develop the habit of not saying anything that is not edifying and knowing when to keep quiet. We can filter the things we say through the love of God and the Word of God by asking ourselves, "Is what I am about to say edifying? Will it bless others and build them up?" If not, then it may be better to not say anything at all, or change our words and our tone to say something that is helpful to build others up according to their needs that it may benefit those who listen.

Dear Heavenly Father, help me today to not let any unwholesome talk come out of my mouth, but only what is helpful for building others up according to their needs, that it may benefit those who listen. In Jesus' name, amen.

November 18

The Bread of Life

"Then Jesus declared, 'I am the bread of life. Whoever comes to me will never go hungry, and whoever believes in me will never be thirsty.'" John 6:35

There was a crowd of people who followed Jesus and listened to his teaching. Members of the crowd asked Jesus for a sign from God. They said that previously God gave a sign by providing bread from heaven for Moses and the Israelites when they traveled to the Promised Land. Jesus responded that God gives the true bread that comes down from heaven to give life to the world. When they asked for that bread, Jesus said, "I am the bread of life..."

Just as God sent bread from heaven to provide for the Israelites on their journey, God sent his Son, Jesus, to come down from heaven and live life as a man, to die on the cross, and rise from the dead to save us from the penalty of our sins and give us eternal life.

We often turn elsewhere to satisfy the hunger and thirst in our souls such as relationships, pleasure, material things, position, popularity, and achievements. All of those things may provide some temporary sense of satisfaction, yet without Jesus, there is still an emptiness inside of us that only he can fulfill. Jesus is the bread of life that gives us strength and nourishment to our souls. He satisfies the yearnings of our souls so that we will never hunger or thirst again. Jesus is the true bread from heaven. Jesus is our bread of life.

Dear Jesus, you are the bread of life. I need you in my life each and every day. Fill my heart and my soul with your love today. Only you can satisfy the hunger in my soul.
In Jesus' name, amen.

November 19

A Cord of Three Strands

"Though one may be overpowered, two can defend themselves. A cord of three strands is not quickly broken."
Ecclesiastes 4:12

A husband and wife are bound together with the love of God. We need God's help and God's love in our marriage relationships. We just can't do it on our own. A cord of three strands is a great illustration of a Christian marriage. The love of God, the husband, and the wife all come together to create a strong bond of love.

A husband and a wife who are committed to Christ have received God's love for themselves first and can share God's love. We can be filled with the love of God in such a way that his love overflows into our relationship with our spouse and others. The presence of the love of God makes a huge difference in a marriage relationship. God's love provides supernatural strength in the love we share with our spouse.

God created us with the capacity and need for a spiritual love relationship with him. The Lord has also created us with the capacity and need to have an intimate love relationship with our spouse. The experience of love in a Christ-centered marriage brings joy and fulfillment to a deep part of our soul. God is pleased and honored when we share his love in a committed marriage.

Dear Heavenly Father, I thank you that a three-strand cord is not easily broken. Fill me with your love today so that your love overflows through me to others. In Jesus' name, amen.

November 20

Pray for Me

"I urge you, brothers and sisters, by our Lord Jesus Christ and by the love of the Spirit, to join me in my struggle by praying to God for me." Romans 15:30

The apostle Paul urges his brothers and sisters in Christ to pray for him. We benefit by learning to ask for prayer from others when we need it. When people pray for us, they intercede to the Lord on our behalf. The Lord answers prayer and we benefit from the prayers of others through the hand of God working in our lives in response to their prayers. We pray for our own needs and challenges, but we get spiritual aid and strength when others are praying for us as well. The prayers of the saints make a difference in our lives especially when we are facing challenges. Many of us believe in the power of prayer; we take the time to pray for other people, yet we hesitate when it comes to asking for prayer for ourselves. Whether it is pride or timidity, we need to shake off whatever stops us from asking for prayer from others because we all need prayer. The Lord does not intend for us to live our lives isolated and detached from the help and prayers of other people. The Lord will bless us by putting prayer warriors in our lives. We can turn to those people and ask them to pray for us. We need all the help we can get to draw closer to the Lord every day and do mighty things for God. We draw closer to the Lord and other people in the body of Christ when we are praying for each other and having the humility and courage to ask for prayer when we need it.

Dear Heavenly Father, thank you for the people you have put in my life who pray for me. Help me to ask others for prayer when I need it. In Jesus' name, amen.

November 21

God Shows Us the Way

"I will instruct you and teach you in the way you should go; I will counsel you with my loving eye on you."
Psalm 32:8

The Lord shows us the way we should go. We do not have to wander aimlessly through life. The Lord has a purpose and a plan for each of our lives and he is faithful to guide us according to his will. The Lord has provided his Word for us in the Bible. God's Word shows us the way we should go. The Bible teaches us how to live a fulfilled life in the will of God. The Bible provides moral teachings and instructions for our lives. The Lord helps us to live healthy and upright lives according to the instructions and teachings in the Word of God. The Lord is with us to help us to live according to his Word. He knows we need his help. He has given us his Holy Spirit to be inside of us to teach us and to help us follow his way. The Lord has also anointed and appointed his church as his way to instruct us and teach us in the way we should go. The church is the body of Christ. When we join a church, we are under the spiritual leadership of the pastors of our church. The Lord will use them through the preaching and teaching of his Word to instruct us and teach us in the way we should go. When we become Christians, we make a commitment to abide by the commands and teachings of the Bible. We can do this with God's help. The Lord watches over us with a loving eye to guide us and to help us to live in the way we should go.

Dear Heavenly Father, I pray that you will use your Word and your Holy Spirit to instruct me and teach me in the way I should go; counsel me with your loving eye on me.
In Jesus' name, amen.

November 22

An Attitude of Gratitude

"Rejoice always, pray continually, give thanks in all circumstances; for this is God's will for you in Christ Jesus."
1 Thessalonians 5:16–18

The Thanksgiving holiday is observed on the fourth Thursday of November in the United States. This is a day to give thanks to the Lord for his many blessings in our lives. Many businesses and schools are closed for this holiday. Traditions for the Thanksgiving holiday include having family visits and enjoying a big meal together. This is an enjoyable holiday to have time off, spend time with family members, eat a delicious meal, and focus on being thankful for the Lord's goodness in our lives.

For Christians, every day should be a day of thanksgiving. We have so much to be thankful for! We are thankful to God for Jesus dying on the cross to save us from our sins. We are thankful for the new life we have in Jesus Christ. We are thankful for the promise of eternal life! We can go on and give God thanks for so many things in our lives. The Bible instructs us to give thanks in all circumstances. We can be thankful in the good times and also in the difficult and challenging times. We benefit by having an attitude of gratitude when faced with trials and challenges. Gratitude overcomes negativity. Rather than complaining or feeling sorry for ourselves, we think about the good things in our lives that we are grateful for and give God thanks.

Dear Heavenly Father, thank you for the many blessings in my life. Help me to give thanks in all circumstances and to always have an attitude of gratitude. In Jesus' name, amen.

November 23

Both Sides of the Story

"In a lawsuit the first to speak seems right, until someone comes forward and cross-examines." Proverbs 18:17

We may become influenced by information someone tells us. However, we need to refrain from jumping to a conclusion and withhold from making a decision until we hear both sides of the story. When we hear one person's perspective, that perspective may be limited to their own experience. We may make the mistake of making an incorrect decision because we do not have all of the facts. It is important for us to hear both sides of the story before we draw a conclusion and make a decision about a situation or a person. When we take the time to hear both sides of a story, we may find that the two perspectives are very different from each other. We do not get the whole story until we hear both sides of the story. It is wise for us to wait and be open-minded to a broader perspective rather than being close-minded and quick to judge. We can practice wisdom and grace by giving people the benefit of the doubt rather than making decisions based on hearsay rather than facts. We practice God's love when we hope the best for others rather than thinking the worst toward them. We can be wise and cautious without being judgmental and dismissive toward other people. Our culture is so quick to criticize and judge anyone with whom we have a disagreement. We can go against the grain of our culture by hoping for the best in others, giving people the benefit of the doubt, and always hearing a person out before making a decision about them.

Dear Heavenly Father, I pray for your wisdom and insight to hear and understand other people before making decisions about them. Give me the grace and love to hope the best for others and to give other people the benefit of the doubt.
In Jesus' name, amen.

November 24

Lay It Out before the Lord

*"Hezekiah received the letter from the messengers and read it. Then he went up to the temple of the L*ORD *and spread it out before the L*ORD*. And Hezekiah prayed to the L*ORD*:"*
Isaiah 37:14–15

Sennacherib, the king of Assyria, was preparing his army to attack Jerusalem. He sent a messenger with a letter to King Hezekiah threatening Hezekiah and the people in Jerusalem. The letter also ridiculed the Lord and stated that the Lord could not protect Jerusalem from Sennacherib and Assyria. King Hezekiah took the letter to the temple and laid it out before the Lord. He prayed for the Lord's help and protection. The Lord sent the angel of the Lord to put to death eighty-five thousand Assyrian soldiers. King Sennacherib withdrew and returned to Nineveh, where he was killed with a sword by one of his own sons.

Although this is a brutal story of war, this account demonstrates the Lord's mighty power to fight and win our battles for us. This also demonstrates the importance and power of prayer. King Hezekiah's response to the murderous threats was to take it to the Lord in prayer. Just as Hezekiah laid out that threatening letter before the Lord, we can lay out our burdens and struggles before the Lord in prayer. God already knows our burdens and our troubles. It is an act of faith and trust on our part to lay those troubles before the Lord and entrust them to his help and care. Most importantly, when we pray, we open up our hearts and lay our concerns out before the Lord in faith and trust in him and his mighty power to save.

Dear Heavenly Father, just as Hezekiah laid that letter out before your presence, I lay out my troubles and struggles before you. I open my heart and lay it out to you in prayer. I love you and I trust you. In Jesus' name, amen.

November 25

Hate What Is Evil

"Love must be sincere. Hate what is evil; cling to what is good."
Romans 12:9

When we become Christians, we continue to press into our relationship with Jesus and cling to what is good. We have a passionate pursuit of the Lord that continues in our lives as believers. We can grow closer to the Lord and become more mature in our faith as we set our hearts to pursue the Lord and cling to him and his goodness.

As we grow in our love for the Lord, it will help us as well to learn to have a hatred for evil. A casual attitude regarding sin and evil runs the risk of compromise, thus allowing sin to get a foothold in our lives. In this spiritual battle we are fighting, our best offense is the Lord and his power. We also need a strong defense by having a good healthy hatred for sin and evil. It seems at times that we allow sin to come back into our lives as though it were an old friend that we missed and have not seen in a while. There was nothing good or innocent about our sinful past, so we need to learn to hate sin and evil to prevent allowing sin back in our lives. We can remember the pain that sin caused us and the harm it brought to our relationships with loved ones. Remembering the pain and misery caused by sin can develop an anger toward sin that will help us stay away from it and not go back so easily. We can pray that the Lord will help us hate sin and evil to overcome temptations that deceptively present sin as harmless and pleasurable. It benefits us to have that hatred for evil rise up inside of us to keep us away from sin, as well as our deep love for God to cling to him and want more of him in our lives.

Dear Heavenly Father, help me to hate evil and to cling to you in love. In Jesus' name, amen.

November 26

Turn in Faith

"But I trust in your unfailing love; my heart rejoices in your salvation. I will sing the LORD's praise, for he has been good to me." Psalm 13:5-6

Psalm 13 is an example of a psalm of lament. David expresses his anguish before the Lord, complaining that the Lord has forgotten him. He pleads for the Lord's help with a sense of urgency and crisis. David pours out his anguish before the Lord. Then, in a change of focus, he turns from his anguish to his faith in God. This is a pattern that David practices in his psalms. He pours out his heart and articulates his anguish over his problems and his pain, then he turns his focus away from his problems and his pain and onto his faith in God. David ends the psalm by declaring his trust in God's unfailing love and praising the Lord.

This sets an example for us in our prayers and our walk with the Lord. We can learn from David to be emotionally expressive in prayer and pour our hearts out before the Lord. We can let it all out and tell God how we feel. God is loving and compassionate. He wants to hear our heart and he can handle it when we let it all out. Then we can follow David's example and turn from our emotions to our faith in God. Rather than remain in our anguish, we remember God's goodness and his unfailing love. We rejoice in the Lord's salvation even in the midst of trial and anguish. We can choose to turn in faith to God and praise the Lord. The Lord gives us strength through his presence, even in the most difficult times.

Dear Lord, in the midst of my struggles and my anguish, I trust in your unfailing love. My heart rejoices in your salvation. I will sing to you, Lord, for you have been good to me.
In Jesus' name, amen.

November 27

Disciples Make Disciples

"And the things you have heard me say in the presence of many witnesses entrust to reliable people who will also be qualified to teach others." 2 Timothy 2:2

As Christians, we are disciples of Jesus Christ our Lord. A disciple is a follower. We are followers of Jesus when we surrender our lives to him as our Lord and Savior. A disciple is also a learner. After we accept Jesus as Lord, we need to learn how to live our lives as Christians. The first disciples had the blessed privilege to learn directly from Jesus. They followed Jesus and listened to his teachings. They were eyewitnesses to his miracles and his example of love and holiness. Before Jesus ascended to heaven, he told his disciples to go into all the world and make disciples. Jesus taught them how to be his disciples, then he commissioned them to teach others. This process of teaching others how to be followers of Jesus is the ministry of discipleship. Participation in our church plays a vital role in our discipleship. We need to be taught the truth in God's Word and how it applies to our lives. We are taught the fundamentals of being a Christian in today's world. The Lord will use other Christians to teach us how to live the Christian life. Then we can turn around and teach others as well. This is the pattern set forth by Jesus and practiced and taught by the apostle Paul and other New Testament leaders. The Lord continues to use this pattern of discipleship today. We need to be connected to learn from other Christians how to follow Christ, and then we can also help teach others who are new to the faith.

Dear Jesus, I am your disciple. Help me to learn from others how to follow you, and then show me how I can also help make disciples for you. In Jesus' name, amen.

November 28

The Alpha and Omega

"I am the Alpha and the Omega, the First and the Last, the Beginning and the End." Revelation 22:13

In the apostle John's vision written in the book of Revelation, Jesus declares that he is "the Alpha and the Omega." "Alpha" is the first characterof the Greek alphabet. "Omega" is the last character of the Greek alphabet. Jesus goes on to say that he is the Beginning and the End, and that he is the First and the Last. This provides context for what Jesus meant by saying that he is the Alpha and the Omega. Jesus repeated his point three times in different ways. Repetition is a poetic element used in the Scriptures to make a point and to teach a concept with different variations.

Jesus is the First and the Last, and he is everything in between. Jesus is the eternal God. He always was and always will be God. Jesus is the same yesterday, today, and forever. Jesus is our God from everlasting to everlasting. Jesus was present with God the Father when they created the earth. The Bible reveals that the earth as we know it will pass away, but Jesus will remain forever. The eternal nature of Jesus is supernatural. The eternal nature of God is a divine mystery. This is one of the many things about God that we can neither completely understand nor explain, but we believe by faith in God. Jesus is infinite; he has no beginning and no end. We are finite. Our minds are limited by our finite nature. Our souls, however, are eternal, and we will be with our Lord Jesus forever in heaven.

Dear Jesus, you are the Alpha and the Omega; you are the First and the Last; you are the Beginning and the End. I love you and I worship you. In Jesus' name, amen.

333

November 29

Go against the Flow

"Do not follow the crowd in doing wrong...."
Exodus 23:2

As Christians, we are called to be separate from the world. We do not do what everybody else is doing. Some practices are common in our society and our culture but are contradictory to the Word of God. The Lord has given us his Word with instructions and guidelines on how to live. The Bible tells us what to do and the Bible tells us what not to do. As followers of Jesus, we remain dedicated to the values of the Word of God even when everyone around us is not. We go against the flow of this world by being committed to our faith even when it is not popular. Just because "everyone is doing it" does not mean that it is okay for us to do. We always ask what the Bible says about the things we do and we want to glorify the Lord in everything we do. We cannot follow the crowd even though the world around us may influence us. With God's help, we can exercise the courage to speak up and say, "No, I am not going to do that" when following the crowd would lead to wrongdoing. If the people we are spending a lot of time with are constantly doing wrong and trying to influence us to do the same, then perhaps we should spend less time with them and find friends who share our values and want to honor the Lord with a lifestyle of obedience to him and his Word. As Christians, we are not perfect; we are not better people than those in the world around us, but we are followers of Jesus, not followers of the crowd.

Dear Lord Jesus, I am committed to following you. Help me to make the right choices to follow you and not follow the crowd in doing wrong. In Jesus' name, amen.

November 30

The Ministry of Mentorship

*"To Timothy my true son in the faith: Grace, mercy, and peace
from God the Father and Christ Jesus our Lord."*
1 Timothy 1:2

In the salutation of his letter to Timothy, the apostle Paul calls Timothy his "true son in the faith." Paul's relationship with Timothy emulates what we would describe as a mentor relationship. Paul became a spiritual father to Timothy and helped him personally and spiritually. Paul took Timothy under his wing and encouraged him in his faith. Just as Timothy was blessed and encouraged by his relationship with Paul, we can benefit by having a spiritual mentor in our lives. Our mentor may not be a pastor, but a mature person in the Lord who is further along in his or her faith walk than we are and can help us on our spiritual journey. A mentor will pray with and for us. A mentor is someone from whom we can receive biblical wisdom. A mentor can be a source of accountability to provide support and encouragement for us to stay on track with the Lord and make right choices.

After Paul first became a Christian, he was mentored and encouraged by Barnabas. Later Paul became a spiritual mentor to Timothy and others. In our faith journey, it is important for us to have a person like Barnabas as well as a person like Timothy; a mentor as well as a mentee. Our mentors and mentees may change in time and seasons of life. These are relationships for us to seek and embrace on our faith journey.

*Dear Heavenly Father, I pray that you would show me someone
who can be a mentor for me in the faith. I also pray that you will
show me someone whom I can mentor as well.
In Jesus' name, amen.*

December 1

Understanding the Times

"from Issachar, men who understood the times and knew what Israel should do—200 chiefs, with all their relatives under their command..." 1 Chronicles 12:32

Before David became the King of Israel, an army gathered around him at Hebron. Groups from various tribes and families of Israel joined him. The sons of Issachar were distinguished among the other families because they had an understanding of the times, to know what Israel ought to do.

The Lord can grant us this ability to understand the times and to know what to do. The Lord is with us and in us through the presence of his Holy Spirit on our journey of life. The Lord grants us wisdom, understanding, and discernment as we look to him. The Lord has provided timeless truth and wisdom in his Word. As we read, meditate on, and study the Word of God, the Lord grants us spiritual insight and understanding. He grants us the understanding of how to apply his Word in our daily lives. With the Lord's help, we can have a clear understanding of the world around us as people, circumstances, and needs change. The Lord will help us to respond according to his will. The Holy Spirit can guide us regarding the decisions we make as he helps us to understand the times and to know what to do. The world around us may seem crazy and confusing. When we turn to the Word of God and ask the Lord in prayer, he will help us to understand the times and to know what to do.

Dear Heavenly Father, help me to understand the times and to know what to do. I pray for your wisdom, insight, and discernment as you guide me today according to your will. In Jesus' name, amen.

December 2

Finish the Work

"Now finish the work, so that your eager willingness to do it may be matched by your completion of it, according to your means."
2 Corinthians 8:11

Procrastinating and putting off the completion of doing things we believe the Lord wants us to do may stagnate our growth in the Lord and the accomplishment of his purposes in and through our lives. It may be that the Lord's plans are unfolding in front of us as we complete the tasks that he has already given us. We practice obedience by following through on what we know the Lord wants us to do. As Christians, part of our integrity and testimony is that we do the things we say we are going to do; we finish the things we start. We may have experienced setbacks or delays in doing what we believe God wanted us to do, but that does not mean that we give up. We can complete the vision or plan that the Lord put on our hearts according to our means. We do not have to rely on some unattainable occurrence to move forward, we can do it with what we now have. Rather than accept the disappointment and regret of failure or continued procrastination, we can finish the work or achieve that goal that the Lord put on our hearts if we do not give up. We can lay a foundation and set a pattern in our lives of obedience and completing the things we started that will build momentum for us and put us in the position to accomplish new things that the Lord wants us to do in the future. With the Lord's help, we can finish the things that he wants us to do.

Dear Heavenly Father, I pray for your help to finish what I know you want me to do. I pray that my eager willingness to do it will be matched by my completion of it, according to my means. In Jesus' name, amen.

December 3

Go the Extra Mile

"If anyone forces you to go one mile, go with them two miles."
Matthew 5:41

In his Sermon on the Mount, Jesus taught that if anyone forces you to go one mile, go with them two miles. The people listening to Jesus may have associated this instruction with a scenario involving a Roman soldier. Historical tradition suggests that under Roman law, a soldier was able to commandeer a Jewish person and require that person to walk with the soldier and carry his gear for one mile. This paints a picture of responding to offense with gracious kindness, generosity, and love. Jesus reinforces this concept by providing two other examples. He said, "If anyone slaps you on the right cheek, turn to them the other cheek also. And if anyone wants to sue you and take your shirt, hand over your coat as well." All three of these examples teach us to treat offensive behavior with gracious love.

We can be so quick to defend ourselves, demand our rights, and lash back at those who offend us. Jesus teaches us to be more loving, more forgiving, and more gracious to those who hurt or offend us. Jesus came down from heaven to die on the cross to save us from our sins. Talk about going the extra mile! He did not resist or fight back when he was arrested, tortured, and hung on the cross to die—and yet we become angry when someone cuts us off in traffic or goes in front of us in line at the store. With God's help, we can go the extra mile by showing his grace, his forgiveness, and his extravagant love to those who offend us today.

Dear Heavenly Father, help me to forgive and show your love to those who offend me. In Jesus' name, amen.

December 4

Encouraged in the Lord

"Tobiah the Ammonite, who was at his side, said, 'What they are building—even a fox climbing up on it would break down their wall of stones!'" Nehemiah 4:3

When Nehemiah and the people of Jerusalem started rebuilding the wall around the city, they were opposed by their enemies. At first, the opposition mocked and ridiculed them for their efforts. One man said that the wall was so flimsy that even a fox could knock it down. It is a challenge for all of us to deal with ridicule, mockery, or criticism. This can be discouraging and cause us to want to give up or give in. It hurts our hearts to hear discouraging comments. But we do not have to receive those discouraging comments! Rather than taking it to heart, we need to recognize that those statements are not true. Instead, we can reject discouragement and focus on our faith in God. We also can surround ourselves with positive and encouraging people who pray with us, pray for us, and believe in us. For every person who did something great for the Lord, there was likely someone who told them that it could not be done. When the Lord puts something on our hearts that he wants us to do, he is the one who will make it happen as we put our faith and trust in him. Other people may not have the faith or the vision that the Lord gave us. Our faith and confidence are not in ourselves but in the Lord! Nothing is impossible with God! We can do all things through Christ, who gives us strength.

Dear Heavenly Father, I reject the hurtful, discouraging, and critical things that are said by other people. I turn to you for hope, for help, for strength, and for success.
In Jesus' name, amen.

December 5

Breakthrough Prayer

"During the days of Jesus' life on earth, he offered up prayers and petitions with fervent cries and tears to the one who could save him from death, and he was heard because of his reverent submission." Hebrews 5:7

Jesus set forth an example to us in many ways through his life as a man. The Gospel narratives reveal the pattern of the prayer life of Jesus. He regularly withdrew to spend time alone in prayer. The writer of Hebrews reveals the passion of Jesus' prayer life. Jesus prayed in reverent submission with fervent cries and tears. Jesus modeled a passionate prayer life and intimate relationship with our Heavenly Father. This is the type of prayer life that breaks through to the heavens and touches the heart of God. A shallow, casual prayer life results in a shallow, casual relationship with God that has little spiritual impact. We can have an effective prayer life when we press in to the Lord and pray through the spiritual process of connecting our hearts with the Spirit of God. A breakthrough prayer is a passionate prayer. We pour our hearts out completely before the Lord in surrender and reckless abandon in reverent submission to him. Breakthrough prayer connects with the anguish of the battle of life and death that is on the line as we pray for souls and a desperate dependence on the Lord for our own lives and spiritual needs. God have mercy when we approach our prayer time with the same casual attitude we have when we place an order at a drive-through at a fast-food restaurant! Instead, may God help us to follow our Lord Jesus in a passionate, reverent, submissive prayer life with fervent cries and tears.

Dear Heavenly Father, I pour out my heart to you in prayer in reverent submission with fervent cries and tears. Help me to have a passionate prayer life. Help me to have breakthrough prayer. In Jesus' name, amen.

December 6

There Is Joy in the House of the Lord

"I rejoiced with those who said to me, 'Let us go to the house of the LORD.'" Psalm 122:1

When we go to church, we go to the house of the Lord. Life is busy and demanding with stress, work, and challenges; but there is peace and refuge in the house of the Lord. This is a special place where we can worship the Lord in his holy presence. We praise the Lord with music and singing together with other believers. There is freedom in the house of the Lord. The Holy Spirit has his way in our midst. We are safe in the house of the Lord. We are accepted in the house of the Lord. We are not alone. We feel the love of God and the love of his people, our spiritual family. We are glad to go to the house of the Lord because we hunger for his Word. We hear our pastor preach and teach the Word of God. The Lord speaks to our hearts and gives us encouragement and spiritual strength in his presence through his Word. The house of the Lord is a house of prayer. We pray with and for others, and other people pray for us. God does powerful things when we come together in his name in his house. The house of the Lord is a lighthouse in our community. All are welcome. None are turned away. Souls are saved and lives are changed in the house of the Lord. God blesses us when we come together as the body of Christ in his name. There is joy in the house of the Lord.

Dear Heavenly Father, I rejoiced with those who said to me, "Let us go to the house of the Lord." In Jesus' name, amen.

341

December 7

Faith in Jesus

"Immediately Jesus reached out his hand and caught him. 'You of little faith,' he said, 'why did you doubt?'" Matthew 14:31

When Peter saw Jesus walking on the water, he asked Jesus to let him walk on the water as well. When Jesus invited him, Peter stepped out onto the water, going out to meet Jesus. But it was not long before Peter saw the wind and he became afraid. That is when he started to sink. Immediately, Jesus reached out his hand and caught Peter. This describes an experience that is similar to something we might experience—we may step out in faith for something new and exciting, and then once we get started, we experience unforeseen circumstances. At first, we were focused on the Lord, but then those troubling circumstances can divert our focus and challenge our faith. Then we can become troubled and afraid. We can begin to sink in our fears and doubts. That's when Jesus reaches out to us. Jesus is there with us through his Holy Spirit when we feel alone and afraid. Jesus is there for us through the promises in his Word. We can hold on to the presence of God and the Word of God when we feel ourselves becoming overwhelmed by troubling circumstances and emotions. The Lord is always there for us. He loves us so much that he will not let us sink. He will save us, he will rescue us, he will reach out his hand and catch us.

Dear Heavenly Father, help me to keep my eyes on Jesus and not allow circumstances or fear to weaken my faith. Thank you for your saving grace and your strong arm to reach me wherever I am. In Jesus' name, amen.

December 8

The Blessings of Obedience

"The LORD will make you the head, not the tail. If you pay attention to the commands of the LORD your God that I give you this day and carefully follow them, you will always be at the top, never at the bottom." Deuteronomy 28:13

Moses recited the blessings of obedience to the Israelites as they were traveling to enter the Promised Land. The importance of obedience is emphasized throughout the Bible. The Lord has saved us, forgiven us, and delivered us from our sin. Our response to the Lord is to obey him. Obedience is foundational to our lives as Christians. We are responsible to know the Word of the Lord and to follow it in our daily lives. As we do so, God blesses our obedience. Our obedience keeps us under the Lord's covering to receive his blessings. The Lord keeps us in his loving care, watchful protection, and generous provision. The blessings of obedience include the promises that we would be the head and not the tail; that we will be at the top, and never at the bottom. This is in contrast to the experience of the Israelites as slaves in Egypt. They knew what it was like to be oppressed and exploited. This is also similar to our past lives as slaves to sin. We were in an unfavorable and dishonorable position of defeat in our sins. Because of the victory of God through Jesus Christ, we are freed from the slavery of sin. The Lord blesses us with victory, honor, and favor through our relationship with him. When we live in obedience to God, we are blessed and highly favored.

Dear Heavenly Father, I thank you that when I pay attention to the commands in your Word and carefully follow them, that you will make me the head and not the tail; and I will always be at the top, never at the bottom. In Jesus' name, amen.

December 9

A Terrible Trade

"See that no one is sexually immoral, or is godless like Esau, who for a single meal sold his inheritance rights as the oldest son."
Hebrews 12:16

The writer of Hebrews refers to an event that was recorded in the Old Testament. Esau went out hunting. When he returned, he encountered his younger brother, Jacob, who had cooked a pot of stew. Esau said he was famished and demanded a bowl of stew. Jacob told Esau he would give him a bowl of stew for Esau's birthright. Esau agreed and he received his bowl of stew. As the older brother, Esau's birthright was to be the head of the family and to receive a double portion of the inheritance when their father Isaac passed away. Esau traded his inheritance for a bowl of stew. He said he was so hungry that he did not care about his inheritance. He wanted that stew more than anything else.

The writer of Hebrews compares Esau's impulsive and reckless decision to sexual immorality. Sexually immoral behavior dishonors the Lord and causes harm to our relationship with the Lord. Sexual immorality results in hurting others and ourselves. It causes severe damage to relationships. It brings damage to a person's reputation and possibly to their career and their future. It is not worth it to bring such severe and long-term hurt and consequences to fulfill a need or desire for the moment. This is as sad and absurd as Esau throwing away his inheritance for a bowl of stew. With God's help, we can have the self-control and obedience to follow the Lord's commands in his Word and live self-controlled and upright lives while denying the immediate gratification of sexual immorality and other sinful desires.

Dear Heavenly Father, I pray for your strength, faith, and self-control, to resist sexual immorality or any other sinful desires that would harm my relationship with you. In Jesus' name, amen.

344

December 10

God is with You

"Have I not commanded you? Be strong and courageous. Do not be afraid; do not be discouraged, for the LORD your God will be with you wherever you go." Joshua 1:9

No matter what we do, no matter where we go, God is with us. We are not alone. We can always be comforted by his presence. We may encounter troubling circumstances during our day, but the Lord is there with us and he will walk with us through our troubles. We can take comfort in his presence. The Lord's presence brings us courage and strength. We have security in the Lord. He is our rock. He is our refuge. He is our hiding place and our strong tower. There are moments that our fears may rise up inside of us. It is in those moments that God's love can cast out those fears. We can be strong and courageous because our confidence is in the Lord, not in ourselves or other people. God watches over us with his loving care. Our trust is in him. The Lord has given us his Holy Spirit inside of us to give us his strength. He is faithful. We remember his faithfulness in our past and are assured of his faithfulness in our lives today. We have courage because our faith is in him and we know that we are not alone. We remember that if God is for us, then nothing can stand against us. We are encouraged by his presence and the promises in his Word rather than becoming discouraged by our own fears or worry. The Lord wants us to be assured and encouraged by his love and his presence today. We do not give up or shrink back. We step forward in faith and confidence today because God is with us wherever we go.

Dear Heavenly Father, today I will be strong and courageous. I will not be afraid, I will not be discouraged, for you are with me wherever I go. In Jesus' name, amen.

December 11

The Seven Pillars of Wisdom's House

"But the wisdom that comes from heaven is first of all pure; then peace-loving, considerate, submissive, full of mercy and good fruit, impartial and sincere." James 3:17

The Lord grants us his wisdom to make decisions in life. Wise decisions take into account the long-term impact of our choices. James provides seven qualities of wisdom from heaven. With God's help, we can prayerfully consider these objectives in our choices.

To be pure is to be void of maleficence, negativity, ungodliness, or selfish motives. To be peace loving is to seek reconciliatory paths that cultivate healing and unity. To be considerate is to be mindful of the positions and feelings of all people involved. To be submissive is to respect and value the input and leadership of others rather than imposing our own agenda. To be full of mercy and good fruit is to refrain from courses of action that will cause hardship for others, but to be intentional about beneficial results for all. To be impartial is to be fair and equitable in our choices, rather than showing favor to a particular person or group. To be sincere is to be authentic about our intentions, not fake and phony in any way.

If our decisions oppose these principles, then perhaps we are not making wise choices. With God's help we can take the time to pray and consider these objectives in the decisions we make. We can ask ourselves if our choices align with these qualities. We can make decisions with wisdom from heaven.

Dear Heavenly Father, I pray for your wisdom from heaven. Help me to be first of all pure; then peace-loving, considerate, submissive, full of mercy and good fruit, impartial, and sincere. In Jesus' name, amen.

December 12

Stored up Blessings

"How abundant are the good things that you have stored up for those who fear you, that you bestow in the sight of all, on those who take refuge in you." Psalm 31:19

God loves us so much that he stores up good things for us. He has great plans for us. The Lord has supernatural resources at his disposal and he has blessings stored up for us because he loves us so much and he is happy to see us be blessed. The Lord miraculously blesses us with his favor and his goodness in all areas of our lives, including our relationships, our family, our jobs, our health, our finances, and our spiritual relationship with him. The Lord stores up blessings in our lives out of the abundance of his goodness and his love for us. The Lord may also store up blessings as a result of our prayers. The Lord hears our prayers and sees our tears. His response to our prayers may not be immediate, but as we keep praying, the Lord is storing up good things in response to our prayers. That deliverance, that divine appointment, the salvation of a loved one, the provision for a need, that opportunity that we have dreamed of, and so many other good things for our lives are stored up for us. The Lord will open up his storehouse and pour out those blessings in our lives in his perfect time. The greatest blessing that God has stored up for us is our eternal life in heaven in the presence of Jesus our Lord. We continue to pray and enjoy his presence. Our trust is in the Lord. God is so good.

Dear Heavenly Father, how abundant are the good things that you have stored up for those who fear you, that you bestow in the sight of all on those who take refuge in you. I love you and I trust you as I wait on you. In Jesus' name, amen.

December 13

Set Apart by Truth

"Sanctify them by the truth; your word is truth."
John 17:17

Jesus prayed for us that the Lord would sanctify us by his truth. God's Word is truth. We stand on the Word of God as our source of truth for life in this world. God's Word gives us insight, understanding, and guidance. God's Word provides the basis for us to navigate life. God shows us how to live according to his Word. This world that we live in presents concepts and beliefs that oppose the Word of God. We can be influenced by the world around us in such a way that interferes with God's will and his plan for our lives. The Word of God helps us to be separate from the world and not get wrapped up or drawn into worldliness or ungodliness. If we do not hold on to God's Word and adhere to it, we could get swept away by the lies and falsehoods of the world and the evil one. It can be disheartening and confusing to hear about the troubles and craziness in the world around us. But we have the Word of God to keep us from getting caught up in the confusion of the world. The Lord uses his Word to set us apart from the world and keep our hearts and our minds on him. The Word of God brings stability to our minds and our thoughts because the truth from God's Word is the basis of our beliefs. When we spend time reading, studying, and meditating on the Word of God, the Lord is working in our hearts and minds to set us apart from the world and draw us closer to him and his plans and purposes for our lives. The Word of God renews and transforms the attitudes of our minds. God's Word sets us apart from the world for the Lord.

Dear Heavenly Father, sanctify me by the truth today. Your Word is truth. In Jesus' name, amen.

December 14

No Other Gods

"You shall have no other gods before me."
Exodus 20:3

The Lord makes it clear in the first of the Ten Commandments that we are to have no other gods before our Heavenly Father who made the heavens and the earth. In the society and culture we live in today, we may not experience the presence of false idols and false gods around us in a religious sense. However, the principle of the first commandment is that we should not allow any person, place, or thing to interfere with or take precedence over our relationship with God. When we allow other interests to oppose the commandments of the Lord or take us away from our passionate dedication to the Lord, then it is as if we have allowed another "god" before our Lord. The Lord wants us to love him and worship him with all of our hearts. If something is stopping us from doing that, then we are putting that value before the Lord. This is something we need to be aware of as we navigate life. We cannot allow the responsibilities, activities, or interests in our lives to interfere with our devotion to the Lord. The greatest indication that we have allowed something to go before God is when this other interest leads us to disobey the Word of God in any way. With God's help, we can be vigilant about the many distractions and issues in our lives that vie for our attention and may pull us away from our devotion to the Lord. We worship the Lord with all of our hearts and we do not allow anyone or anything else to go before him.

"Dear Heavenly Father, I love you and I worship you with all of my heart. Help me to not allow anyone or anything else to come before you. In Jesus' name, amen."

December 15

Spiritual Authority

"You, dear children, are from God and have overcome them, because the one who is in you is greater than the one who is in the world." 1 John 4:4

The Lord has given us spiritual authority to be overcomers in spiritual battles. Our authority is in the name of Jesus Christ, who conquered the devil, death, hell, and the grave when he rose from the dead after dying on the cross to save us from our sins. Because of the death and resurrection of Jesus, we have access to the power and authority of our Almighty God. When we accept Jesus as our Lord, the Holy Spirit resides in us with power and authority. As followers of Jesus Christ, we do not have to be pushed around and bullied by the spiritual forces of evil in this world. We stand on the power and spiritual authority of God. Jesus is the source of our authority. When we pray in Jesus' name, we pray in the authority of Jesus. This is not our personal authority to do with what we please, but it is the power of God to stand firm in his strength to accomplish his will. We stand in a relationship with Jesus in a position of strength, power, security, and victory. The Lord has given us his Word to overcome the lies and falsehoods of our spiritual enemy in this world. We take spiritual authority when we stand on the truth and obey the Word of God in our lives. We overcome the lies, temptations, and spiritual attacks against us in the name and authority of Jesus Christ our Lord.

Dear Heavenly Father, your Holy Spirit in me is greater than the spiritual forces of evil in the world. I pray for your victory in your authority and power in the name above all names, Jesus Christ my Lord. Amen.

December 16

Sweet Sleep

"When you lie down, you will not be afraid; when you lie down, your sleep will be sweet." Proverbs 3:24

It is so important for us to get a good night's sleep. Good sleep refreshes and renews our bodies and our minds for good health and helps prevent sickness. One of the many blessings we experience from the Lord is that he can help us to lie down in peace and have sweet sleep. The Lord gives us rest when we come to him. We allow time to get the rest we need to take care of our health. When we lie down to sleep, we do not have to toss and turn because we are upset, worried, afraid, or angry. When we are having troubles in our thoughts before we go to sleep, we can talk with the Lord about it in prayer as we lay down. We go to sleep at night with a clear conscience knowing that we are living right before the Lord. When we lay down to sleep, we can thank the Lord for another day and for his goodness in our lives. We can meditate on the Lord's goodness and his Word. We can review and meditate on Scripture that we are memorizing so that the Word of God ministers to our minds and our hearts before we go to sleep. We can do some reading from the Bible or a Bible-based book. We can listen to worship music and have a heart of worship before we go to sleep. Because of God's blessing of peace and rest in our lives, we can sleep in peace. Thank the Lord that he gives his beloved rest and sweet sleep.

Dear Heavenly Father, thank you that when I lie down, I will not be afraid; when I lie down, my sleep will be sweet because of you. In Jesus' name, amen.

December 17

Walk in the Way of Love

"Follow God's example, therefore, as dearly loved children and walk in the way of love, just as Christ loved us and gave himself up for us as a fragrant offering and sacrifice to God."
Ephesians 5:1–2

The Lord has lavished his love on us and his love flows through us to love others with the love of God. We follow God's example when we walk in the way of love. Love is an attribute of God. When the Holy Spirit resides in us, God's love is our attribute. Love was God's motivation to give his Son, Jesus, to save us from our sins. Jesus loves us so much that he gave himself up as a sacrifice to God for our sins. The love that God shows us is a giving, sacrificial love. To walk in the way of love is to live a life of selflessness and sacrifice. Our lives as Christians can reflect sacrificial love for God and for others. We put the Lord and others before ourselves and give our lives to serve the Lord and others. Love is the greatest commandment. Love is God's royal law. Love is the fruit of the Holy Spirit. Walking in the way of love is evidence of being filled with the Holy Spirit. Others know that we are Christians by our love. God's love fills our lives and flows through us back to the Lord and to others. We have been loved and forgiven much. We respond by loving and forgiving others much. When we share sacrificial love with others, we turn to the Lord and he fills us every day fresh with his love. This is walking in the way of love through the grace and enabling of the Holy Spirit.

Dear Heavenly Father, help me to follow your example as your dearly loved child and walk in the way of love, just as Christ loved me and gave himself up for me as a fragrant offering and sacrifice. In Jesus' name, amen.

December 18

Built on the Rock

"Therefore everyone who hears these words of mine and puts them into practice is like a wise man who built his house on the rock." Matthew 7:24

Jesus taught that everyone who hears his words and puts them into practice is like a wise man who built his house on a rock. When the storms came, the house was still standing because it had a firm foundation. But everyone who hears the words of Jesus and does not put them into practice is like a foolish man who built his house on the sand. When the storms came, the house fell down with a great crash.

The difference between the wise and the foolish man is that the wise man put the words of Jesus into practice. They both heard the words. Knowing what the Word of God says is not enough. We have to put God's Word into practice in our daily lives. The Word of God provides a firm foundation for us to build our lives. We build our lives on that firm foundation when we live a lifestyle of obedience to the Word of God. When we are faced with hardship, adversity, or struggles, the foundation of our lives provides strength and perseverance for us to withstand those trials while keeping our hope and faith in the Lord. Yet a lifestyle of disobedience that neglects the commands and teachings of the Bible does not provide a foundation for us and will not withstand the storms of life. Without that firm foundation, adversity and difficulty will cause devastating effects, and our lives will fall apart. Although a lifestyle of obedience to the Word of God takes effort and sacrifice on our part, that obedience is building a foundation of strength, security, and success in our lives.

Dear Jesus, help me to be like the wise person who hears your words and puts them into practice. Help me to obey your Word today. In your name, Jesus, amen.

December 19

Peace on Earth

"Glory to God in the highest heaven, and on earth peace to those on whom his favor rests." Luke 2:14

Christmas brings a celebration of the peace of God through Jesus Christ. When the angels announced the birth of Christ, they proclaimed a message of peace.

Jesus brings us peace with God. Sin separates us from God by placing a wall of hostility between us and God. Jesus mended our broken relationship with God by dying on the cross to save us from the penalty of our sins. He rose from the dead to lead us in a new life on earth and eternal life in heaven. We have peace with God through Jesus Christ.

Jesus brings us peace with others. The love and forgiveness we receive from God through Jesus is shared with others. The Lord does not want us to be mad at each other and in broken relationships with family and friends. With God's help, we share his love and forgiveness and we have peace in our relationships with other people.

Jesus brings us peace within our own hearts. When we become worried and upset, stressed out, or angry, the peace of God can overcome the distress in our minds and emotions.

This Christmas, we can receive the spiritual message of peace. Rather than getting caught up in the hustle and bustle of the holiday, we can focus on having peace with God, peace with others, and peace within ourselves.

Dear Heavenly Father, I thank you for the peace that you brought through Jesus. Dear Lord, I pray for your peace in my relationship with you, in my relationships with others, and within my own heart. In Jesus' name, amen.

December 20

To Us a Child Is Born

"For to us a child is born, to us a son is given, and the government will be on his shoulders. And he will be called Wonderful Counselor, Mighty God, Everlasting Father, Prince of Peace." Isaiah 9:6

This beautiful Messianic prophecy written by Isaiah points to the birth of Jesus. These promises of the coming Messiah were a source of hope and comfort for God's people. The promises in the Word of God continue to be a source of comfort and hope for us as believers today. Just as the Lord fulfilled his Word and his promise through the birth of Jesus, the Lord is faithful to fulfill his Word regarding the return of Christ. Our celebration of Christmas is a celebration of the faithfulness of God to fulfill his Word.

This prophecy about the birth of the Messiah provides a description of who Jesus is and what he does. Jesus is our Wonderful Counselor. Jesus is our Mighty God, our Everlasting Father. Jesus is our Prince of Peace. "The government on his shoulders" describes the authority and sovereignty of Jesus. Jesus is the King of Kings and Lord of Lords. There is no government, ruler, or authority that is greater than Jesus.

This Christmas season we thank the Lord for his faithfulness in fulfilling his Word and his promises. We reflect on who Jesus is and what he does in our lives and in our world. Jesus is the reason for the Christmas season.

Dear Jesus, I praise you for being the King of Kings. All government is on your shoulders. You are my Wonderful Counselor, Mighty God, Everlasting Father, and Prince of Peace. In your holy name, Jesus, amen.

December 21

The Word Became Flesh

"The Word became flesh and made his dwelling among us. We have seen his glory, the glory of the one and only Son, who came from the Father, full of grace and truth." John 1:14

Jesus is the eternal God, the second member of the Trinity. He came to earth to save us from the penalty of our sins and grant us eternal life. The beloved apostle John describes the birth of Jesus in spiritual terms. John states that "the Word became flesh...." Jesus is the embodiment of the Word of God. He is the fulfillment of the promise of God. The miraculous event of God becoming a man is called the incarnation of Christ. Jesus emptied himself of his divinity to take on a human form. He could have appeared as a strong grown man, but he did not. He came as an infant child born of a virgin. Jesus became one of us to stand in our place when he suffered and died on the cross to save us from the penalty of our sins. Jesus loves us so much that he became a man and died for us. The birth of Jesus signifies God reaching down to save us by giving us his Son.

We celebrate Christmas as the greatest expression of God's love coming down from heaven so that we may have eternal life. Christmas is the celebration of the fulfillment of God's promise to send a Messiah to bring salvation to the world. The miraculous impact of the birth of Christ carries on through his death on the cross to save us from our sins, his resurrection from the dead to lead the way for us to heaven, and his promised return to earth in his glory.

Dear Heavenly Father, thank you for the gift of your Son who became flesh and made his dwelling among us so that we may be forgiven for our sins and have eternal life.
In Jesus' name, amen.

December 22

The Lord's Purpose Prevails

"But you, Bethlehem Ephrathah, though you are small among the clans of Judah, out of you will come for me one who will be ruler over Israel, whose origins are from of old, from ancient times." Micah 5:2

The prophet Micah provided this Messianic prophecy regarding the birthplace of Jesus. Micah predicts that the Messiah would come out of Bethlehem. About 700 years after this prophecy was written, Mary became pregnant through the power of the Holy Spirit. She was betrothed to be married to Joseph. At the time she was carrying, they had to travel from their home in Nazareth to Bethlehem to register for a tax that was ordered by Caesar Augustus. This provides an outstanding example of Old Testament Messianic prophecy being fulfilled by Jesus as recorded in the New Testament. This also provides an example of God working behind the scenes in mysterious ways during difficult circumstances. Joseph and Mary were going through extremely challenging circumstances. They had to deal with the stigma of Mary being pregnant before they were married, they had to register to be taxed by the Roman Empire, they had to travel while Mary was expecting, and when they arrived in Bethlehem, they could not even find a place to stay so Jesus had to be born in a manger. Yet despite all of those challenges and difficulties, the Word of the Lord was being fulfilled. God's plan for salvation for all humankind was unfolding in a miraculous way. Right in the midst of all that trouble, the greatest gift to humankind was being born. The events that occurred in the account of the Christmas story remind us that even in the midst of trouble, discomfort, and tragedy, God has a plan and his purpose will prevail.

*Dear Heavenly Father, my trust is in you as your purpose prevails in the midst of difficulty and hardship.
In Jesus' name, amen.*

December 23

Humble Beginnings

"While they were there, the time came for the baby to be born, and she gave birth to her firstborn, a son. She wrapped him in cloths and placed him in a manger, because there was no guest room available for them." Luke 2:6–7

Jesus was born in humble circumstances. He could have been born into a wealthy, glamorous, or powerful family, but he chose to be born into a poor family and he was born in a manger where animals were kept because there was no room for them at the inn. Jesus is our eternal, glorious, powerful God, yet he came to earth with meekness and humility. Jesus became a man to represent all humans to take the penalty of our sins. Jesus represented all people to be part of the atonement and salvation brought to us by dying on the cross and rising from the dead. Jesus did not come just for the prosperous, the rich and famous, the well-to-do. Jesus came for the poor, the lonely, the forgotten people among us. Jesus' humble life on earth sets an example for us of humility. As followers of Jesus, we do not seek fame and fortune or riches and glamour. We seek to live our lives in humility and with simplicity the way that Jesus did. As we celebrate the Christmas season, we want to remember that the birth of Christ was a humble event. It was not fancy and glamorous. We do not need to make the celebration of Christmas complicated and sophisticated when the birth of Jesus was simple and humble. With God's help, we can celebrate Christmas with the simplicity and humility that encompassed the birth of Jesus.

Dear Jesus, thank you that you came humbly in a manger to save me from my sin. Help me to follow you in your example of humility and simplicity. In Jesus' name, amen.

December 24

Miraculous Birth

"Therefore the Lord himself will give you a sign: The virgin will conceive and give birth to a son, and will call him Immanuel."
Isaiah 7:14

This Old Testament promise was written by the prophet Isaiah about 700 years before the birth of Jesus. It foretells a miraculous part of the Christmas story—that the promised Messiah would be born of a virgin. Jesus was born as a baby like any other baby, yet he was not conceived by a human father. His birth mother, Mary, was overshadowed by the power of the Holy Spirit and she gave birth to Jesus even though she had never been with a man. Jesus is and always was the eternal God. He took on the form of a baby to be born a human while he was still God. The name Immanuel means "God with us." Jesus was fully human and fully God. He lived a sinless life and died on the cross as a representative of humankind to save the world from the penalty of our sins. He rose from the dead to lead all of us who follow him in resurrection power over sin and in eternal life with him in heaven.

Christmas is a time to celebrate the miracles of God. The eternal God taking on the form of a baby born in a manger through a virgin birth are miracles of Christmas. We believe these miracles by faith because ours is a miracle-working God. We celebrate the miraculous sinless life that Christ lived as a man as well as the atonement for our sins made through his death on the cross and the miracle of his resurrection and our promise for eternal life with him. This Christmas we celebrate the God of miracles and we continue to believe for his miracles in our lives today.

Dear Heavenly Father, thank you for the miracle of Christmas. I pray that you continue to work miracles according to your great love and great power. In Jesus' name, amen.

December 25

Treasure up These Things

"But Mary treasured up all these things and pondered them in her heart." Luke 2:19

Jesus was born in a manger in Bethlehem. Just about nine months earlier, an angel appeared to Mary to inform her that she was going to have a child conceived through the power of the Holy Spirit. Now that the child was born, Mary looked into the eyes of her baby, Jesus, who was a true miracle from God. Angels also appeared to nearby shepherds and announced the birth of Jesus. The shepherds hurriedly came to find Mary and Joseph and the baby Jesus in a manger. They were so excited and praised the Lord for this great miracle. This was an amazing occurrence of heaven coming down to earth. Mary treasured up all these things and pondered them in her heart.

This Christmas season we can treasure up the spiritual significance of the birth of Jesus and ponder the gift of Jesus in our hearts. Jesus, who is the eternal God, became an infant child, born in a manger. He lived a sinless life and he died on the cross to save us from the penalty of our sins. The birth of Jesus is the greatest gift of love by God to the world to save us from our sins and give us eternal life. It was on the morning of Jesus' birth that hope was born. The birth of Jesus gives us hope and is a sign of our faith that Jesus loves us so much that he sacrificed his life to save us. The birth of Jesus is a reminder of the truth of God's Word and the fulfillment of his promises. The birth of Jesus Christ is a celebration of joy for the greatest expression of God's love.

Dear Heavenly Father, I thank you for the greatest gift in the world that you gave your Son, Jesus, to save me from my sins and grant me eternal life in heaven. In Jesus' name, amen.

December 26

The Compassion of Christ

"A bruised reed he will not break, and a smoldering wick he will not snuff out...." Isaiah 42:3

Isaiah provides a poetic description of the compassion of Jesus in this prophecy about him. He will not break a bruised reed or snuff out a smoldering wick. A reed that is bruised looks like it might not make it, but rather than discard us when we are bruised and we feel like we might not make it, Jesus has compassion on us. He heals our brokenness and helps us to be restored to a place of strength. A smoldering wick has a flame that is barely burning and it is about to go out. Jesus gently and carefully fans that little flame back to a strong flame. When we are struggling and we feel like we are falling apart, Jesus has compassion on us and gently loves us, and helps us to revive our lives in him. Throughout the Gospel narratives, we encounter the compassion of Jesus to be a driving motivation for his ministry and his miracles. Jesus is rich in compassion for the lonely, the sick, the wounded, and the broken among us. When we are hurting, Jesus has compassion for us. He wants to draw close to us in compassion and love to bring his healing and restoration to our lives. We can receive Christ's compassion in our lives today and treat ourselves with compassion rather than being so hard on ourselves and beating ourselves up. We can turn the compassion of Christ on ourselves. Compassion is an attribute of Jesus that we can share with others around us. We show compassion when we are touched and moved by the pain of others and we reach out to help others with mercy and love.

Dear Jesus, thank you for your compassion in my life. Help me to show your compassion to others and myself.
In your name, amen.

December 27

The Kingdom of God

"Once, on being asked by the Pharisees when the kingdom of God would come, Jesus replied, 'The coming of the kingdom of God is not something that can be observed, nor will people say, "Here it is," or "There it is," because the kingdom of God is in your midst.'" Luke 17:20–21

God's kingdom is an everlasting kingdom. Although we live here on earth and are subject to the authorities in this world, the kingdom of God is not of this world. The kingdom of God is at hand because of the access that Jesus brought for salvation by dying for our sins and rising from the dead. When we accepted Jesus as Lord, we submitted ourselves to his kingdom and we recognized his rule and reign in our lives and over all creation. The kingdom of God will be culminated and ultimately fulfilled when Christ returns and we are in eternity in his presence. We live our lives here on earth as members of the kingdom of God. Although we live in this world, we are not of this world. Our citizenship is in heaven. We are kingdom-minded. We are set apart from the kingdom of this world in our dedication to holiness and obedience to Jesus our King despite the forces of sin and evil and the ways of the world around us that oppose the message of the gospel of the kingdom of God. In the midst of our struggles and spiritual battles, we look with hope toward the consummation of God's kingdom through the return of Jesus and eternity in his presence. Until then we are kingdom builders as we share the gospel of Jesus Christ and see others enter the kingdom of God.

Dear Heavenly Father, help me today to be kingdom minded in my dedication and obedience to you despite the opposing influences of sin and evil in the world around me. Use me today to build your kingdom by sharing your gospel and your love with others. In Jesus' name, amen.

December 28

With God's Help

"With your help I can advance against a troop; with my God I can scale a wall." Psalm 18:29

The Lord gives us strength, courage, and faith to do things that we cannot do on our own. Our own limitations hold us back. We have doubts, fears, and insecurities. We lack the confidence to take on tasks that seem challenging or insurmountable. David had faith in God to know that it was the Lord who gave him strength. Our confidence and faith are not in ourselves, our faith is in God. When we trust the Lord, we too can have that confidence that we can do all things through Christ who gives us strength. We do not allow our doubts or fears to hinder us because the Lord is our light and our salvation, whom shall we fear? We do not allow the challenges or opposition to intimidate us because we know that if God be for us, who can be against us? The Lord is mighty in power. Nothing is impossible with God. When we put our faith in the Lord, we have the courage and confidence to step out in his power to do things we would not think of doing on our own. When we know that the Lord has called us to do something, we have faith in him to provide the means to carry it out. We move forward despite our own reluctance because we know that God is able to do immeasurably more than we could ever ask or imagine according to his power that is at work within us. We have peace and security under his covering of love that dispels our fears and allows us to trust in him. With God's help, we can scale that wall and advance against that troop today.

Dear Heavenly Father, with your help, I can advance against a troop, with my God I can scale a wall. I can do all things through Christ who gives me strength. In Jesus' name, amen.

December 29

Living Love Letters

"You yourselves are our letter, written on our hearts, known and read by everyone. You show that you are a letter from Christ, the result of our ministry, written not with ink but with the Spirit of the living God, not on tablets of stone but on tablets of human hearts." 2 Corinthians 3:2–3

We are living love letters from Christ, written to the world around us. The Lord has inscribed his love on our hearts and he has changed our lives because of it. In him we live and move and have our being. His love overflows through us to the world around us. God's light shines in our hearts and is reflected through our lives in the world around us. We have read the Word of God. The Word of the Lord has renewed our hearts and our minds. We have hidden God's Word in our hearts. The Word of God has become part of us. With the Lord's help, we obey the Word of the Lord and follow the instructions and teachings of God's Word in our lifestyles. We have become living examples of God's Word. Our lifestyles reflect the Word of the Lord through our example of obedience to God in action. We may be the first Bible that someone reads. They see our lives and how we live. Our life can be a demonstration of what it means to be set apart for the Lord in the world of sin around us. Our lives are an expression of God's love for the people we encounter. Our lives have become a love letter from God to the world around us.

Dear Heavenly Father, you have written your Word on my heart, not with ink but with the Spirit of the Living God, not on stone tablets but on the tablet of my heart. Help me Lord, to be a living love letter from you to others around me today.
In Jesus' name, amen.

December 30

Fight the Good Fight

"I have fought the good fight, I have finished the race; I have kept the faith." 2 Timothy 4:7

The apostle Paul looks back at his life as a Christian and compares it to a boxer in a fight, or a runner in a race. He did not compare his Christian life to a picnic in a park or a vacation at a resort. He did not say that he buckled up and enjoyed the ride. He compared his life of faith to very strenuous, competitive sports that require extensive strength, endurance, and exertion. When we fight the good fight as Christians, we may have to bob and weave, we may bounce off the ropes, we may take some hits, we may even get knocked down, but we are not knocked out. We get back up before the count. We keep swinging by being consistent to do what God called us to do and we live according to his Word. With God's help, we even see the devil get a black eye through the Lord's victories. Jesus already knocked the devil out when he died for our sins and rose from the dead. We just need to stay in the ring and not throw in the towel. When we run a good race as Christians, we also do not give up. The race we are in is a marathon, not a sprint. We keep going even when we are exhausted. The Lord gives us strength to carry on. Our eyes are on the finish line, which for us is heaven. Until then, we know we are fighting a good fight. We are running that marathon race. With God's help, when it is time for us to be with Jesus in heaven, we want to look back and say, "I have fought the good fight, I have finished the race, I have kept the faith."

*Dear Heavenly Father, give me your strength today to fight the good fight, to run the race, and to keep the faith.
In Jesus' name, amen.*

December 31

The Conclusion

"Now all has been heard; here is the conclusion of the matter: Fear God and keep his commandments, for this is the duty of all mankind." Ecclesiastes 12:13

The book of Ecclesiastes is likely to have been written by King Solomon. This book is a narrative of his search for the meaning of life. Solomon had vast resources and the means to pursue whatever his heart desired. He sought fulfillment and meaning in life through pleasure, relationships, accomplishments, learning, wealth, power, and in material things. Yet in all of his experiences, he sadly found that these pursuits were meaningless, that they did not bring fulfillment to life. At the end of the book, Solomon makes this conclusion: "Fear God and keep his commandments, for this is the duty of all mankind."

We learn an important lesson from a man who had it all and tried everything. Only God can bring the fulfillment and meaning in life that we are all searching for. The Lord loves us and created us to be fulfilled in a love relationship with him. We have forgiveness and salvation through our Lord and Savior, Jesus Christ. We find fulfillment and meaning in life through Jesus Christ our Lord. As this year comes to an end and we are reflecting on our goals and purpose for the new year, we keep our chief duty as our priority—to fear God and obey his commandments. When we live a life of reverence and obedience to the Lord, he gives our lives meaning and purpose for our time on earth and eternal life in heaven.

Dear Jesus, you are my meaning and purpose in life, you are my all in all. As we begin a new year, help me to always fear God and obey your commandments. In your name, Jesus, amen.

Scriptural Index

368

2:42......................2/26
Romans
1:17..................... 10/31
1:28.......................9/14
5:1 ....7/24
5:8.......................8/10
6:4 ....2/23
6:23 ....9/1
7:15, 19..................8/29
8:1 ....5/29
8:28.......................10/3
8:38–39..................2/14
10:9 ....1/4
10:17....................7/27
11:33.................. 11/10
12:1 ....4/27
12:9 .... 11/25
12:18....................9/10
13:7 .... 11/11
15:30 .... 11/20
1 Corinthians
1:26–27..................6/9
1:30–31................7/13
3:6–7 .... 10/15
10:13....................3/11
10:23.................. 10/21
10:31....................5/31
11:23–25................3/26
12:27....................2/12
13:1 ....11/5
13:11....................7/25
14:33....................9/20
15:3–4...................4/11
15:33......................8/8
2 Corinthians
1:3–4....................7/11
3:2–3 .... 12/29
4:8–9.....................1/23
4:17–18..................8/20
5:17.......................1/21
5:18........................1/9
5:21.....................10/1
8:11.....................12/2
10:5......................4/22
12:9.......................1/28
13:14......................3/9
Galatians
1:10.................. 10/13

2:20 ....4/2
3:28 ....1/15
5:1 .... 11/15
5:16–17...................2/21
5:22–23.................6/18
6:1 ....9/17
6:9 ....5/11
Ephesians
1:19–20..................4/12
2:8–9.....................5/22
2:10......................9/25
3:20–21..................6/24
4:15......................6/20
4:22–24..................5/10
4:26–27..................6/23
4:29 .... 11/17
4:30 .... 10/12
5:1–2 .... 12/17
5:18.......................11/3
5:25.......................8/15
5:25-26..................8/16
6:4 ....9/6
6:12 ....5/2
6:18......................2/13
Philippians
1:3.......................5/26
1:6.......................7/17
2:3–4.....................2/22
2:5.......................3/19
3:10–11...................3/30
3:13–14..................1/25
4:8.......................11/9
4:12 .... 10/17
Colossians
3:23......................4/18
1 Thessalonians
4:13–14..................7/12
5:16–18.............. 11/22
5:23........................8/4
5:24......................3/16
2 Thessalonians
3:3.......................5/28
1 Timothy
1:2 .... 11/30
2:1–2....................2/20
2:5 .... 10/24
2 Timothy
1:7 ....6/17

2:2 .... 11/27
2:4 ....8/18
2:15......................7/10
2:24......................2/17
3:16–17...................1/7
4:7 .... 12/30
Titus
2:11–13..................7/3
Philemon
1:10–11..................5/19
Hebrews
1:14......................8/25
4:12 .... 11/12
4:15......................3/10
5:7 ....12/5
10:24–25................1/30
11:1 .... 10/19
11:8......................8/27
11:24–25................9/27
12:2......................4/3
12:15.....................5/24
12:16....................12/9
13:5......................2/24
James
1:2–4.....................6/29
1:5 ....1/24
1:13–15..................2/28
1:17......................2/4
1:19–20..................4/29
3:17 .... 12/11
4:7 ....9/29
5:11......................7/29
5:16......................6/16
1 Peter
1:3.......................4/14
3:9.......................1/22
4:1 ....3/29
4:8.......................7/16
5:7.......................1/17
2 Peter
3:9.......................8/2
1 John
1:9.......................5/9
2:20 .... 10/28
4:4 .... 12/15
4:7–8.....................1/31
2 John
1:6.......................6/4

Topical Index

Ministry of 7/19
Miracles of 8/6, 9/8, 11/14
Redemption by 4/10, 11/15
Relationship with 1/2, 1/10, 3/3,
    3/6, 4/2, 5/14, 5/15, 5/17,
    8/13, 8/14, 11/18
Resurrection of 3/27, 3/28,
    3/29, 3/30, 3/31, 4/3, 4/4,
    4/7, 4/8, 4/9, 4/12, 4/13,
    4/14, 6/30
Return of 3/30, 7/3, 7/28, 8/2
Righteousness of 5/9, 10/1,
    10/31
Sacrifice of 8/10, 8/15
Servanthood of 7/23
Sinless life of 3/10
Suffering of 3/29, 4/1, 4/3
Teaching of 1/6, 1/13, 1/26,
    2/27, 7/2, 3/13, 3/24, 3/28,
    4/23, 6/10, 9/10, 9/12, 9/23,
    9/28, 10/26, 11/2, 11/7,
    11/18, 12/3, 12/18
Triumphal entry of 3/25
Victory of 8/31
Virgin birth of 12/24
Joy, 11/4
Jubilee, 7/28
Justice. See God, Justice of
Justification, 7/24
Kindness, 2/17
Kingdom of God, 12/27
Labor Day, 9/3
Lies, 7/15
Light, 2/7, 7/31
Listening, 7/27
Love, 1/6, 1/31, 6/4, 6/20, 7/16,
    8/15, 10/26, 11/5, 12/3,
    12/17, 12/29
Loyalty, 3/21
Lust, 2/15, 9/2
Marriage, 11/19, 8/15
Martin Luther King, Jr., Day, 1/15
Materialism, 8/22
Maturity, 7/25
Meditation, 1/9, 2/1, 8/9
Memorial Day, 5/26
Mentorship, 11/30
Mercy, 5/23, 6/9

Messianic prophecy, 3/7, 3/25,
    3/31, 4/4, 4/9, 4/10, 8/1,
    10/9, 12/20, 12/22, 12/24,
    12/26
Ministry, 5/19, 6/10, 7/21
Mother's Day, 5/8
Music, 4/17
National Day of Prayer, 5/1
New Covenant, 3/26, 4/7
New things, 6/28
New Year's Day, 1/1
Obedience, 2/2, 5/13, 5/20, 5/25,
    6/4, 6/6, 6/7, 7/5, 8/27, 9/8,
    9/9, 9/26, 11/16, 11/29,
    12/2, 12/8, 12/18, 12/31
Original sin, 4/9
Palm Sunday, 3/25
Parenting, 2/9, 9/6
Passion, 1/20, 10/11
Passover, 3/27
Past, the, 10/8
Patience, 7/9, 10/18
Peace, 8/23, 12/19
Pentecost Sunday, 6/2
Perseverance, 1/25, 5/11, 6/29,
    7/29, 9/15, 12/2, 12/30
Pilgrimage, 8/14
Politics, 4/15
Praise, 7/20, 9/16
Prayer, 1/5, 2/13, 3/4, 3/22, 4/30,
    5/1, 5/8, 5/17, 6/16, 9/19,
    9/22, 9/23, 11/6, 11/20,
    11/24, 11/26, 12/5
President's Day, 2/20
Pride, 9/13, 10/30, 11/8
Procrastination, 12/2
Prudence, 6/12, 11/13
Purity, 11/1
Racial Equality, 1/15
Reconciliation, 1/9, 9/10, 9/12,
    10/18
Regeneration, 1/13, 1/21, 3/20, 4/2,
    4/26
Relationships with people, 4/30,
    5/4, 5/5, 5/14, 8/8, 9/10,
    9/12, 9/22, 10/13, 10/18,
    10/22
Repentance, 2/27, 6/1, 11/1

373

Made in the USA
Monee, IL
09 December 2023

47758036R00214